WANDERINGS

IN

BALOCHISTAN

WANDERINGS
IN
BALOCHISTAN

C. M. MACGREGOR

GYAN

Published by

Gyan Publishing House
5, Ansari Road
Daryaganj, New Delhi-110002
Phone: 011-47034999, 9811692060
E-mail: books@gyanbooks.com

Distribution Network
gyanbooks.com
India, USA, Canada, UK, Australia

ISBN: 978-93-6433-603-1 (PB)
First Published, 1882

2nd Impression 2024

Printed at: Gyan Press, Delhi.

WANDERINGS IN BALOCHISTAN
Author: C. M. MACGREGOR

WANDERINGS IN BALOCHISTAN.

Captain R. B Lockwood,
3rd. Punjab Cavalry.

WANDERINGS

IN

BALOCHISTAN.

BY

MAJOR-GENERAL SIR C. M. MACGREGOR,

K.C.B., C.S.I., C.I.E.,

BENGAL STAFF CORPS, QUARTERMASTER-GENERAL IN INDIA,

AUTHOR OF

"NARRATIVE OF A JOURNEY THROUGH THE PROVINCE OF KHORASSAN."

LONDON:

W. H. ALLEN & CO., 13 WATERLOO PLACE,

PALL MALL. S.W.

PUBLISHERS TO THE INDIA OFFICE.

1882.

WANDERINGS IN BALOCHISTAN.

INTRODUCTION.

When I was returning through Khorasan in 1875, after my attempt to reach Herat, one resolve was uppermost in my mind, that "nothing would ever induce me to travel in these countries again." The fact was, all the salt had then gone out of that trip. I had undertaken it with a definite view in the interests of Government, and Government, rightly or wrongly, had interfered with me, and the trip had thenceforth no more interest for me, and the stages through the dreary wastes of Khorasan seemed interminable; the sun appeared to increase its fervour; the people became more uninteresting; nothing looked bright but a little spot in the old country, where my wee bairn was living; and having the meeting with her in prospect I lived in the future and forgot the present, always repeating, "Nothing will induce me to come again." Alas for the frailty of human resolves! here I am at it again! I cannot conceive how it has come about, for if there was one thing on which my resolve was fixed, it was that Central Asia should see my face again no more. I continued in this frame of mind all through the winter of 1875, during which no more dangerous subject could be broached to me. In the spring of 1876 I could bear a little to hear about it; in the summer my interest almost revived; in the autumn I was on my way, and now, ere a second winter is over, I am again in the thick of it. I think a good deal of this state of affairs is owing to an idiosyncrasy of mine, for the sight of a map with blank spaces on it produces in me a feeling of mingled shame and restlessness. Of course it is not any particular fault of mine that maps have blank spaces on them, yet I always feel the glaring whiteness of the blanks is looking reproachfully at me. Major St. John's map of Persia is, in this respect, particularly aggravating, for all over it is written "unexplored." Judging from my own feelings, I think it would be a good plan if the Geographical Society were to have all unexplored tracts painted on their maps some conspicuous colour, say scarlet, as the sight of these burning spots, thus prominently brought to their notice, would, I feel sure, rouse much of the latent energy of young Britons, and perhaps divert a good deal of it from mooning about the Row, to more useful wanderings in unknown regions.

But to explain how it all came about that I again found myself so soon on the move. I may mention that Lord Salisbury had been particularly considerate towards me in the expression of his views about my late travels in Persia, and such kindness, coming at a period when I was somewhat sore at the result of my journey, led me to wish to make some return, if possible, for the encouragement thus received. And so it happened that in an interview I had with him, when we were discussing, with the map before us, my late travels, I said that, though I had had enough of travelling in such wild countries, I should be very glad to go anywhere and to do anything he might think me capable of undertaking, and I particularly suggested certain regions in Mekran as a field of exploration. Lord Salisbury said that any information about the comparatively unknown locality in question could not fail to be interesting, and he promised to consider whether he would allow me to travel in those regions. On a subsequent occasion his Lordship informed me that he had obtained the assent of the Council of India to my returning to duty *viâ* Balochistan, with the view of procuring detailed geographical information of the districts through which I should pass.

So it happened that the autumn of the year of our Lord 1876 was again destined to see me on the road to the East.

All preliminaries being settled, I was to have left London on the 23rd September, 1876, but a bad attack of fever rendered it necessary to put off my departure till the 25th of the month, when Lockwood and I moved out of Charing Cross station, our hearts brimming over with excitement at the work before us.

CHAPTER I.

PARIS TO PUSNI.

There being no particular reason for hurrying, but rather the contrary, we travelled slowly, taking a last regretful share in all the delights of Paris, Vienna, and Pesth. It cost us a severe wrench to tear ourselves away from the last, so full was it of those amusements and pleasures which one never finds in the East. But it had to be done; so steaming down the Danube, we reached Rutschuk, there took rail for Varna, and on by steamer to Constantinople.

From this queen, if not of cities, at least of sites, we made our way across the Black Sea, which certainly kept up its name of "Fana Kara Denghiz" (detestable Black Sea) while we were on its bosom, as I never got such a tossing about before in my life, and we were very glad to find ourselves lying outside the beautiful town of Trebizond.

Here by the kind assistance of our friend Mr. Billiotti, whom Lockwood would persist in calling William Otty, Esq., as being, he thought, more respectful, we were soon able to get horses for our journey to Erzeroom.

The ride was most delightful; we had capital horses, and made excellent progress. On arrival at Erzeroom, we were met by the Pasha's carriage, and drove on in state to the house of our hospitable friend, Mr. Zohrab. Here the kindness we received will long remain a bright spot on my memory. We went carefully all over the fortifications, and making a trip to Kars, performed the same duty there.

Starting on the 10th of November, we had an awful, in fact quite too awful a journey over the mountains of Armenia to the Tigris. The winter was early, and snow had fallen before we got off, and so for ten days we went through the snow, and arrived each night at hovels which baffle description; not, I regret to say, to sit down to a frugal meal, but to sit down and be made an anything but frugal meal of by——the memory is too much for me.

Arrived at Jazira we at last had some peace, and travelling on a raft on the Tigris seemed, by contrast, the most supremely luxurious mode of getting about I had ever experienced. In five days we reached Baghdad, and then went on to Basrah and Bushire; but as a description of this part of our travels does not enter into the purpose of this book, I pass them by lightly.

Leaving Bushire we made for Jask, a spot on the Mekran coast where the Indo-European Telegraph Company have a station. It is not a beautiful place, nor do I think any human ingenuity could make it an acceptable residence for any ordinary mortal. The only materials for a landscape are a glaring, glittering, glabrous sea for a foreground, a glaring, shining, sandy plain for the mid-distance, and bare volcanic hills for the background. Add to this, heat which must make a nervous sinner most apprehensive, and the fact that you never see a soul of the outside world, and only get letters twice a month, and I think I have given sufficient reason for any one to be a little more impressive and feeling than usual on saying farewell to any friend going to Jask. But of course there is no place so bad on this earth that somebody won't swear by it, no man so bad that some woman won't speak up for him and cling to him, and so no one need be surprised to hear there are some people who say "Jask is not half a bad place." I have heard the same said of a malarious swamp in Assam, of a burnt-up crater surrounded with cinders, of a spot where you are snowed up for months in the year, and of another where it rains eternally for about 360 days out of 365. Not a bad place! no place is a bad place, I suppose, if you only know how to live in it; as the Scotch gardener said of his much-abused garden made on a rock, "She's no a bad gairden gin ye doong her weel." I fully expect when I get to that place Dadur, of which the poet said, "Al khuda bawakt kih dadur bud chira duzakh sakhtah?" ("Seeing that there is Dadur, why did God make the infernal regions?")—yet to hear some one say of it also, "It's not half a bad place."

So that when I found, as of course I soon did, that Major Mockler said Gwadur, the next stage we reached, was a very nice place, I was not in the least surprised. There's no doubt that if the bitterest enemies were to be made to live alone together for four years they would end by being bosom friends, —*i.e.*, if they did not kill each other at first; so that as Gwadur has failed to kill Major Mockler for four years, of course that officer praises it.

And, I do not know why exactly, but it seems to me I should like Gwadur better than some other

Gwadur Bay.

Gwader

places I have seen, such as Fao, Bushire, Bandar Abbass, Maskat, and Jask.

There is something picturesque about it; on the south the hill rises straight up to a height of 480 feet, and to the north the fantastic shapes of the Koh-i-Mahdi make it take one's eye more. The town is not a very large one, but I believe it is rising, and moreover it seems to me to be the natural commercial outlet for a very much greater extent of country than it now drains. Altogether it is a place with more of a future than a past. One of the peculiarities of Gwadur seemed to me, the number of flagstaffs. I am aware that the erection of a ship's mast with a flag on the top of it in season and out, is regarded by her political officers as one of the outward and visible signs of Great Britain's power, but generally British agents are content with one such emblem of majesty, provided only that it is higher and more unwieldy than any other by which it is surrounded; but here there are four,—let us hope, then, they are a sign of the coming greatness of Gwadur.

We arrived at Gwadur on the 1st January, 1877, and at once disembarking, went with Major Mockler, who had kindly come with us from Jask, on purpose to be in a position to help us to the utmost of his power. I had telegraphed from Bushire regarding most of my wants, which were in reality but few, for we had come provided with all necessary outfit. The chief necessaries were some good riding camels, and a trustworthy man or two to go with us. The first, Major Mockler had already arranged to supply, by letting us have some of the camels belonging to his own escort; and if he did not give us the second,

I fancy the reason was because, there being no demand for such an article as trustworthiness in and about Gwadur, there was no supply.

All the 2nd was occupied in making up our packages into proper loads, writing letters and arranging for receiving them, and in enquiring about the country we were to traverse; but it soon became evident that no information was to be procured at all of the country beyond Panjgur, so that there was no way of getting it except by going to that place ourselves.

The first question which presented itself for solution was in regard to the routes which we should follow between the sea-coast and Panjgur. I was of course anxious that we should get complete information regarding all the practicable routes from the sea-coast, in order that we might start from Panjgur with the thread of our onward journey taken up complete.

A consideration of distance rendered it unnecessary to enquire about any route east of Sonmiani; that is to say, our enquiries were limited by the mouth of the Dasht River on the west, to Sonmiani on the east.

From between these points many routes lead into the interior; the easternmost from Sonmiani itself, goes by Bela and Wudd to Nal, and has been traversed frequently by British officers, who have recorded more or less complete information regarding it; from Nal to Kharan there is, however, a hiatus which should be filled up. That from Ormarah by Kolwah to Panjgur was followed by Captain Miles in 1873, and all the numerous routes which lead from Gwadur itself had been seen either by Ross, Lovett,

St. John, or Miles. From Gwadur there are no less than four routes: the first, which is known as the Talar road, goes by the village of Kuppar to the Talar pass, a rugged track over broken ridges of sandstone; from this it turns to the north-west by Amulani to avoid the end of the spurs thrown out to the west by the southern range of the Kej valley, and also because water is not procurable in a more direct line. From Amulani the road goes over a level plain for some twelve miles, when it enters a series of low hills, crossing which in a northerly direction, it reaches the town or village of Miri in the Kej valley. The Faleri route goes by Seroki on the Dasht River, and the Durdan route lies to the north of this, and finally the Tankh route joins on the Talar road. All these had been traversed at various times by our officers, and so it was not necessary again to go over them. There only therefore really remained two routes which had not been visited, namely that from the mouth of the Dasht River, and that from the village of Pusni. My attention had been particularly called to the first by Major Lovett, who described it as probably a very suitable line for an advance of a force into the interior; and I therefore asked Lockwood to go and have a look at it, while I myself undertook the exploration of the second.

But before we start into the interior, I will say a few words regarding the points on the Mekran coast at which it would be possible to land in numbers; yet in considering what I shall say, it will always be necessary to bear in mind one fact, viz., that landing on the Mekran coast cannot be effected anywhere without considerable danger and difficulty, before the end of September or much after the end of March. Even during the fine weather the whole of this coast, being quite open, has a surf on it, which is often so high as to render landing very difficult; and as this is due to local causes, the exact times at which this inconvenience will occur cannot be foreseen. Moreover, as the coast is generally formed of low hills which come down to the water's edge in abrupt cliffs, the selection of landing-places must be confined to the various bays, which alone can be considered suitable points for disembarkation.

Commencing from the west, the first we come to is Sonmiani, regarding which and the following place I cull some information from a capital little work by Commander Stiffe of the Indian Navy, called "The Persian Gulf Pilot."

Sonmiani Bay extends from Ras Muwari to the Hara range of hills for nineteen miles, with a succession of rocky points and small inlets. On the east, there is about ten fathoms of water three miles off shore, and the depth thence decreases regularly to four fathoms at low water, quite close to the bar off Sonmiani, and within a mile of the shore east of that place. The village itself consists of a few hundred mud houses, but no supplies can be obtained, and only some bad water is here procurable.

Ormarah, the next point, has two usual anchorages, one called by the natives Demezarra (or East Bay), with only a depth of three and a half fathoms, about two and a half miles from the village, the water shoaling rapidly, and making landing inconvenient at low water. This bay is open to easterly winds, which blow strong at times from December to February. The west bay, or Padazarra, is similar, but is shoaler, and is seldom visited.

The Residency, Gwadur.

Pusni, which lies to the west again, is an old telegraph station. The bay here is shallow, and the anchorage is one and a quarter to one and a half miles from the shore, in three to three and a half fathoms, the soundings shoaling regularly, and the bottom being sandy. There is considerable surf here after April, and it is then difficult to land. No supplies can be got here, but fresh water is procurable from some three miles up the Shadi Khor.

Gwadur is the principal town on the Mekran coast, and stands on a sandy isthmus to the north of the Gwadur Head, a rocky promontory similar to but not so high as that of Ras Ormarah. It contains about five thousand inhabitants, and is built in great part of mat huts, but it has a square fortlet in the middle. The population is a very mongrel lot, chiefly Baloch, who live by fishing. Many boats belong to this place, probably not less than two thousand five hundred, of which some thirty are large sea-going boats, which trade with Kurrachi, Maskat, Bandar Abbass, Bombay, and the Malabar coast. The traffic with the interior by caravans is, for this part, considerable, and is chiefly with Kej and Panjgur. The principal imports are piece goods, sugar, rice, timber, etc.; the exports, cotton, wool, ghee, salt fish, and shark fins, and, lastly, the only really fine product of all Mekran,—splendid dates from Panjgur.

It is a residence of a British political officer, and there is a telegraph office; as, too, the mail steamers call here once a fortnight, it cannot be considered altogether cut off from the known world. Further, as supplies are procurable, and good water, and it is about twenty times larger than any other place in

Mekran, a wild Baloch from the interior naturally looks on it much as a Yankee does on Paris.

The East Bay, in which an anchorage on good hard bottom, with a depth of about three fathoms, can be had some one and a half miles from the shore, is well sheltered from south-west winds and sea, but on the monsoon the long, low swell rolling round the point of Gwadur Head causes a vessel to roll violently, and in easterly winds it is sometimes difficult to communicate with the shore, though the gale is never strong enough to endanger a ship. In the west Gwadur Bay there is good anchorage in four fathoms, with a sandy bottom, about two and three-quarter miles east of the telegraph office, and in an easterly gale a vessel would find shelter here.

Before my arrival on the coast of Mekran, the mouth of the Dasht River had never been explored; but, as I have said, my attention having been called to it by one of Major Lovett's reports, I asked Captain Lockwood to visit it. He found the bar of the Dasht River to be quite dry at low water, and to have about one fathom over it at high tide. The river at its mouth is about four hundred yards broad, with flat, sandy banks, almost flush with the water. For four miles up the river, the depth at flood varies from two to three and a half fathoms in the deepest places, and the width gradually lessens to one hundred yards. At six miles the width still further diminishes to eighty yards, and the depth to six feet, and this continues to the tenth mile. From this the depth goes on decreasing till, at the fifteenth mile from the mouth, three feet can hardly be got at high tide. Therefore a spot about a mile below a place called Mars, which is itself three and a half miles below Surian Jump, is the highest point which can be reached under the most favourable circumstances. At this place the river has a hard, sandy bed, with clay banks, which are, however, very high in places, and would have to be cut down. From the foregoing, it is evident that though it might be practicable, by taking advantage of the tide, to make use of this river, the precariousness of its depth, and the extra trouble of transferring men and stores, would make the advantage to be derived from its use problematical.

The points on the coast, therefore, at which it would be possible to disembark are Sonmiani, Ormarah, Pusni, Gwadur, and the Dasht River. Between these, regarded as places of debarkation, there is not much to choose; all are indifferent, and therefore any selection would have to be determined more by the convenience of the routes leading into the interior,—a consideration which would reduce the number of suitable landing-places to only two, viz., Pusni and the Dasht River.

Sonmiani, though comparatively a good port, has the disadvantage of being situated very far to the east, while Ormarah and Gwadur have certain advantages with counter-balancing disadvantages. Both are doubtless the sites of towns, the inhabitants of which would be able to give a certain amount of assistance in the way of labour and supplies, and they have good water. But it is pretty certain that the people would flock to whatever point work was secured to them, and therefore their first advantage would cease, and their water supply is not sufficiently good to compensate for the comparative unsuitability of the roads leading to the interior.

All our packages being ready, we sent off our servants and traps early on the morning of the 3rd; we ourselves followed in the afternoon, determining each to make a short march the first day. Captain Lockwood took a course to the west, round the head of the west bay; while my course lay north, along the shore of the east bay. We were both loath to part from each other and from our kind host, Major Mockler; three months of sufficiently wild and trying travels had sufficed to rub off from us that crust of selfishness and priggishness which all civilized beings interpose between each other, more or less, in their intercourse, and we had got down into the real stuff beyond, and appreciated it; and in the case of our host, six days' constant intercourse had not shown us in him anything but what was gentlemanly and kind, thoughtful and considerate. And now we were all three to part, while at least two of us could not say when we should see an English face again. I do not know that we were very sad, for our hearts were beating high in the thought that we were actually beginning the enterprise we had come thousands of miles to commence; but I think there was just a little lump in our throats as, with the undemonstrativeness of our race, we shook hands and uttered the one word on which more people ponder than on perhaps any other in our language—Good-bye. So I turned east and Lockwood west, and we had started. My road lay at first over the seashore, and the refreshing sound of the waves kept my thoughts cheery; for to me there is nothing sad in the sea waves,—as long, that is, as they break on the shore; they seem, in their ceaseless life and bustle, to read one a lesson that it is always well to be up and doing something; for a man who lets himself remain still, either mentally or physically, stagnates like standing water. No, there is nothing sad in the sea waves as long as one is on shore, but if boxed up in a ship it is quite the contrary, and to me there is nothing more dreary and dismal than an interminable waste of waters seen from the deck of a ship leaving the beach. The track, then, led over a hard, level plain, covered with innumerable little shells; and at the fifth mile we came to one of the mud volcanoes which are, I believe, peculiar to this part of the coast.

This one, the name of which was Durrya Cham, is very small compared with the great mud volcano of Chundra Gup described by Captain Hart, but in its characteristics it is similar. It consisted of a crater formed of dried mud, and within on the centre was a basin of liquid mud, which ever and anon bubbled up with a faint sound. While I was there the bubbles were very small, and at long intervals; but the man with me said that sometimes the mud rose up and ran over the sides of the crater; these latter, indeed, being composed of evidently the same mud baked by the sun, testified to the accuracy of the fellow's assertion.

I notice that Captain Ronald Campbell mentions that the Mohammedans believe that the working of these volcanoes is affected by the tides, and Colonel Goldsmid confirms this theory, believing that the sea is the immediate agency in creating the bubbles, and he thinks that many of the "Shor" hills which abound on this coast probably exhibited similar appearances to these mud volcanoes until the receding waters of the ocean ceased to act on them.

Uninfluenced by such causes, they fell into shrivelled and furrowed heaps, bored through and through with cavities.

Going on from this we soon came to the broken spurs of the Koh-i-Mahdi, a singular-looking hill, which forms a most picturesque item in the landscape round Gwadur. This hill, which is about four hundred feet high, is formed of clay, and its sides have been so "furrowed and scooped out" by rain, and, perhaps, also crumbled by the intense heat, that it now assumes the most fantastic shapes, rising, as Major Lovett says, into pinnacles and towers, looking in the distance like the ruins of some vast decaying town or fort. The highest peak is a sugar loaf rock at the east end, nearly four hundred feet in height, and from its furrowed sides resembling the remains of some Gothic architecture, it is now known as the Cathedral Rock. This range, which is about four miles in length from east to west, is quite isolated, and probably owes its origin to some volcanic eruption.

Winding through rugged and sharp-edged ridges of water-worn mud, we came to our camp on the other side of the Koh-i-Mahdi hill. It was placed in a little open space, with a few stunted trees near a small pond of water,—the only excuse for halting at such a spot. From it there is a good view of the Nigor plain and the Durram Koh ridge, which here runs parallel with the sea-coast, about twelve miles distant. The highest point is called Mukh, and it is said to be 1,550 feet in height. It decreases in height north of the Mahdi ridge, and ends suddenly in a remarkable notch, or rather two perpendicular steps called Gurr. From the west, at the point where the

The Koh-i-Mahdi, Gwadur.

Durram Koh

Tankh route turns it, to where the road from Kuppar goes between it and the Chilari Koh, a distance of not less than forty miles, this range cannot be crossed, unless, perhaps, by footmen, cutting off the Kolanch valley from the Nigor plain on its south.

On the 4th January we did not get off till rather late, owing to the dilatoriness of the sowar, Gholam Kadir, who had been sent with me by Major Mockler. This gentleman did not appreciate early rising, and so delayed the start as much as he could. The road lay over a dreary, hard plain, of the nature called "pat" in Sind. The sun was very hot, and to make it more pleasant, at Barambab, a ravine with a little water in it, I had to wait for nearly two hours before my camels came up to enable me to have breakfast. This ravine, which emanates from the Durram range, falls into the sea about twenty miles east of Gwadur. When I was there, there were some pools of brackish water, in one of which I bathed, or rather tried to bathe; but before I got far into the pool I sank so suddenly in the mud, that it was only with a tremendous bound that I got out of it again. So I then contented myself with taking water from the edge, and there laving my heated limbs, without again trusting to its treacherous bottom.

Going on from this, we soon crossed the bed of the Kurwad Khor, a ravine which joins with the Barambab before it reaches the sea; and then got into a labyrinth of low hills, from which we did not emerge till the eighth mile was accomplished, when crossing a low ridge the trees of the village of Kuppar were seen about a mile distant. This is a miserable hovel, but as that goes without saying regarding any place in Balochistan, I will not worry my readers by the damnable iteration which would be necessary if I gave a true account of every collection of hovels met with in my travels in this country. It was not long before I found that no more favourable adjectives could be applied to any place in this region than "miserable" or "wretched;" and that whatever is worth seeing—and that is little enough in Balochistan—is not owing to man, but nature. The chief (?) of this place is one of the natives who are paid by our Government for looking after the telegraph line, which passes close by to Pusni, and he was sufficiently civil to me, doing what he could, which was little enough. However, if he did not do much for me, I had the great satisfaction of feeling I had done a good deal for his people. I had probably spent the largest sum ever known to have been expended in his village, except, perhaps, by two or three former travellers; and I had afforded all of them the greatest intellectual treat they had enjoyed for years. An opportunity of this sort was not to be lost, so the whole village came and sat round me in rows, drinking in the amusement afforded by my sayings and doings slowly and pleasantly, and, let us hope, also with becoming benefit to their mental appetite.

5th January.—To-day Gholam Kadir, who had been nominated my factotum, managed to start by six, having the night before called all his gods to witness that he was determined to get off before four. In fact, as he said, "Four! what's four? if you wish me I will go at two! one! now!" The reason of this order for an early start was, I hope, a pardonable dislike to sitting in the sun for two hours, an infliction I endured the day before, while waiting for breakfast;

such basking must be condemned alike in the interests of one's digestion, temper, and health. Not having slept a wink all night, I was enabled to feel what a struggle was going on in Gholam Kadir's mind as the dawn gradually broke. The night before he had asserted that any hour was the same to him for starting; he was now no less consistent—Irish fashion, it is true—in that he still remained of the same opinion, but his reckoning was reversed; seven would do as well as six perhaps, he now thought. However, when I put my head out of the tent he was gone, and the first bit of news which greeted me was that one of the camels had run away, and I was thus left to provide another at the last moment. Turning to one of my friends of last night, it was satisfactory to find he was equal to the occasion; he would, he said, provide a camel or camels—on payment, he added. "Of course," I remarked, "on payment." I readily consented, and enquired what I had to pay. "Five rupees," he answered modestly. No doubt some millionaire had been travelling in these parts, for the rupee had become most seriously depreciated. As far as I could see, the rupee in Balochistan is equal to about sixpence; a depreciation which, if it extends to India, will cause the English to follow Gladstone's considerate advice to the Turks, and be "off bag and baggage."

Leaving a representative behind to conclude as little a one-sided bargain as he could, I went on, and passing between the mat hovels of which the village is formed, soon came to the low ridge which encloses Kuppar on the east. The nature of these hills cannot fail to strike one forcibly.

This is a country in which there certainly is a minimum of rainfall, yet the whole country affords endless proofs of having been shaped by water. This is especially the case with the hills; they are generally composed of a whitish clay (which is very slippery when wet, and when dry forms into a perfectly impalpable powder on the slightest pressure), and the wonderful shapes into which they are worn can only have arisen by the action of water. Beyond this ridge is a plain stretching without intermission to the Kondasol ridge, which, though really twenty miles off, looked quite near. About half way, the Sowr creek is crossed. It is passable at low water by a slippery ford, but when the tide is in it is converted into a deep insuperable obstacle some seventy yards wide. Here I halted to have breakfast, and luckily I had some sweet water with me, as all here was quite salt. In Balochistan it is, indeed, a very necessary precaution always to take with you on every stage as much sweet water as you can carry.

The heat of the sun during the nine miles I had to go after breakfast was very trying, and the glare on the white plain traversed very great. At Kumbi I waited under a tree in the hopes my other camels would come up in time to enable me to go on a few miles further, but as they did not do so till past three, it became impossible to begin another march, and so I halted at that place.

From here I sent off a letter Mockler had very kindly given me for Mir Kamalan, a Gichki chief whom he had strongly recommended to me as a pleasant companion and a trustworthy follower for my journey. The amount of negotiation which proved necessary before any one could be procured to undertake to carry this letter would have sufficed to settle the Eastern Question.

Up to this it seemed that my powers of description would not be called much into requisition. The whole country is composed of a white clay, which in the hills assumes the most diverse and fantastic shapes, while on the plains it makes up for its previous contortions by assuming an unvarying dead level, which would satisfy the greatest advocate of a seniority system. The villages, too, do not give one a chance; in the first place there are none, and in the second the few hovels seen are invariably formed throughout of very dilapidated matting, which no word-painting can colour into picturesqueness.

I had now come fifty miles from Gwadur, and had only passed about ten hovels, and there was not the slightest sign of any villages between the sea and the hills.

What water these people do use (and the consumption, seeing that no one ever washes, and much drinking would bring on dysentery, cannot be great), they seem to collect by the construction of very rude dams on the lines of drainage. Yet there is probably abundance of water to be had for the digging, and as the soil is good, there appears no reason why these desolate and unpeopled clay plains should not one day teem with life. The climate too, so the head man of Kuppar said, is not so bad, *i.e.*, he means there *are* worse places. Kej, he says, is hotter, and I should think the whole of Upper Sind was greatly more so.

But with all the disagreeables of this uninteresting country, I was certainly much better off here than I was on our trip through Armenia. Here I have very decent servants, there I had a fiend named Husain, whom I am sure could never have got so many bad qualities into his small body without some dealings with the devil. What more need be said? It is strange what apparent trivialities change the whole nature of things. We all know the enthusiastic lover of nature who regards, or says he regards, not food, or sleep, if only he may enjoy nature's majestic scenes. Yet what heaven could be heaven long where—everything else perfect—one had to eat Husain's "pillaos" at eight, and be eaten at nine by—Armenia's unrivalled breed of fleas!

6th January.—On waking this morning the pleasing intelligence which must so often have been conveyed to former travellers in these detestable regions, was brought to me,—"One of the camels is missing." I was in a philosophical state, induced by a long night without sleep, so all I said was, "Then get another." Another was got, after I had left a man behind for the purpose, and he had paid down five rupees for the day's march of about thirty miles, *i.e.*, about 1,000 per cent. more than the most extortionate camel driver in India would ask. I don't know why it is so, but I believe it to be a fact, that the more apparently unsophisticated a savage is, the harder bargain he will drive with you. True sometimes in savagedom you get things wonderfully cheap, but that only proceeds from ignorance; let the noble aboriginal once get an inkling that his sheep has a value, and he will ask a price that would never even suggest itself to the most rapacious London butcher.

Having got under weigh, at last we made for the south end of a queer-shaped ridge called Kundasol, and rounding it, entered on an interminable plain only broken by the isolated hill of Jabl Zerin, which appeared like a speck in the far east. This ridge, I have no doubt, was once a plain unpretending offshoot from its parent range the Chakuli Koh, but it has been converted by some convulsion of nature into a state of the most extraordinary confusion, looking as if charges of dynamite had been placed at intervals along its whole length, and, exploding, had upheaved what was once a uniform ridge into a series of lateral ridges like a fallen flight of steps.

From this the road went for twenty miles over a level plain of hard white clay thickly encrusted with a layer of shells. It then entered a series of sand hills, over which we floundered painfully right into Pusni. Though we were only at the beginning of January, the heat of the sun and the glare from the white plain combined made the ride most disagreeable, and I was glad once more to see a sign of civilisation in the spacious buildings erected by the British Government near the seashore for the staff of the Persian telegraphs. One hears of dynasties of Boledis, Gichkis, etc., in these parts; of their power, and their magnificence; yet there can be no doubt that none of these, in their highest glory, or even in their wildest dreams, could ever have imagined, far less accomplished, the erection of such a building as this, built simply for a few telegraph clerks.

Arriving here, I took upon myself to appropriate to my own use whatever the building contained, and though it was only three days since I left the hospitable roof of Major Mockler, I thoroughly enjoyed the luxury of having somewhere withal to put what nature had provided me to sit upon, while, too, admitting one can get through the night lying on the ground, I must confess a bed is preferable.

I had hardly arrived, and had not yet had a bath, when the principal man of these parts came to pay his respects, and to have a stare at the newly-arrived Faringi.

This gentleman, Mir Bahram by name, was chief of the Kulmuttis, and is said by an enthusiastic official who visited Pusni some years ago, to boast a descent of 2,000 years,—an antiquity before which even I, as one of the "ancient MacGregors," must bow. I think when one talks of a chief of such antiquity coming to pay one a visit, the average stay-at-home reader is apt to imagine an individual of noble and dignified mien, arriving, say, on a blood Arab mare, with gorgeous trappings, and surrounded by a glittering galaxy of wild but magnificent-looking warriors, with a few slaves bearing his jewel-inlaid arms and shield and pipe. On this occasion, at all events, this was not the case, and truth demands that I should say that Mir Bahram was an elderly and sufficiently good-looking gentleman, but dressed in a long dirty nightgown, followed by some thirty others also in nightgowns, which were likewise far from clean. After exchanging the usual Baloch salutations, which, notwithstanding that I had been learning them by heart the day before, I had some difficulty in emitting, we proceeded to more mundane matters. The modes of address common amongst the Baloches are unusually long and tedious, as is apt to be the case with people to whom time is no object, to whom, in fact, any way of killing that said commodity is a god-send. First you say "Salam alik," and receive as an answer, "Salam alik." Next comes "Wushut," but as this is Greek to many of my readers, I will give it in English. Say A and B meet, they say simultaneously, "Peace be with you," "On you be peace"; then, "Welcome." Then they plod through the regular string of questions "Are you well?" "Are you quite well?" "Is it yourself that's well?"* "Are your people well?" "Is your brother well?" "Is your wife well?" Then one says, "Khabar dih" ("Tell us news"), and the other answers, "By the grace of God all is well," and so on. This excessively long mode of salutation could not, of course, survive a day among people who had anything to do, and even in the East it is often considered a bore; the only thing the people really want to know being the news.

7th January.—Next morning the first thing I did was to rid myself of Gholam Kadir, who had proved a regular incubus, weighing heavily upon me for the last four days, and thwarting all my arrangements. Major Mockler, with the best intentions, had very kindly furnished me with this man as a sort of orderly, and I had agreed to double his usual rate of pay, advancing him one month before starting; in return for which he was to act as interpreter and make himself generally useful. This agreement he appeared to consider sufficiently fulfilled if he took my best camel for his own sole use, and rode ahead of me so far that I could never speak a word to him; and when I ventured to remonstrate, he informed me, in an insolent manner, that he was doing what he agreed to, and if I did not like his ways he would be glad to return; so return he did. The fact is, from reading the reports of St. John, Lovett, and others, I was prepared to expect something of this sort, and I had

* Traces of Hibernia here.

originally therefore telegraphed to Kurrachi to have some Sind camel-men sent to me; but dissuaded by Mockler's assuring me I should have no bother with the men of the country, I weakly yielded, and started trusting to the good graces of this gentleman.

Afterwards I went out to have a look round. I was at first unable to see anything but sand hills; but having got the general direction of the village, I at last found it, nestled in a labyrinth of sand heaps. I notice a former traveller describes Pusni as a miserable spot, and I certainly quite agree with him; I should call it *the* "most miserable spot" if my memory did not remind me I had so often thought that of other places; and then to say a place is the most wretched place one ever saw, would not be very intelligible without a foot-note giving a few specimens of the disagreeable places one had seen; at all events, I may say I cannot recall at this moment a more uninviting locality. Yet it is said by the well-informed to have been one of the points at which that most sorely tried of admirals, Nearchus, touched as he was wending his weary way along the unlovely shore of Mekran. Beyond this tradition there is nothing, I think, of any interest in the place, and the most wonderful fact that I can chronicle regarding it is, that there is said to be an officer of the Telegraph Department, who, having been here once, wishes to come again. I do not vouch for the truth of this report, and am inclined to doubt it, as the officers of the telegraph I have met have always been sensible persons.

I had now to engage other men to look after the camels, and I wished also to buy another riding camel or two. In order to accomplish this I had to go through a most tedious amount of negotiation. Bargaining is a great nuisance at the best of times, and I always think a people more or less civilised according as they abstain from it, and content themselves with naming one price; but bargaining with a Baloch is of all kinds the worst; first, if he understands any known tongue, such as Persian or Hindustani, he always speaks it in a fashion that no one can comprehend him; then he is densely stupid, except when he sees his way to getting a shilling for three pennyworth. Several camel-drivers presented themselves for service, and I at last took an old man who declared he had been with the British in the Afghan campaign, and also in Sind in the Miani days. He did not seem to know anything, and I was not very much taken with my bargain, which was to give him three times more than he was worth; but he assured me that after I had tried him for a few days I should wonder at my luck in possessing such a treasure.

I had thought of taking a picture of Pusni, and got out my apparatus for the purpose; but the utter mockery of the thing then struck me, for to photograph a sand-hill would be mere waste of time and material. Any of my readers can make a model of Pusni for himself next time he visits the seashore, or I dare say his bairns would do it for him with pleasure. On one side is the sea, and as this is the same anywhere, you have half the picture; then make a lot of sand-heaps of any shape, any size, in any position you like, and you have Pusni.

In the evening the chief of the ancient clan of Kulmuttis came again to see me, this time with fewer be-nightgowned followers. If his hair was cut, his beard trimmed and allowed to remain its natural white, this old gentleman would be quite nice-looking; his features are good, and his expression when speaking open and pleasant. According to his account, his kingdom does not bring him in much: he has some precarious cultivation up the Shadi Khor, and he owns one boat; but his largest source of revenue is the payment he receives from the Telegraph Department for not knocking down the line. This amounts to about fifty rupees per mensem—an enormous sum in these parts. He was very anxious I should buy one of his camels, only paying twice its value; and perhaps I might have been green enough to have done so, had he not actually proposed I should pay for it first and have it sent after me. I confess I am generally easily taken in. If any one tells me a fairly lucid and consistent lie, with sufficient earnestness, I always credit the man. In fact, one of my pet theories is, You should always believe in people till you find them out, and then never again trust them. But Bahram's proposal was too much even for my verdancy. Fancy the splendid animal that (if any) would have come hopping out to me on three legs!

Talking of Bahram's allowance reminds me of a report I have been reading, in which I was much amused to find him recommended for a share of the payments which were to be made for the care of the line, because, in the opinion of the official who made the suggestion, "it would be nice to encourage the descendant of people who saw Alexander's fleet anchor in their bay"! Well, well, many a man gets on far better than he deserves because one of his ancestors once did something sufficiently famous, or infamous, to be rewarded with a peerage; but this is carrying the claims of blue blood a little too far.

CHAPTER II.

BALOCHISTAN WILDS.

8th January.—I got off this morning with some difficulty. It is always troublesome to move servants out of good quarters, and it was 7.30 before we started. The road goes up the bed of the Shadi Khor the whole way, and is very good indeed. There is plenty of excellent water on its bed after about five miles from the coast, and there is a great abundance of fuel and camel forage. The latter is taken from the "Gaz," or tamarisk, and acacia trees. There are also a great number of the "Jaor" bush, which has a very pretty pink flower, but which has the evil reputation of being poisonous to camels. I only made about ten miles to-day, in a direction generally north, as I had to wait for a camel which I wished to buy. We passed one or two miserable patches of cultivation, which were all withering up from want of rain, or rather from lack of sufficient enterprise and intelligence on the part of the cultivators; for close by, not more than twenty feet below the level of these fields, was an ample supply of water in the river. The name of our camp was Laz Bent, situated just under the Talo hill, and a curious off-shoot of it called Koh-i-Sukhta. From here a road goes by a bit of cultivation called Gazdar to Kalmat, a place to the east of Pusni on the coast.

Mir Bahram rode out with me, and asked me for a letter setting forth the important services he had performed for me. As, however, he had done nothing at all, it was somewhat difficult to word such a letter, strict regard being had to the truth. However I gave him one, which I tried to model on a celebrated testimonial which the late Major James once gave to some chief on the Peshawur frontier. He evidently could not say much for his moral character, as he was reduced to certifying that the bearer was a very fine-looking fellow. So I recorded that Mir Bahram was a very pleasant-mannered old gentleman, and *seemed* very open and honest. Much good may it do him! After all, one pens these sort of testimonials more for the sake of those who may come after one, in the hope that they may receive a little extra civility in return. I also gave him a very nice clasp knife, which I should have been very glad to have received as a present myself; but he evidently did not think much of it or of me. I suppose some gentleman backed with the wealth of the Government of India had been bestowing upon him better things; so I shall be regarded in Bahram's heart of hearts as a somewhat stingy individual. This Indian custom of tendering presents every time you go near a chief is a very silly one, which it is high time should be abolished. If presents are really given as a reward for some service done, or from the same source as gratitude is said to spring, well and good; but it seems to me that Government is a steady loser by the system. At all events, in these countries it makes it very difficult for a private traveller to get along at all without half ruining himself. I often felt in Persia that such and such an individual expected a present, which I was not always able to give. In fact, as one never can spare one's own articles, so unless one lays in a regular supply of presents before starting, one is obliged to ignore the "donative" part of the business. Thus it was in Persia; I was on arrival at the Caspian completely cleared out; my watch, my sword, all my guns, and my pistols, besides numerous little things, had disappeared.

9th January.—My march to-day was from this somewhat fertile spot, called, as before stated, Laz Bent; the latter word meaning cultivation in the Baloch dialect. The road was very good for the most of the way, going up the Shadi Khor, till we got abreast of the Talo ridge, when it left the river, and then crossing a plain covered with tamarisk, entered a labyrinth of low hillocks, called Andarok, through which it wound. Here it was in places very narrow, but it could easily be widened to any extent, as the soil is very soft and friable. This ridge once passed, another small plain is crossed leading again to the river, which had made a bold sweep out to the east to round the ridge, and then, foiled as it were in its attempt to find an outlet in this direction, it came back west, hugging the north foot of the Talo ridge. At the point where the road regains the river is a place called "Dokani," *i.e.*, shop, a name probably given to it by some jocose Baloch,—on the same principle that a negro is often called snowball, there being of course no sign of any shop anywhere. The banks of the ravine at this point are very high and steep, so much so that the bed becomes a defile; but the road was very good. From Dokani a road goes off to the south-west to Kolanch.

On the way I passed, in more than one place, curious circles of stones, with two or three set up in the centre. These, I was told, it was the custom to place round happy bridegrooms on their way to be married. The fortunate youth stands in the centre, while musicians and friends play round him, and offer him ironical congratulations on his luck; and then stones are arranged to commemorate the event. Continuing up the ravine, I arrived at Ghoramani Bent in fourteen and a half miles. The ravine latterly became more and more filled with the "pish" (dwarf palm), a shrub which is as useful to the Baloch as the bamboo is to the Burman. From this the former makes ropes, sandals, pipes, matting, and a variety of other articles for his house, etc. The matting is for the most part of a good description, but I cannot say I admire the sandals, which wear out in a day's march, and the rope also never lasts more than a day or two. The fact is the Baloch is a philosopher; he says, if a bit of rope will last two or three days, what more do you want? who knows what will happen in four? The pipe is a very novel article, and I commend it to the Editor of that invaluable book, "The Art of Travel." It is made by rolling a leaf of the "pish" in a conical form, and then holding it in the hand to smoke.

10*th January.*—The road to-day commenced by going up the Shadi Khor ravine for an hour, when it left it and got on to some high ground to the north. I was very glad to find myself once more able to look round; travelling in a defile has a depressing effect, and it is fatal to survey operations. Once on the high plateau which lies above the ravine, I got a capital view in every direction, and saw that the Talo ridge is continuous with a range to the north, which seems to be the third ridge between us and the Kej valley. To the south-east, a range stretched away to the east from Dokani, apparently as far as the Dasht River. Crossing this terrace in a north-west direction, in half an hour I came abreast of the first of the three ridges mentioned above, and in an hour further arrived at the second. Before, however, entering this latter, we descended into a ravine called Gharki Khor, which had great abundance of good water, and an inexhaustible supply of fuel and camel forage, and also some coarse grass. Here I breakfasted in the shade of the scarped bank.

Soon after starting again, we entered the second range, and continued wandering about over successive ridges for three hours, descending occasionally to cross ravines, some of which appeared to come from the high range beyond, and some smaller ones to convey the drainage of the second range. As there was a difficulty about one of the camel loads, I was unable to get further than the Sohraf ravine, distant 18 miles 5 furlongs, though I had hoped to reach Pidark. I found afterwards that I ought to have gone up the Gharki Khor to Tump, whence there is a more direct road to Balgatar.

On the way, I made the acquaintance of one of those queer characters one only meets, I think, in Asia,—a wandering Hindu Guru, who had been in these parts for thirty years, and who had, according to his own account, travelled nearly everywhere between the Oxus and the sea. Whether he had done so or not, I cannot say, but he certainly showed a wonderful knowledge of the parts he declared himself to have visited; and as Orientals do not go through much geographical instruction, the only way he could have heard of the places he mentioned, and regarding which his information was, as far as I could judge, accurate, was by having actually been there himself. As he might be useful to me, and he himself professed the most profound indifference as to where he went, I took him in tow, just to test him, and see to what purpose he might be turned. At all events I thought he might be of some use as an interpreter, and if fairly honest, his knowledge of the Baloch character might prove of some service. To-day I was in despair at having lost my shaving brush. I dare say some of my readers will laugh at such an avowal, but we all have our pet luxuries and weaknesses, and I must say I think life always seems to me different if I have been unable to shave.

I forgot to mention an amusing circumstance which happened before I said good-bye to Mir Bahram. I had asked him for a guide who would take me at least as far as Kej, and he had complied, and was giving the man his final instructions in Baloche. I do not speak that language, but it is so like Persian, that I can make out sufficient to follow the meaning to a certain extent, and I think what the old gentleman was saying might be freely translated as follows:—"Now, you are to go with the Sahib, wherever he wants, to Kej if he wishes, or to Kolwah." At this the guide put his two fingers to his eyes, as expressing his readiness to do either.

Then Mir Bahram said, "You know he will ask you the name of every hill, every river, and every hut you see; so mind you tell him." Guide: "What does he want to know for?" Mir Bahram: "Heaven only knows! these sahibs always do that; they ask the name of everything, and then write it down." Guide: "Very good. The ravines, you know, have names, but how am I to name all the hills?" Bahram: "Call them anything you like, he will write it down." However, the sequel proved the guide was not an inventive genius; when he knew the name he told it at once, but when he did not, he showed so evidently he was thinking what the deuce he would say, that I never paid any attention to the information he eventually volunteered. The fact is that, though they have names for the ravines they are in the habit of traversing, and for the halting places and cultivation on those ravines, as well as for many other places connected with some event in local history, they, generally speaking, have no appellations for hills, and especially for ranges, nor have they any idea of the connection of mountains with each other, or of any system of drainage. Indeed, it would be wonderful if it were otherwise, as these hills are most intricate and confused in their ramifications; so much so, that nothing short of a regular, careful survey could give anything more than a general idea of their direction and extent.

11*th January.*—I started this morning much pleased with myself, for I had made an arrangement with the Hindu Guru aforementioned, to come on with me and show the road. I considered in doing this I was performing a most intelligent operation. I was much struck with his apparent knowledge of these parts, and thought to have him with me was a great catch, and so mounting him on a camel he led the way gallantly, and as far as Pidark, some six miles, we went on very well. This, the first village we had seen since leaving Pusni, is situated on the south of an extensive and dense grove of date palms. The houses are all the most miserable constructions of matting, and the people seemed to me about as wretched looking a lot as I had seen. There is a queer-looking fort here, which I suppose is looked on as the very perfection of fortification. Its outline has no particular shape, being something between a square and a circle; but the grand feature is that it is, as it were, three forts within each other. First you enter and find yourself in a sort of circus ride, about forty feet wide; then on a mound is another wall, and inside that again is the fort, which looks like a high house, with a nondescript tower at one of the angles. The walls are all very thin, and are built of mud. They are loop-holed, but would hardly even stop a bullet. I dare say to any ordinary Baloch commander such a place would appear so well-nigh impregnable, that after having fired a shot or two at it, he would retire to the nearest spring and hope to catch a few stragglers from the garrison; having killed them, he would doubtless write a despatch describing a battle.

Leaving Pidark without seeing its chief, who was probably better employed than getting up on a cold morning to welcome a stray Faringi, we came to a Zikri shrine about a mile off to the west, under a hillock called Koh-i-Morad. It consisted merely of a mud dome with a few old flags stuck on it, so that there is nothing peculiar about the shrine, but about the Zikris there is. They are also called Dai Mazhabis, and, as far as I can make out, they do not believe in Mahomed, or in any one else, and some of their rites seem to be of the most bestial nature.

I think a work on the curiosities of religion would be interesting. The varieties of beliefs in the world are never ending and always changing, and what one man honestly thinks will save him, his neighbour has no doubt will damn him; I wonder who is right, Jew, Christian, Mahomedan, Hindu, Feetishman, or Confucian?

From the shrine we reached some high ground from which there is a good view of the country, and I therefore sent on the luggage, and stayed to get some bearings. To the north the view is entirely closed by a long ridge, which runs east and west; and to the south, there is another ridge, parallel to it at a distance of some miles. To the east, again, the view is intercepted by a series of low spurs from the north ridge, which run out beyond Pidark; while to the west all is open, and there is no sign of any range. At the foot of the north range is a long bare glacis slope, extending right down to the Shadi Khor, but it is so much cut up by ravines as to be entirely impracticable except along their beds or on the crests of the dividing watersheds. When I got up to my people they were crossing a ravine, and as there was some water there, I stopped and breakfasted. Starting again, we soon began to rise amid a labyrinth of low hills, till after ascending and descending several spurs we got over the main ridge by an easy pass. Up to this my friend the Guru was leading; then he declared his camel would not go, so I gave him another, but that was no better, and he still continued to lag behind. Forcing him, however, to come on ahead and assume his proper place, he did so with a bad grace, and made a great show of beating his camel, and then seeing him looking about him on all sides, I began to suspect something was wrong, and as he soon began to lead us without any apparent meaning, now right, now left, at last I accused him of not knowing where the road was. He laughed scornfully, and said, "This is the road; you must not expect cart roads in Mekran." Still it seemed to me that we were going a great deal too much west, and as there was nothing in the appearance of the hills to the north to account for this, I felt sure he was at fault. Well, after wandering about for a couple of hours, I took the lead out of his hands, and tried what I could make of it. Before long we came on a shepherd, and learned it was as I had thought,—we had been going in quite the wrong path. The road to Sami was in the direction I had taken, but as it was too far off to reach that night, we had to make the best of it, and bivouac by the first water. This was the end of my friend the Guru; he said no more about his knowledge of the country, and afterwards confessed he had lost the way an hour before I spoke to him. We ought to have turned off north-east at the pass over the main range, and gone by a road called Kapot Karung, which led almost direct to Sami; as it was we went north-west, and had to double back in the direction of Shahrak, a small village on the right bank of the Kilkhor. About four miles west from Sami, whence a road goes by Shoraki and Keysak over the north range of the Kej valley to Koshk.

After crossing the ridge there are two roads, one called Lakori and the other Maskkani,—both equally bad.

12*th January.*—This morning, by the aid of a friendly shepherd, we very soon found the way out of the hills, and then we discovered that we were not more than four miles east of the village of Dowlut, but had still a long march before us to Sami. I was disappointed to find this part of the Kej valley, which I had heard described in glowing terms, a most utterly desolate waste of stones, varied, rather than relieved, by scattered "pish" bushes. When some three miles off Sami I halted, and sent my man on to give notice of my arrival, while I had breakfast. After which we had not gone far up the ravine when I was met by a man sent to show me the way. I found a servant I had despatched in advance had not given any notice, and so my tent was pitched in the open, on a very bad and public spot, where all the villagers had to pass to and fro in front of it. Ere long, however, an old man came with some others, made his salaam, and introduced himself as Mir Kamálán. When he first arrived he had his face covered up with his turban, after the usual manner of Baloches, but after a bit he took off his coverings, and displayed a very benevolent, straightforward-looking countenance, which made me think that Mockler's recommendation of him had not been too favourably worded.

This individual is the Naib, or Deputy of Mir Isa of Panjgur, with whom he is connected in some way. He was very civil to me, and did all he could to make me comfortable, and put out sentries to keep off the village crowd from incommoding me.

The next day, the 13th, I went all round the fortifications of Sami, but as they were neither very extensive nor very intricate, it did not take long. The village is situate in a dense grove of palms, and consists of the usual wretched mud and matting architecture, common to this part of the world.

Here I bought another camel, which turned out a very good one. I paid, I think, only eighty rupees for it.

On the 14th I started again, and went first of all to look at a place in the Ghishhor ravine which Mir Kamálán said made it perfectly impracticable. We went for some six or eight miles over the stony bed of the ravine, and then came to one of those places which they call in these parts "abgirs," and sometimes "gat." It consisted of a large deep pool, with the hills on either side coming right into it perpendicularly. So seeing this place was quite impracticable, I determined on trying the road through Balgatar which Mir Kamálán recommended, and we turned south-east and crossed the bed of the river to Hirok, a place with a small patch of cultivation on the left bank of the Kilkhor. I went down in the evening to the bank of the river to have a talk with Mir Kamálán about the people of Panjgur. I did not give him the slightest hint as to what I was going to do, but wished to find out what sort of people I would have to deal with. He was very communicative, and told me all he knew, and that a report had come in to say that Azad Khan of Kharan had come down, and was attacking the Khan of Kalat's Naib in the chief village of Panjgur. This news was important and disagreeable, as Azad Khan was said to be an enemy of ours, and would very likely throw difficulties in our way, even if he did

Kirok.

nothing more disagreeable. Still I saw no way of accomplishing my object except by starting from Panjgur, and I determined to risk it. When we were down at the river that evening, there was not a drop of water in it, but during the evening it came on to pour in torrents, and we all passed a most wretched night, as I had to have the whole party into my tent.

15th.—In the morning I went down to the river, which I could hear roaring in the night, and found a torrent not less than a quarter of a mile broad, going at a pace which put all idea of fording it out of the question, so we had to wait till it ran down.

Besides, after such a night it would have been absurd to have gone on. Even if I had so wished, humanity to the wretched drenched natives demanded a halt, besides the fact that everything I had to my name was soaking wet, and though my camels could carry the things when dry, they could not lift them when wet. Therefore we got everything out on to the ground, and sat down to clean up all the guns, etc., and warm ourselves. The sun was so delightful, that I basked in it for hours, and wrote half-a-dozen letters, little thinking of any after evil effects from my imprudence.

This place Hirok is for Balochistan rather pretty; the extensive foreground of green foliage making the monotonous brown of the hills less oppressive than usual, and the torrent which roared and foamed a short way off added a new feature to this scene. The cultivation here extends for a length of about three-quarters of a mile, by a quarter of a mile broad, along the left bank of the river, and it was the largest cultivated tract I had yet seen in the country.

On the road we passed a village named Kalag, situated about a mile off under the hills, and surrounded with a date grove. At Hirok two ravines come down from the hills called Chari Gwadur and Tari Gwadur; up the former a road goes south over the main ridge, by the Koh-i-Haft Tabaki to Tump, but it is said to be only practicable for footmen. To the north of the Kilkhor is a range called Koh-i-Kanarak.

Next day, the 16th January, we did not get away very early, as I had to send a man to ascertain whether the river was fordable. He came back and said the first ford was practicable, and he thought the others might be; so I determined to make a try, getting off about nine. We had a very fatiguing march, all up the bed of the Khor, crossing and recrossing by fords so deep and swift that each seemed impracticable. On leaving we found two small ravines from the south called the Chari Gwadur and the Tari Gwadur, by which the Hirok cultivation is irrigated. We passed through an immense deal of long grass for four miles, and the jungle was thick enough to make it not very easy to pick our way through. At the fourth mile we traversed a patch of cultivation called Orali Bent, and at the sixth another named Tejaban, which is well supplied with water; indeed in one part there is a very rare sight in Balochistan—a considerable reedy swamp. Certainly one peculiarity of this Kilkhor is the immense quantity of vegetation on its banks, consisting chiefly of camel forage, which grows luxuriantly, showing that the water is everywhere pretty near the surface. As far as I had seen yet, it seemed a peculiarity of this country, that all the water-courses are filled with vegetation of some kind or other. In fact, to give an exact picture of the Kej valley, you need only draw a thin green stripe to represent the "Khor," with broad brown stripes on either side, intersected transversely with faint green streaks to indicate the minor drainage lines. We went on up the Khor for about sixteen miles, crossing the Karki, Bungar, Seh, and Chakuri Khors successively, when we came to a halt at a place called Machekhor. I then scrambled up on to some high ground to take a view of the country and get some bearings. Nearly due east there was a narrow opening of not more than ten degrees, and all the rest of the horizon was shut in between hills. North and south ran the two parallel ridges which bound the valley of Kej in these directions. That on the south seemed to end not far off, but the line was taken up by another ridge, running about north-east to south-west; and between these there seemed to be a considerable ravine, which Mir Kamálán informed me was called the Soraf Khor. At the foot of the far range to the south-east is an extensive tract of apparently thick jungle, called Ushaf, and at the foot of the second are grazing-grounds known as the Thal and Shisharedan; but there is no cultivation, nor are habitations visible as far as the eye can see. When thus employed in looking round me, I felt the wind striking very coldly on me, so coldly that I soon bethought me of the cause, and looking at my finger tips I found them quite white, and then I knew I was in for a bout of fever. I was quite unprepared for it; having been free of it from the last day I was in England,—that is, nearly four months,—I thought I was safe, and this belief was strengthened by the splendid state of health I was then in. But the fact is, on the night of the

14th we all got a good ducking, and I had to sleep on the damp ground with wet clothes, in a tent filled with wet natives. Then as we could not move on owing to the height of the river, I seized the opportunity of drying everything. While my tent was being made fit for me, I had to sit in the sun all day, and though I did not feel it at the time, I found now, when it was too late, how imprudent I had been. There was nothing for it but to creep off to my tent, and throwing myself on the still damp ground, to have all my blankets and clothes heaped on the top of me, and endure it as best I could.

17*th*, *Balgatar*.—After passing the night in a high state of fever, I was very glad to see the dawn breaking and to rout up the servants. We got away by six, and went along the banks of the river for over two miles to a place called Rahgiwara, where the road to Kolwah goes on, while our path turned up north to the hills. From this the well-wooded appearance of the river bed changed, and our road lay over a stony slope for two and a half miles to Chetkula, a halting-place with plenty of water, forage, and fuel. From this glacis slope we had a fine view of the country to the south, which was ended by lines of hills,—one range, which we had crossed, to the west, between Pidark and Sami, running pretty nearly east and west, and another apparently distinct range having a direction north-east to south-west. I do not, however, think this last is really a separate ridge, but that it is connected with the other range to the south, behind where they overlap each other. Between the two there is a considerable valley caused by a ravine called the Soraf, and at the foot of the east range is an extensive tract of jungle called

Balgatar.

Ushaf. Further west, at the foot of the other range, is a glacis slope called Thal; and, again, in the same direction, another called Shisharedan. All these slopes are seamed with ravines, and are merely grazing-grounds. There are no villages, and though there may be people scattered about in tents, there are but few, if any, signs of life. A mile further on we got into the Katagehkhor, and went up its bed for more than three miles to the Katag Pass. The road is very easy, the ascent being most gradual. About half way up we came to water, and kept it with us to the top. Here I had two surprises; we were going up very quietly, and it seemed to me we were yet some way off the crest of the ridge, when quite suddenly we popped over a little rise about fifty feet high, and descended. I took the height of this, though I did not think it was the top; but I knew how deceptive these hills are, and I was looking out to see if we did not ascend again, when the guide stopped, and pointing, said, "The road is blocked with water." I looked, and as far as the eye could scan, I saw in the plain below one long sheet of water. Turning to Mir Kamálán for explanation, for I had not expected to see water, he said, "The Kapf is filled by the rain." "Kapf," I afterwards learnt, meant a depression.

Descending the range as easily as we had come up it, we got into the Balgatar plain, a larger expanse of cultivated soil than I had seen since entering the hills from Pusni. As we were riding over this plain I felt the sun very much, my knees began to ache, and I yawned incessantly,—all signs that I was in for another bout of fever. However, I struggled on as long as I could, till we had done eighteen miles, and then I thought "sufficient for the day is the evil thereof," and stopping by a pool of water, I took my blanket and fur-coat off the horse, and putting them over me, lay down in the scanty shade of a tamarisk bush, and laid up. Why describe these delightful moments? Any one familiar with the East knows all about it; the song, "Shivery Shaky, the man that could not get warm," always occurs to me at such moments. We halted at a mound with ruins of an old fort on it, called Kala Dumb. The usual road went due north to Tash, but this was all now blocked by water. All round this basin were hills; on the east the Koh-i-Mahlur, and on the west the Koh-i-Lop.

CHAPTER III.

AZAD KHAN THE BANDIT.

18*th January: Tash.*—As the regular road was impassable, owing to the water, I was obliged to get a guide to take me round it. After the usual amount of delay, one was procured from the neighbouring tents (Khalk), but he, on arrival, quietly sat down, and expressed his determination not to move further till he knew what his "hak" (payment) was to be, and after a good deal of haggling, I agreed to give him two shillings, and so got off by 7.15 a.m. The road led out over the plain nearly due west for six miles, right up to the hills bounding the Balgatar basin on the west, whence it went on over the shoulder of the Koh-i-Lop to Boleda. On the way we passed an encampment of nomads, who came out to see the novel sight of a Faringi, and all, especially the fair sex, passed their remarks with the most perfect candour and want of prudery. We then left the path which goes on to Boleda by the Ghisakhor, and turned a little more north, passing a graveyard. One does not really frequently come across these cities of the dead, but it seems as if one did, as there is so little to notice in this country. For instance, one of my predecessors in Baloch travel argues from what he deems the frequency of the graveyards, that the country was formerly more thickly populated. It may have been, but there is nothing about the graveyards to give colour to the belief, for they only occur, on an average, once in fifteen miles, and they are by no means larger than can be accounted for by taking them to be, what I believe they are, simply the burying-places of the wandering tribes.

Having reached the hills, we skirted round the base of them, where the water had reached its limit, and we now and again had to cross over low ridges, which seemed, like many of the ranges in Balochistan, to be formed of a loose, disintegrated sandstone. One of these low passes was curious, inasmuch as the road went over the top of, and nearly at right angles to, the upraised strata; *i.e.*, supposing the road to be represented by the two lines below, the top strata ran as is represented by the dotted lines.

After following the edge of the water till we had come round due north of our halting-place of last night, we turned north-east, and arrived at Tash after a march of twenty miles, the direct distance not being perhaps more than ten.

The fact is that Balgatar is a lake basin, as it has no outlet anywhere, and it is only because of the small amount of rain, the heat, the proximity of the water-sheds of the surrounding hills, and it may be the absorbent nature of the soil, that there is not a lake there always. The depth of the temporary lake is nowhere great, and it could easily be forded were the bottom not composed of very soft sticky mud, which would prevent any one attempting it. I noted my surprise yesterday at seeing before me a lake, when I had been led to expect no such thing. Both Colonel Ross and Captain Miles had visited Balgatar before me, yet there is not a word in their reports to show that they were at all aware of such a natural feature. I mention this, not by any means in a spirit of carping; on the contrary, I think it shows, what has long been clear to me, that the most careful traveller by no means exhausts the information about a country, and that the best of us are apt to make mistakes. It is true that when these officers were here there was no water in the basin, but still one would imagine they must have been aware of a depression which, at certain seasons, is covered with water for an area of several miles. However, the matter is easily explained; there certainly is a depression, and when pointed out so patently as it was to me, and tested by the aneroid, it was plainly evident. But the fall and rise is, nevertheless, almost imperceptible, and, unless one's attention was called thereto, it would be easy enough to pass by without noticing it; the native guides are so dense as never to be likely to bring such a matter to notice. Though this lake is formed entirely by rain water, and though there is no sign of saltness of the soil along the edges, where it had already dried up when I was there, the ground underneath must certainly be intensely salt, as, though the rain had fallen only two days before, the water had already become so impregnated as to be quite brackish. The plain of Balgatar is very thinly cultivated, though there is little doubt that all of it, above the level of the salt ground, might easily be made to yield good crops, and thus become, what Major Lovett erroneously supposes it already to be, a granary for the surrounding districts. The supply of water, too, would not be an insuperable difficulty, for the formation of the hills, and the gentle slope of the ground, are peculiarly favourable for the construction of any number of reservoirs. But of course all this requires population.

It is rather amusing listening to the conversation between wayfarers, in those parts, for the Baloch is a dead hand at "gup," or gossip, and after he has got safely through his ridiculously lengthy salutations, he always enquires the news. One man to-day, when asked for tidings of Panjgur, said laconically, "Fighting as usual."

I passed a caravan of donkeys going with dates to Kej, and many were the enquiries, "Who is that with the hat?" One individual, on receiving the usual reply, "Faringi," said, "What does he want here?" Reply: "He's come to see the land; he writes down everything. I suppose we shall have these Faringis taking the country soon." "Who's he got with him?" said one ruffian-like scoundrel. "Mir Kamálán," was the reply. "Lucky for him," and then they all laughed. Perhaps it was lucky, yet, as far as I could discover, the country was as safe as a church everywhere,—not a sign of a thief or robber did I see; but it is impossible to say how much of this I owe to the "ikbal" of the Faringi. At all events, I am sure one could not travel with greater safety among the Baloches on our own frontier.

My camp on this day was situated on a most dangerous spot, being right in the mouth of a pass, down which when there is rain a torrent comes raging; but there was no other decently level ground for my tent, and with only a choice between sleeping across the strata of upheaved sandstone and being washed away, I preferred the latter. It certainly was a bad place for a camp, for there was no camel forage very near, no grass whatever, very little fuel, and the water was brackish. By this time, however, I was getting quite accustomed to this last drawback; the water always seemed more or less saline; even when a Baloch swears it is sweet as mother's milk, to an European it tastes bitter. One gets used to this, though one does not by any means appreciate it; but when it is your fate habitually to drink salt water, you cease to think of fresh, and never dream of wine. So it is with our virtues and our vices, our likes and dislikes; by a merciful dispensation of Providence it becomes "out of sight, out of mind." Take the case of a man who has passed a lifetime braving dangers; let him lie by a time and rust, and he will soon get to doubt his own pluck. And so with our favourite vice; just let the cause of that vice be removed for a time, and your hankerings will soon cease. Thus it is I drink my salt water resignedly, if not with much gusto.

19*th January.*—Providence, I am glad to say, watched over me during the night, at least in so far as not to let the torrent come down. Still, I had a return of fever, and after this was over, I was dozing in a fitful way when I jumped up thinking I had heard one of my men, Haidar, call out, "Khor amad!" ("The torrent is coming!") but I found my light burning peacefully, and no sounds of rushing water in the distance. One gets into a weak state of nerves after four nights of fever.

This contretemps had, however, one good effect, for it kept me wide awake and ready to turn out the servants early, and consequently we got off before sunrise. The march on this day was most perplexing, but by careful survey I got a fair idea of the lay of the country. The whole of the hills run east and west, and the connecting spurs north and south; and in order to get north the road goes dodging about the hills, sometimes running due east to pass a spur, then due west on the other side, then north to cross a ridge round which there is no way. The whole road is quite easy, and there is water in more places than one on it. At starting we went east for a mile to water, then north, down the Korochi ravine to a halting-place with water called Poglu; from this we crossed a low ridge and got to the Hingol Khor, and then another into the Gwatka Cham plain. Here a stiff ridge appeared right before us with no apparent way over it, but we found a road by a narrow defile called Gat-i-Gwatka Cham, going through which we came to another halting-place with water, and some forage called Zeh. From this the road passed a ridge, the second between us and Balgatar, by an easy pass called the Choki Goran, and descended into the Lashkari Khor ravine, a most pleasing feature of which was abundance of cool, clear, sweet, running water. The ravine was almost closed at intervals by walls of stone which come down from both sides and nearly meet in the middle, and in one place there is a very curious mass of isolated rock, running right in the middle of the

Natural wall of rock across the Lashkari Khor.

Abqirat Lamjah.

stream. I think these places must formerly have been the sites of waterfalls, when the river was at higher level than it is now, and gradually, as it has worked its way down, the loose earth or stones has been washed away, leaving a wall of rock, composed of upheaved strata, right across the stream. In time, the water has broken a way through these, but in the case I have mentioned, it must have got round the isolated mass on both sides, leaving it standing in the middle. Another of these places, which the Baloches call Abgirs, by name Jangijah, was the scene of a famous fight between the Gichkis and some people who came from the Garmsel tract on the Helmand, and as the hills on either flank are quite impracticable, and these rock walls nearly meet right across, with only a deep pool in the middle, it must have been a very pretty spot for a fight. This place, when the river is full, is impassable, but there is a difficult path to the left bank, by which camels can be got round it.

Ascending out of this over a low pass, we came to a shrine called Pir-i-Sargar, and then got in amongst a labyrinth of hillocks, which we crossed, till we got to a ravine termed Gwani Khor, where there is a plentiful supply of water, but nothing else. Just before reaching this, we passed a bit of level ground about half a mile square, which had at one time evidently been enclosed by a wall or breastwork, and which was called Urdu-ja-i-gagar, *i.e.*, "The Gagar or Kagar camping-ground." Mir Kamálán said there are several such places scattered about in Mekran, but he knew nothing of how the Kagars got here. I fancy the fact is that these wild people call any one unknown to them, coming from the west, Kagars.

I had a long talk with Mir Kamálán in the evening, as to how I was to regulate my movements; and the way he received the intelligence respecting my geographical bearings, gave me great hopes that I would be able to acquire considerable knowledge of regions perhaps less known than any portion of the East.

20th January.—The march to-day was a pleasant one. I had reason to hope I had got over the bout of fever, and the feeling of returning health, with the fine clear bracing air of the morning, combined to exhilarate one. The road went north the whole way to the Goran range, which is reached in five miles. The ascent up this pass is quite easy, but the road is narrow in places, and would be the better for improvement. The forms of the hills on the way up this pass are peculiarly bold and striking, and the colouring of the brown sandstone rocks stand out well against the clear blue sky. The pass is very low, not more than 3,300 feet, but it is the highest point, I believe, on the road from the sea to Panjgur. The top of the pass is quite flat; on the way up there is a good view of the south ridge of Balgatar, which juts forth quite clear, all the peaks, with which the last few days had made me familiar, being clearly visible.

The descent is also very easy, down a small torrent bed, from which soon sprang the Wash-Jaorkhan ravine, along which the road went for four miles. When we got out into the plain of Dasht, at a place called Sahdun, I was somewhat surprised to see still more ranges in front of us, as I thought the tract called the Dasht sloped down to Panjgur; but the low ridge called Kashani Koh cuts off all view to the north. The Wash-Jaorkhan must be the same as

Shāhbāz.

the Jaorkhan which Captain Miles crossed further up, and which falls into the drainage which eventually goes to the Mashkel,—as does all the water shedding on this side of the Goran ridge; it was probably crossed by Major Lovett lower down, under the name of Gwargo or Gwarok. At this point there is now abundance of water in its bed, and the Baloches tell me that its bed is always a sure find for water at any time of the year. From this the road turns north, and in half-an-hour comes to another ravine called Sehdan (which joins the Jaorkhan), where there is always water and grass, while abundance of "pish" fuel can be procured in the bed, and camel forage from the vicinity. Continuing in the same direction for four miles, a low ridge called Band Koh is reached, after which the road turns north-east by east, and goes over an open plain of light sandy soil, with a fair amount of cultivation scattered about, and a good many tamarisk trees, reaching Shahbaz in five miles. This latter is a small fort situated on a mound, in the midst of the plain, and it is, I should say, a strong little place. I notice that Captain Miles says there are no inhabitants, but when I arrived this certainly was not the case, as, when a good long way off, I noticed the whole mound covered with people.

Seeing this, I stopped to peep through my telescope, and as I made out they seemed to be looking in our direction, and to be in some excitement, so I deemed it prudent to reconnoitre a bit before I put myself in the power of the gentleman in command. My dear reader, I am a very great advocate for reconnoitring on all occasions, not only in war, but in peace. I have seen so many people come to grief by not looking before they leap, that I never do anything important now without thus feeling my way, and therefore, while Mir Kamálán has gone ahead to see if all is right, let me air my theory a bit; that reconnoitring is one of the most useful operations in war all commanders know, but I regret all do not adopt it, for the number of distinguished officers I have seen running their gallant heads into messes from the want of a little looking about them beforehand, is remarkable. And not only in war; it is no less necessary in all the games of life,—in love and matrimony for instance. It is said that good matches are made in heaven,—and so perhaps they are; but depend upon it, heaven does not think anything the worse of you, my dear young lady, if you look a little before you leap, and try to test if that brilliant Hussar on whom you are already beginning to set your heart, is entirely made of gold, or if he is only imitation. Well, you see, this is a wild country, and all the information of Shahbaz was that it was small, but in good order, and well situated; and as I knew the *bête noire* of these parts, Azad Khan, was not very far off, there was nothing impossible in the idea which I confess struck me, that he might be in close proximity to us at that very moment. However, Mir Kamálán soon came back with a wild excited Baloch, who appeared so immensely pleased to see me, that I felt quite sorry not to be able to return the compliment, not having that happy knack of looking intensely delighted at the first sight of men I don't know from Adam. His news was that they did not know in the fort who we were, and he had been sent out to see. He had met Mir Kamálán, who of course had told him a Faringi had arrived, and equally of course my friend did not believe a word he said, but came on to find out for himself: for this reason he smiled, when he beheld an individual so unlike any other being he had ever seen, that he concluded I was indeed a Faringi, if not the evil fiend himself.

His "khabar" (news) was that Azad Khan had sent an ultimatum to the Killadar of Shahbaz to tell him if he did not come in and pay his respects, he himself would arrive next day, and with his gun fire at the recalcitrant keeper of the fort. This gun, I must explain, is not a very formidable weapon, being slung on a camel, and carrying only an one pound shot; but it has a great name in this country, and every one knows the moral effect of artillery is greater than the actual results.

When I arrived at the fort I found about one hundred men, very decent-looking fellows, all ready for a fight, and as the place is strong, if Azad did come it seemed there ought to be a very pretty bit of warfare. My great regret was that I could not stay and see the fray, but it would never have done for me to get mixed up in the quarrels of these people. The present commandant of the fort is a rather fine-looking, determined old man, called Dad Mahomed, and he held it in the interests of Mir Gazian, the Naib of the Khan of Kalat, in Panjgur. He said his reply to Azad Khan's summons was, "I know the Khan, I know Mir Gazian, but who are you? You are a thief, and I won't come and make my salaam, or give up this fort." This reply, if true, was calculated to bring down old Azad raging, so I thought it best to make tracks at once for another part of the world. I said to him that the fort seemed a nice little place for a fight, and no doubt if the hearts of his men were as strong, Azad would have to stay outside some time. "Of course," replied Dad Mahomed, "our hearts are stout; have we not got our women and our children to protect? Let Azad Khan come, and he may seize some of our cattle, but he shan't get the fort."

I had several long talks on the road with Mir Kamálán as to what I had better do on arrival at Panjgur. It appears that the quarrel in that valley is owing to Mir Isa having called Azad in to help him to get his revenge out of his brother Gazian, and as Azad is an old enemy of the Khan's, he may be regarded at present as in rebellion. Mir Isa, I heard, protested he had no intention of rising against the Khan, but only wanted his revenge; but of course I felt such a plea would not hold water, and this made it impossible for me to go near him, though he was, I believe, the only man in the plain who could help me; and as the villages to the east were all too near the scene of action, and those to the west were very small, and too far from that of Isai, the only place where there was a bazaar and I could get supplies, I determined the best thing I could do, and Mir Kamálán agreed thoroughly with me, was to go to Thal, which is close to Isai, and was the residence and in the hands of the Khan's Naib.

So I determined to start very early next morning, and make a long detour to the west, to keep out of all chance of coming across Azad Khan or his people.

21*st January.*—To-day, leaving as early as possible, we took a course to avoid the Kashani ridge, though the direct road goes north over it. Before starting, I despatched a letter to Lockwood, telling him not to come to Shahbaz, but to turn off the road at the Wash-Jaorkhan ravine, and then make for the westernmost end of the Kashani ridge. This letter was pretty sure to reach him before he got to Shahbaz, so I trusted all chance of his meeting any of Azad's people would be obviated.

The road went for the first four miles through a pretty thick jungle of tamarisk to a place called Pulabad, and then at the foot of the above ridge got on to a hard gravelly slope, called Kohband, which it first skirts and then enters at eight miles. Crossing three or four insignificant ridges, all with a strike east and west, the road turns north, and then round to north-west, going over the same sort of ground as on the other side, and at eleven miles crosses the Nimag Khor, which is only deserving of notice from its perennial supply of water affording a spot for halting. From this I sent Mir Kamálán on ahead to give notice of my arrival; having in addition despatched a letter to the Naib the day before. In these countries it is always a mistake not to give due notice of one's approach, as the people do not understand your reasons, and naturally suspect you have some hidden object in thus taking them by surprise. This fact I discovered in Persia; at first I used not to be at all careful on this point, but I soon found it would not do, and I recommend all travellers in Central Asia to be careful always to send on word as much beforehand as possible. From the Nimag Khor, the road, after passing a depression with water in it, called Chapkor, goes over a stony plain termed Sorwan, crossing numerous drainage beds and passing some cultivation at Madiani Chah, Jangani Band, and Ghoramani Band (the water for which is supplied by "bands"), right into Isai, which, as usual in this country, is situated in the midst of a dense grove of date palms, so that nothing can be seen of it till you are in its midst. The Khan's Naib, Shahbeg, rode out to meet me, and was civil. He is a mean-looking individual, with small eyes, which seem to open and shut at intervals, without his being able to control them. I found my tent being pitched in an open space close to the village, but as in this spot I should only have afforded amusement to the inhabitants, without deriving any advantage from the arrangement myself, and, moreover, any sort of privacy would have been impossible, I had my quarters moved to a snug little grove, whose walls afforded me some protection from prying eyes, and my things from sticking to the fingers of any occasional visitor. The sun was hot, and the march a long one, while it seemed longer on account of my horse going lame from the loss of a shoe; so I was glad to get into my tent, but it was only by shutting down all the sides and the doors that I could get any privacy at all. Such an interesting subject for amusement, combined with instruction, as the arrival of a Faringi in their midst does not often occur in these parts, and the worthy Isais were determined to enjoy it to the full. No doubt this feeling is quite a natural one,—nay, I think it is commendable; but this does not make it any the less annoying to have to undergo it. However, on this occasion I was not bothered much, as the tent being closely shut they were unable to see anything, and after my servant, Mahomed, had upset one gentleman who had coolly raised the side of the tent and was peeping in, I had peace. I do not think these villagers are half as bad in this respect as English people would be, and the absence of any chaffy remarks on what they see is another point in their favour; though I dare say some reading this, seated in an easy chair, will be inclined to think me unreasonable for objecting to add to the innocent amusement of a wild people, it makes all the difference when you are the primary object of diversion.

22*nd January*.—I found that after one had got up every morning for three weeks at 4.30 a.m. as I had, I entered most fully into that much slandered individual the sluggard's feelings when he entreats to be allowed to "slumber again." To slumber and wake at the usual hour, and hear no camels grunting or growling, no Haidar blowing his nose, no Mahomed entreating and anathematising all neighbouring sleepers by turns, and then to "slumber again" and feel you may do so, is indeed pleasant. I must say, however, I speak of the joys of sleep rather as a reminiscence, as the truth has been dawning on me for the last year or two, that the sleep of my youth has fled; I never enjoy bed now like I did once. I do not say so in the spirit of those superior beings who think there is some virtue in early rising, but I simply record my regrets.

About eight I was informed that a distinguished Baloch chief wished to see me, but still I was awake enough not to be betrayed into any such diplomatic weakness as would have been displayed if I had agreed to the proposed visit. I argued that a man is not a man, certainly not an official man, till he is dressed, and therefore I requested that the Baloch chief might be informed I would see him far enough before I gave him or any one else an interview till a more reasonable hour. I had no fear of this speech not reaching the ears for which it was intended in properly honeyed disguise, because I knew it would be borne by Mir Kamálán, one of the sweetest-tongued old gentlemen I have seen.

When I did get up, the first who came was a fine gentlemanly old man named Muhammad Shah. He had been chief of Sib, in Persian Balochistan, till ousted by the Kagars, and then he was living on the proceeds of a little land he had near Dozanaf, in the Panjgur valley. His visit was very pleasing to me, both because his manners were most charming, and he had been named to me as the man most likely to be able to help me in my explorations. He brought with him his son Mahmud Khan. Both expressed their willingness to do anything I wished, but I did not venture to say much to them, at this first interview, contenting myself with studying the features of both, to see if I could find deceit therein; for a man who is accustomed to wandering is invariably careful of his companions. The scrutiny was favourable, but I wished them good-bye without showing my hand. Next came an uninteresting old man, called Mir Morad, from Tasp, and the burden of his cry was that the Khan was a tyrant, and nothing would make him anything else. I thought on looking at the sleek appearance of my friend, that if this is the result of the Khan's tyranny, if I were your medical adviser I should prescribe daily doses of oppression for you. My master of the ceremonies now left me; and this most unfortunately, for scarcely had he gone when an invasion of Nowsherwanis took place into my tent. A band of these notorious robbers, headed by a very fine soldierly young man, made a rush at my sanctum, and with boisterous cries in Baloche, four of them coolly sat down in my presence, while about twenty squatted outside. I gave Shah Nawaz, the leader, an appropriate snub for the rudeness of himself and his followers, by saying, "I always heard the Nowsherwanis had no manners;" he expressed himself penitent, but his air was insolent throughout the interview. He is the son of Baloch Khan, who is the great enemy of Azad Khan. Indeed, the family history as a specimen of Nowsherwani harmony is worth relating. Baloch Khan and Mir Lala are paternal cousins and brothers-in-law, and, as male cousins sometimes will, they fell out,—the whimsical cause of the quarrel being as to who should plunder the Khan most. When things got to their worst, Mir Lala, having reason to believe that Baloch was arranging an exit from the world for him, fled from Kolwah, where they both then were, to Kharan. There he soon found an ally in Azad Khan, a second cousin of both, who had a family spite to repay Baloch. So having got about three hundred men out of Azad, Mir Lala started with the intention of attacking Baloch. But when he had got as far as Kaldan, he unfortunately neglected to take any precaution to guard against surprise, and so when his whole party were sleeping, Baloch came down on them with eighty men, and commenced immediately to carve them. After a bit, all Lala's men bolted, and he was left to face the enemy he had come to destroy. This he did like a man, but he was soon overpowered, and Baloch at his leisure hacked at him till he thought he was dead. But though he had sixteen wounds, one of his hands being cut clean off, he had only swooned, and eventually lived to have his revenge by bringing

Azad down on Baloch, and in inducing the latter's own son to turn against him. This son was Shah Nawaz Khan, and though his manners cannot be commended more than his unfilial conduct towards his father, still I must say he was as nice looking a young fellow as I had seen. His features were particularly handsome, and he had a fine clear bold eye, which, combined with his handsome figure and erect bearing, made me itch to carry him off and enlist him in India.

It was thus evident that these were very ticklish times in these parts, and I longed to get away. It was difficult to say what that devil's imp Azad might be up to next. Yet it was quite impossible for me to avoid coming to Panjgur, as I had to get provisions for the road, and secure the services of some thoroughly reliable and influential man to go with me. I certainly do not think that it would have been advisable to come here had I not had Mir Kamálán with me. He was a nephew of Mir Isa, and a connection of Azad's; yet owing to his being a brother-in-law of the Khan's, no less than to his well-known peaceful character, he was friends with all, and I was perfectly safe as long as he was with me, and, as it happened, he was the only Gichki of sufficient influence who at that moment could have been secured for the journey. For all Mir Gazian's people were besieged by Azad, and all Mir Isa's were forbidden companions to me.

23*rd January.*—To-day I paid the Naib of the Khan a visit. He is a very mean individual, named, as afore-mentioned, Shahbeg, and was in a great flurry, when told I was coming to see him, to know where he was to receive me; for it is a fact that this governor of that mighty potentate the Khan of Kalat had not got a place entitled to rank with the poorest cowshed in England. The important difficulty was referred to me for solution, and it was half hinted that I might just as well abstain from bestowing such an onerous honour on the Naib; and under ordinary circumstances I most certainly should have willingly complied, but on this occasion it was necessary to mark, as clearly as I could, that the Naib was the only individual I acknowledged, and that I paid my respects to him as the deputy of the Khan.

Accordingly I went, and after winding through the filthy village, we arrived at a low door, which I was requested to enter. Immediately I had done so, I noticed that it was locked behind us, and I confess a sort of cold shudder passed through me, as I thought of the possibility of my having been entrapped; but on looking at the cringing, timid bearing of the Naib, I was more than reassured.

The place he had selected to receive me in was, I must conclude, the best at his disposal, and yet it was only a filthy stable-yard, a part of which had been cleared to make room for a bed for me to sit on, and for a carpet for his other visitors. The conversation was, as usual, of the most inane description, and after giving him a pair of binoculars I left. I understand the Naib did not appreciate the present, for which I was sorry; but I confess I had been quite mistaken in my selections of presents for these Baloches. Judging from my Persian experiences, I had brought with me some guns, watches, telescopes, and knives, which I found the Persians appreciated thoroughly; but these Baloches are too utter savages to care for either watches or telescopes.

As Mir Kamálán, who, though his manner is better and his disposition generally more kindly, is nearly as great a savage as the others, said to me, "A watch! what's the good of a watch?" I replied, "To tell the time,—the time for prayers, for food, etc." He rejoined, "Every one knows the time for food, and ought to know the time for prayers, without a watch; which, as far as I can see, is no use at all except to stick by your side: two rupees each is better." I offered old Muhammad Shah a telescope, but he declined, saying, "I dare say it is a very good thing for those who possess a fort, on the tower of which they could then sit and watch for their enemies; but I have no fort, and thank God all here are my friends." Of course these people like having guns given them, but I think it is quite wrong to bestow presents of such value for every trifling little service. The best thing a traveller can do, if he is so insane as to come to such countries for his own amusement, is to turn himself into a sort of perambulating cloth merchant, and measure out yards of broadcloth and longcloth, according to the merits of the individual, or the amount of opposition or obstruction you expect from him.

After the visit to the Naib was over, I sent Mir Kamálán to Dozanaf, to bring Muhammad Shah, and when he came I told him where I wanted to go. He expressed himself quite willing, and entered into the proposal with considerable spirit. It was agreed on all hands that it would be sufficient to take twenty good matchlock-men, which number, with Mahmud, his brother Gholam Rasul, and cousin Mirza Khan, and our own guns (rifles), would produce about thirty guns. To take more would increase the difficulties of providing transport for their supplies, and less would not be sufficient guard, while thirty determined men of one mind can make very good head against much larger numbers who are undecided and not expecting them. One great difficulty was the procuring of camels. These are never very plentiful in these parts, and now, owing to Azad's presence, nearly all had been driven off to safer grazing grounds. I wished, if possible, to mount all the men, but from what I heard at first I almost despaired of getting more than ten animals at the outside, so that one-half the men would have had to march. I tried to impress on Mir Mahmud the absolute necessity for making proper arrangements for food and ammunition, and he promised to see that every one was provided with one month's supply. I was, however, not to be put off in this way, and meant of course to inspect their supplies carefully before starting, and to carry, besides, a reserve of provisions myself, not to be indented on till the end. For water, we should have to rely on what we carried in "mussucks"* from place to place. The agreement I made was, I was to pay each of the matchlock-men one rupee per diem, and the two officers four rupees per diem, the reward of Mahmud himself being left till the trip was over. I gave them all five days' pay in advance, and they agreed the rest was to stand over until I returned to some place of safety. These terms were perhaps high, but the service, if they performed it properly, was well worth it, for after all it would only amount to about 850 rupees, excepting anything extra Mahmud got for himself.

An immense deal of mystery had to accompany

* Leathern skins for holding water.

the giving the advance money to Mahmud, and by advice of Mir Kamálán I did "it darkly and in the dead of night," so that nobody might know; but of course everybody did know at once. I suppose Mahmud, when he was enclosed in whatever answers for the four-poster in a Baloch nuptial chamber, imparted the fact of his being in possession of so much money to his "sposa," who of course said, "Oh, of course I won't tell: you know I never do," and thereupon spent a sleepless night, thinking to whom she should impart the news the first thing in the morning.

With the view of providing myself with an excuse for being in this part of the world, I gave out that I was making inquiries into the rights of the Kuhak boundary question. I therefore sent for Mir Morad, and inquired of him all I could learn about the matter, and induced him to promise to have the whole case written out, so that I could forward it to my Government for consideration. He was much pleased at this, and with the ignorant cunning a savage so often shows, thought he would make hay while the sun shone, and thereupon he began a complaint about his being the rightful owner of some land in Panjgur. But I soon stopped him by saying I had nothing to do with that, but was only enquiring into the frontier question of Kuhak.

24th January.—I received yesterday a letter from Lockwood, who said he was coming up from Belor, and would probably arrive on the 25th. I wrote at once, and begged him to be careful not to go to Shahbaz, but turn off the road before getting there; in fact, what I wrote the other day.

This morning, before I had finished breakfast, I

was sitting outside my tent, when a swaggering individual came up, and coolly sat himself down, saying, "The Sirdar sends his salaam,"—meaning Azad Khan. Of course I could do no less than thank him and enquire after the Sirdar's health. I then found that this gentleman had evidently been sent to question me in the usual manner with these people, and also to pump me. I did not mind in the least telling him my name, etc., or whence I came, and where I was going; all of which information I therefore imparted to him. Next he said, "The Sirdar says, if you want to traverse any of the countries near, he is better acquainted with them than any one, and will be very happy to tell you." I answered, "Thank the Sirdar very much for his kindness; it is, I know, notorious that he is acquainted with the whole country, but as I am only going to places that are well known, there will be no necessity to trouble him." I did not get out of the next query quite so easily. My questioner said, suddenly, "Why don't you go and see the Sirdar?" This was evidently a feeler to ascertain if I could be induced to visit Azad, when he would be able to point to my presence as a proof of his not knowing he was doing wrong in attacking the Khan's villages. I answered, "How can I go when there is fighting going on? At any other time I would be glad to see the Khan." Then he said, "Niaz Muhammad, the Jemadar of Artillery" (the whole park consists of one 2 Pr. camel gun!) "sends his salaam, and says, if you are enlisting men he would like to serve under you." "Present," I replied, "Niaz Muhammad with my best compliments, and say that I have already enough domestics, otherwise I would have been very happy to have taken him as a servant;" and then I changed the conversation, in order not to give him a chance of reply.

Shortly after, Mahmud brought his cousin Mirza, to introduce him. He seemed a very bright, intelligent-looking young fellow, and was the same man whom St. John mentioned as having come to confer with him about the Kuhak question. Since those days Kuhak has passed into the hands of the Kajars, after some fighting, in which he was present.

My dear reader, suppose you were in a wild country like this, where there is no law, and where a man's life is not regarded as of any value, you would naturally be a little on the *qui vive.* But suppose you had for a few minutes forgotten where you were, and were engaged in writing, as I was, a childish letter to your only child, your thoughts turned solely on peace and love, and suppose at that moment a wild ruffian suddenly turned the corner of your tent and came up to you with a pistol in his hand, what would you do? I know what I would have liked to do,—bolt into the tent and shut the door; but not being able to adopt this more safe course, I put on an air of determination and went up to him, and asked who he was, keeping my eye on him the while. I saw him quail. I don't know why he should have done so, but he did, and after a few words he put the pistol into his belt. I noticed the while it was capped. I suppose I shall never know whether he had any idea of shooting me. Afterwards he talked to me for some time; he was a man of Azad's, and said he had been sent also to give me his salaam; and while he talked, I formed resolutions to wear a pistol in future. The old story: a lot of good my resolutions would have been if that man had fired. He was an intelligent fellow, and talked well, and so I forgave him the shock he had caused my weak nerves. He said Azad had told him to say Kuhak did not belong to the Kajars, but the English. I replied, "It does not, of course, belong to us, but it certainly is not the Kajars' by right. They have taken it by force." After this interview I almost determined to leave Panjgur next morning, and go to Kalag. Azad as yet had certainly shown no sort of disposition to be uncivil, but he was a wild devil, and one could no more be sure of a man like that, than of a mule.

CHAPTER IV.

GWADUR TO PANJGUR.

I WILL now turn to Captain Lockwood's journey. The same day as I did, that officer proceeded on his wanderings. Clearing Gwadur, for seven and three-quarter miles he followed the beach of the west Gwadur bay, first going in a northerly, and then gradually circling round in a westerly direction. The beach was flat and shelving, the isthmus on the right being a level, sandy plain covered with tufts of grass. At seven and three-quarter miles the road left the beach at an old telegraph post put up to mark the place, and turned to the right, in a northerly direction, over the sandy isthmus. This place was called Zahri Kanag. One mile further on the Ankora Nulla was reached. It was some two hundred and fifty yards broad, with easy broken banks and a firm sandy bed, nearly always dry, the tide never rising high enough to make it impassable. Two miles further on he arrived at a halting-place near a tree on the banks of the Jati ravine, which joins the Ankora some miles to the south. There was plenty of good water in this ravine after rain; the supply, however, being uncertain. Good forage for horses and camels is here procurable all the year round, but no fuel except dry grass, and no supplies of any sort or kind. The Ankora halting-place is some three miles to the north, while the ravine of that name forms the boundary of the Arab settlement at Gwadur. Bar. 30·3.

Next day he went from Jati to Pishikan, seventeen miles south-west, in four hours and thirty-three minutes. Leaving Jati, the road took a south-west direction, crossing the Tazani ravine, which comes from the Tuzdan hill, immediately on leaving. This was two hundred yards broad, with broken easy banks and a firm sandy bottom, and contained pools of brackish water. At three miles he passed a bit of low swampy ground, covered with water dependent on rain, and then skirted close to the south of the Tuzdan, a mud hill some three hundred feet high, surrounded with broken ground, which extends for eight miles. The road then continued in the same direction to get round the Faleri ravine, which is impassable for three miles from the sea; having crossed this it took a more southerly direction, and passing Shabi, a mud hill to the left, at twelve miles, and Koh-i-Fasu and Gird Koh to the right and left respectively, at fifteen miles, arrived at Pishikan at the seventeenth mile.

This latter village consists of eight or nine matting huts, inhabited by fishermen who call themselves Pishikanis. It is two hundred yards from the sea, and some fifty feet above it. The soil is very fine sand, covered with tufts of camel thorn and grass. There was one well, eighteen feet deep, with two and a half feet of water in it on his arrival; but it was reported nearly dry a couple of hours afterwards, the water having been exhausted in supplying a flock of sheep. There were also two or three other old wells of the same depth, which had fallen in. Grass is plentiful here, and might be collected to any amount from the neighbouring villages, and the whole country round is good for camel grazing. There is no fuel here, wood being brought from Chatani Bal, a village fifteen miles distant. The inhabitants describe the place as healthy, and not so feverish as Gwadur. Pishikan belongs to the Arab Wali of Gwadur, but the people pay taxes to Mir Morad, Khan of Tump. The west Gwadur bay is described by the people here as more sheltered than the east, and according to the chart the anchorage is as good, if not better. Any amount of water could be got by digging wells in the Drabalo ravine, three miles west, where the water is only three feet from the surface, though they say it gets slightly brackish in dry weather.

4th January.—From Pishikan the road ran in a westerly direction over very fine sand covered with tufts of grass. At three miles it crossed the Drabalo ravine, which comes from the hills a mile to the right. This was a hundred yards broad, with easy rounded banks, and a firm sandy bottom ; it is always dry, except immediately after rain. Plenty of excellent water is to be got in its bed by digging two or three feet. The road following the above direction passed for six and a half miles under mud cliffs, a hundred and fifty feet high, cut into fantastic shapes by the action of the water, when it gradually circled to the left, and arrived at Gaz, in fourteen miles from Pishikan. The road to this was over some undulating sandy ground till it joined the above cliffs, when it passed under, and, between them and the sea, about one mile distant to the left, over firm, gravelly soil to Gaz. No habitations or cultivation were passed on the way.

Gaz consists of eight or nine matting huts of fishermen close to the sea shore. Water is got from wells, twelve feet deep, dug in the sand, and is brackish in dry seasons. From Gaz the road turned west, and, breaking through the cliffs to the right, ascended by a rocky, rough pass, and again descending, arrived at a glen some half mile broad, which it followed for three and a half miles to a patch of trees and cultivation, called Labu, when it issued on to a plain, and circling to the left, arrived at Panowan in nineteen miles from Pishikan. The village in question consists of a few trees and five or six matting huts close under the hills. There are two wells of good water fifteen feet deep, one of which they say cannot be drawn dry. Bar. 30·3.

5th January.—Leaving Panowan, the road went west for a quarter of a mile till clear of the hills, when it turned to the left, and followed close under cliffs to the left for one and a half miles; it then commenced a very gradual ascent over hard, gravelly soil up the high ground lying between Ras Kalagar and Gwatur bay. It then ran along the top, about two hundred feet above the sea, for two miles, when it again descended, and passing through cultivation pretty thickly covered with trees, arrived at the village of Junri in six and three-quarter miles. This place consists of about thirty matting huts, inhabited by Sahibzada Baloches and fishermen, and is situated on the east shore of Gwatur bay, two miles north of Ras Junri. There is a plentiful supply of water from wells fifteen feet deep, and any amount more might be dug. There is here about one square mile of land covered with wood, that would be useful for fuel. Four native boats were anchored out at sea on their return from fishing. Fifty or sixty sheep and goats could be got here, and perhaps twenty camels.

Captain Lockwood, on the 6th January, left Junri at 8.25 a.m., in a native sailing boat thirty feet long, drawing seven feet of water; and after two hours and five minutes' sail (ten miles), anchored in one and a half fathoms of water, a quarter of a mile from the mouth of the Dasht River. He then got into a queer and dangerous contrivance answering to the captain's gig, which drew about three feet of water, and after about five minutes' paddle he got on to the bar, and with some difficulty shoved the boat over about fifty yards of knee-deep water into one fathom. The tide was on the rise, and five hours before flood. His boatman told him there were two fathoms of water on the bar at high water, but at low it is quite dry, with only a small channel six inches deep. The river at its mouth is about four hundred yards broad, with flat, firm, sandy banks, almost flush with the sea. For four miles up the river the depth varies from one to two and a half fathoms in the deepest places, and the river gradually narrows to a hundred yards broad; this was four hours before flood tide, when there would be at least one fathom more. At six miles the breadth diminished to eighty yards, and the depth under the steepest bank to five feet, shelving off to nothing. At nine miles the river was eighty yards broad, and in places six feet deep, the stream being nearly full flood. At fifteen miles the tide was at its highest, and on the turn, and he had great difficulty in finding a passage for the boat, but managed to get it up to sixteen miles, three and a half miles south-west of Surian Jump. The river to this point has a hard, sandy bed, and firm, dusty banks, in places ten feet high at low tide. Nothing could be more dreary than the aspect of the surrounding country. Captain Lockwood passed a few camels grazing in the tamarisk jungle on the banks, but there were no permanent villages. The distances given, and the direction of the river, are only approximate, while its course winds a great deal more than shown on the route map.

At Surian Jump the river was three hundred yards broad, with a firm bed, with pools of fresh water. The tide comes to here, but the fresh water is drinkable soon after it goes down. The highest point the tide appears to reach in the hot weather is Kuldan.

Surian Jump consists of a few matting huts of Bihari Baloches. Cotton and wheat are cultivated here in small quantities. Water is procurable from the Dasht River, and wells in its bed, which are two or three feet deep in the dry months.

Nigor, the subdivision through which he then passed, is a district situated north of Dasht, and divided from it by a hill about one thousand feet high, called the Karosa Tankh. It contains the following villages (all of them being made of sticks and matting), with the annexed number of houses:—

Pitok	50
Hotachat	50
Druch ka koh	30
Mucha Chat	60
Shai Zungi	60
Talui	30
Bal	150
Kai Rin	50
Gwarag	30
Sichig	24
	534 Houses.

The subdivision of Nigor belongs to Tump, and pays revenue to Morad Khan. It is inhabited by Kaudai Baloches, who are Zikris by religion. Kauda Dad Muhammad, the head man, has been to Hindustan, and speaks English!! Water is procured from wells which never dry. Perhaps not less than one thousand camels could be got out of it, and it is said that it sends two hundred camel loads of wheat to Gwadur yearly for sale. It may here be stated that long, rank grass in the Dasht River is called "kek," but the twisted grass which is found about Pishikan is termed "baraka."

Leaving Surian Jump, the road went north-east for a little more than one mile over a dusty "pat" soil covered with camel thorn, to Kuldan, a few huts situated under a mud hill a hundred feet high. It is inhabited by Bihari Baloches, who procure their water from the bed of the Dasht River, one and a half miles off. The road then turned slightly east, and at about two and a half miles over the same style of country, passed under the telegraph line. A little more than a mile further on it wound to the left, where there are a few matting huts, called Seroki, inhabited by Shahzada Baloches. The water of this village is also brought from the bed of the Dasht River. Continuing in the same direction, and over the same style of country, in five miles it arrived at Kulatu, a few matting huts of Hot Baloches, situated one mile south of the Dasht River. It has a conspicuous mud tower perched on the top of a fifty feet high mud hill overhanging the village. From this, three-quarters of a mile over broken ground brought one to a ravine from the Koh-i-Tankh, a hill about six miles to the right. After this, the road, continuing in the same direction, stretches over a country broken up by dams and cultivation, and covered with low trees and bushes, and in thirteen miles arrives at Dumb, close on the left bank of the Dasht River.

The road the whole way passed up the left bank of the Dasht River, and never two miles distant from it. The surrounding country, with the exception of a few mud mounds to the right, is perfectly flat and open. At Dumb the Dasht River was one hundred and fifty yards broad, and thirty feet deep, with a firm, muddy bottom; there were also large pools of good water in the bed. The tide never reaches so high as this.

Leaving Dumb on the 8th January, Captain Lockwood crossed to the right bank of the Dasht River, and then followed the road, which, taking a north-easterly direction for two miles, ran between low, isolated mud hills, about fifty feet high, and continued among them for nearly three miles. It then crossed to the left bank of the Dasht, which was here a hundred yards broad, with steep ten feet banks; its bed covered with tamarisk jungle and long coarse grass. The road then wound, about three-quarters of a mile from the river bank, under low hills on the right for two miles to Sut-ki-Gaidar, where there were some partially excavated brick ruins. Continuing in a north-easterly direction, two miles further it crossed the Saijdi ravine (fifty yards broad), which broke through the hills on the right and joined the Dasht close by. One and a quarter miles further on the road passed Dadan, which consists of a small tower perched on a mud hill thirty feet high, with a few matting Baloch huts and a little cultivation close to the river. The Gwadur road *viâ* Garok, which comes through the hills, here joined from the right.

The road then, for one mile, ran up a ravine ten feet broad and ten feet deep, with a narrow hill between it and the river; then for a mile went through cultivation and dams, close under the Saijdi hills. From this, going on in the same direction for three miles over open, hard "pat," one arrives at a few huts on the left bank of the river, called Miting. The road the whole way is never two miles distant from the Dasht River.

9th January.—The road, on leaving Miting, for a quarter of a mile went due north, up the bed of the Dasht River. It then turned slightly east, and in a quarter of a mile cleared the tamarisk jungle on the bank, and left Potan, a few huts of Rind Baloches, to the left. Then winding more east, it went for seven miles over open, dusty "pat," covered with a few "kai" and tamarisk trees, till it arrived at the remains of some huts called Sadui Kalat, when it again joined the left bank of the Dasht River. Then turning more east still, it continued for four miles among grass and tamarisk jungle on the left bank of the river, passing Darzain and Zarain Bog, two villages with a few huts inhabited by Hot and Kandai Baloches. The road then crossed to the right bank, up which it ran for nearly two miles, and then returned to the left bank, and cutting off a corner of the river, arrived at Hasadin in four miles. At the apex of the last bend, three miles west of Hasadin, the Gwarag, a large well-wooded ravine, joins from the north.

The country passed over on this march was perfectly level, and bounded on the south-east by the Saijdi Koh range, seven or eight miles distant, and on the north-west by hills eight or ten miles away.

The Dasht was here, as elsewhere, well-wooded with "kai" and "gaz" (tamarisk) trees, and had a sandy bed two hundred yards broad, with large pools of water in it. Hasadin is merely a halting-place on the left bank of the river, on the west edge of a network of ravines and broken ground, cut by the drainage of a low range of hills west of Saijdi.

Leaving Hasadin, the road stretched up the bed of the Dasht River for three-quarters of a mile, when it entered the jungle on its left bank, and turning a little to the left, at three miles reached Langasi, a village two miles distant on the right bank of the river; while to the left, one mile on, it crossed to the right bank of the river, and at three miles passed a few huts called Matilab. One and three-quarter miles further it recrossed to the left bank, which it kept for two miles, when it again crossed the right bank, and turning to the north, quitted the river, and went over hard, dusty "pat" covered with "kai" and tamarisk trees. Then passing an isolated hill to the right, it arrived in two miles at Kuhak, situated on the right bank of the river.

At this point there is plenty of water to be got in pools in the bed of the river, and any amount of fuel and coarse grass for fodder is procurable. Kuhak itself is a wretched village of a hundred houses made of sticks and matting, clustered round the foot of a fort stuck on the top of a rocky mound about one hundred feet higher.

Leaving Kuhak, the road crossed to the left bank, and went north-east in thick tamarisk jungle for five miles, when it passed two or three huts called Kunchaki, inhabited by Rais Baloches, and immediately after crossed the Kasar ravine from the right (twenty feet deep and twenty yards broad), at a little over six miles from Kuhak; it then crossed the Nilag ravine, also from the right, which drains from Pidark, and at nine miles it passed an isolated hill two and a half miles to the right, and a little farther on Ballin to the left. At ten miles the Dasht River was crossed to the right bank. The bed is here two hundred and fifty yards broad, with a sandy bottom and bank six feet deep. There was a thickish tamarisk tree jungle on both banks for one or two miles' distance, two miles beyond which was Kauntadar, situated on the right bank. The road stretched over firm, white "pat," very dusty, much cut up in places by irrigation dams. The route on the whole of this march lay through the tamarisk jungle on one or other side of the river, and was very tortuous, and the view much impeded.

Kauntadar is a village of one hundred and fifty matting houses, inhabited by Kaudais and Rais. Water is procured from pools in the bed of the river. Sulaiman Khan, the head man of the place, has made a garden about three hundred yards from the river bank, which is watered from a well fifty feet deep, the water of which is quite sweet.

On the 12th, leaving Kauntadar, Captain Lockwood went to a halting-place on the Nilag ravine, fourteen and an eighth miles south-east. The road crossed to the left bank of the river, and leaving it ran due east for three miles through thick tamarisk jungle. It then went over some broken ground north of the east end of a low hill called Badari, and turned slightly south over "pat" covered with camel thorn and a little grass. One mile further it crossed a small ravine called Kilai (twenty yards broad, eight feet deep, dry, with low, easy banks), and in another passed Kamerani, a hovel consisting of half-a-dozen huts of Rais Baloches. About one and a half miles on the road the track leading direct from Kuhak to Kej was crossed near some date trees close on the right, called Amalani, which is sometimes used as a halting-place. Immediately after leaving this it passed Sangai (eight huts of Shahid Baloches), situated on the ravine of the same name, which is thirty yards broad, ten feet deep, and drains from the hills south of Kej. Again, in one mile the Haftari ravine, which joins the Nilag, was reached. The Nilag road then came to broken, stony ground under the Miskina Muk hill, and passing among some low mounds running out from it, arrived at the bed of the Nilag ravine, where he halted.

The ravine has at this point no defined bed, but may be some three hundred yards broad, with pools of water and abundance of good grass in its bed.

The march this day ran obliquely across an open plain, bounded on the north by the Kej range, and south by the Miskina Muk hills. The country was a flat "pat," with a little cultivation, where water can be caught by dams, and covered with camel thorn, "pish," and "kai" trees.

13th January, 1877.—Leaving the halting-place, the road ran east by north close under the Miskina Muk hill, with the Nilag close on the left, over hard, firm, gravelly ground. At three miles it crossed the Nalani ravine on the right, here fifty yards broad and ten feet deep, with a firm, gravelly bottom. The hills bounding Kej to the south are at this spot about six miles distant, and they are succeeded by a labyrinth of broken rising ground, which extends down to the bank of the Nilag. This latter was here three hundred yards broad, with well-defined twenty-five feet deep banks, and a great deal of beautifully clear water in its gravelly bed. Leaving this, the road in one and a half miles passed Jamki, a peaked hill to the left, and again entered the Nilag ravine. At this stage there were a few tents of Sangar Baloches, who said they had come from Kej with their flocks for grass, but as it was a bad season, for want of rain, they were going back. Just beyond this the Kanera road from Gwadur to Kej was crossed, and two miles on the track left the Nilag and went along its right bank for a little more than two miles, when it crossed the left and reached some three or four huts of Sangar Baloches. The ravine here splits into three, the most northern being still called Nilag; the next, southward, the Zango; and the southernmost again, the Katlani. Situated ten or fifteen feet above the bed of the river, there was a spring of excellent fresh water, which ran at a good pace, and was six inches broad and one deep. This water is used by the inhabitants of the adjoining huts to irrigate some little cultivation in the Sangar bed. From this point the road passed up the left bank of the Zargo, and four miles on crossed a track from Kej to Gwadur, called the Maluki road. This point is the watershed of the Nilag and Shadi Khors. The former drains west to the Dasht, and the Shadi south-east to the sea at Pusni. About three miles on, Captain Lockwood arrived at the Gilian Kumb ravine, where he halted.

On the 14th January, leaving the above halting-place on the Gilian Kumb, Captain Lockwood went to Jamak, a distance of seventeen and three-quarter miles, in four hours forty-six minutes. The road ran nearly due east between low hills, two or three hundred yards off on the right and left, over black gravel, with lots of "Nadag" grass. At two miles he crossed the track from Dokani to Turbat in Kej, and in one mile came to the Kalerag ravine, which drained to the Shadi. In three-quarters of a mile he crossed yet another ravine, and immediately afterwards the road entered a tract of very jumpy kind of ground, and twisted amongst low mounds and ravines for a quarter of a mile, when the Pidark fort became visible nearly two miles distant below. The road from here descended, and crossing the Shadi Khor, and then, three-quarters of a mile further, the Kalagai Khor, arrived at Pidark in six and a half miles from Gilian Kumb. The road the whole way was over firm, black, stony ground, the hills bounding the Kej valley on the south being about four miles to the left hand (north), separated by broken moundy ground. On the right were two broken ridges, with nearly perpendicular strata, all running in exactly the same strike, *i.e.*, nearly east and west; and in this direction there was no hill of consequence as far as the Saijdi ridge before mentioned. Pidark is a large place for these parts, and consists of a hundred and fifty to two hundred mat huts, and a high fort near a date grove. The head man was named Pahzadin, and the inhabitants were Bardarzai, Barechi, Katagaris, and Kaudas. Some rice is grown here, and perhaps two hundred cattle and four hundred sheep might be raised. The road, with very little work, could be made practicable up to this place. From Pidark to Jamak the track had a general direction of east by north, and ran over the same kind of gravel as the first part of the march, and along the foot of the Sami hills, crossing their southern drainage, and continually going up and down and in and out of broad, deep, stony ravines draining from them; the view being everywhere much obstructed. About three miles from Jamak the track descended from the foot of the hills to a plain in which that place is situated. The distance from Pidark is eleven and a quarter miles, making the whole march seventeen and three-quarters. Jamak consists of a rickety stone and mud tower, with a few mat huts round it. It is inhabited by Bali, Saijdi, and Kosag Baloches. The head man is a Gichki, named Mir Ismail. A good deal of rice is cultivated here, and sold at Kej, the water supply being drawn from five karez (channels). Eight hundred sheep could be got in the place. There is plenty of grass to be obtained from the ravines and surrounding stony country.

On the 15th January, 1877, he went from Jamak to Gwarko, eleven miles east by north, in two hours fifty-seven minutes.

The road was over brown, stony ground, and in a little over three-quarters of a mile passed a grove of date trees to the right of the road, called Kisinag. Three and a half miles farther it came to Mian-i-Kalag, a date grove in a ravine; and two miles beyond this it passed Sarkalag, another date grove in a ravine watered by three karez, which also irrigate a little cultivation in the bed of the ravine. One mile on the track took a more northerly direction, and after three and a half miles arrived at Gwarko.

The road was straight up the Pidark Damag, or valley, along a sort of glacis from the south side of the hills south of the Sami valley, and crossing the drainage of the hills, ran in and out and up and down the steep banks of broad, stony ravines draining to the Shadi Khor. The ground was firm and hard, covered with black stones from six to eight inches in length, and had a little grass in tufts sprinkled about. The hills to the left were about four miles distant, and about a thousand feet above the level of the road. The country to the right was much broken with irregular ridges of low hills parallel to one another and to the Asi hills. North of the sea, as far as could be learned, there is no level ground deserving the name of a valley between. It had rained hard the day before, and there was running clear water in most of the ravines crossed, some of which indeed are, it is said, never actually dry. Gwarko is a mud and stone fort, with some fifty huts situated in a date grove, and watered by four karez. It is inhabited by Kauda and Kosag Baloches, the head man of whom is a Gichki, called Sahibdad, who speaks Hindustani, and was very civil. Five hundred sheep might be raised here. There is plenty of grass to be got out of the surrounding country.

If the road were improved a little, and drag ropes were used, it would be practicable for guns. About half the inhabitants here, as at Jamki, are Zikris by religion. He passed a couple of flocks of goats and sheep grazing, which were said to have come down from Panjgur on account of the fighting there.

On the 16th January Captain Lockwood went from Gwarko to a halting-place on the Talach ravine on the road to Thal, seventeen miles east by north, in four hours fifty-two minutes.

From Gwarko the road led south-east over the stony glacis that surrounds that locality down the Dammas ravine for two miles, passing a date grove called Mashkai, three-quarters of a mile to the right, at about one mile from Gwarko. Continuing the same direction, it then passed Daimachi, another date grove watered by karezes, two and a half miles from Gwarko, to the left. The road then entered the hills, and continued winding in them for two miles, when it again came out into the stony plain east of Gwarko. Two miles on, due east, the road again entered the skirt of the hills to the south of the Gwarko plain, and continued amongst them for the rest of the march, which was nearly in a straight line in an east by north direction. The road was at the foot of a slope five miles broad at the bottom of the south side of the range of hills that bounds the Sami plain on the south. Immediately on the right of the road after Daimachi were broken parallel ranges of hills from two to five hundred feet above the level of the plain, running in a line with the road, which latter was crossed at short intervals by stony, steep-banked ravines that drain from the hills to the left and break through those to the right. There were no villages right or left near the road, and only one, little frequented, footpath, called Rungan Kand, which goes to the Sami valley, crossed the march. At the halting-place, though it had rained hard two days ago, there was some difficulty in finding water, and then only a very little was procured. The road the whole march was very broken, and would require a great deal of labour in clearing and levelling to make it practicable for wheeled carriages. Little or no grass or camel thorn was procurable at the halting-place.

On the 17th January he went from the above halting-place on the Talach ravine to another on the

Ispirod ravine, seventeen and a quarter miles north-east, in four hours thirty-nine minutes.

Leaving Talach, the road went north-east, and gently ascended for two miles over broken stony ground, shut in by hills right and left. It then turned to the right and entered a ravine called Kokeni, the bed of which it followed, still ascending, and then wound up a narrow ravine joining the Kokeni from the right, till four miles from the halting-place, when it arrived at the head of the Gwarko valley, and on the south-west edge of a flat black stony plain three miles broad and four and a half long, called Thal. Continuing in a north-easterly direction, the road crossed this plain, and at nine miles from the halting-place on the Talach, entered low hills, and winding among them for one and a quarter miles, came out into another flat, black, stony plain. The hills that bound the Sami plain to the south here came to an end, and the above plain sloped gently from south to north towards the Sami ravine. The road, continuing in a north-easterly direction across the sloping plain, arrived at the Ispirod ravine in seven miles, or seventeen and a quarter from the halting-place on the Talach Nulla. On this day Captain Lockwood passed on the road five or six large flocks of sheep and goats of some five hundred each, which had come from the north on account of the fighting in Panjgur. The shepherds told him the people of Balor had gone to "salaam" Azad Khan, but their chief at Sami had sent orders to them to turn south. He passed no villages on the road; there was water after rain in the ravine beds, but the supply is not to be depended on. Grass was plentiful the whole way. The road was very difficult, and would require a great deal of labour to make it serviceable. There were no roads crossing the march. Thal separates the watershed of the Shadi Khor from that of the Kej River. From Gwarko there were no signs of habitations or cultivation, and the only frequenters of the ground passed on these two marches were shepherds who came in search of grass. Bar. at halting-place, 28·6 ; min. thermometer at night, 40.

On the 18th January Captain Lockwood went from halting-place on the Ispirod to Balor, twenty-seven and a half miles, in seven hours nineteen minutes.

The road continued over the same sort of black, stony plain, in an east by north direction. At two miles it passed a well to the left, fifty feet deep, but with no water. At six and a half miles there was another well, one hundred and forty feet deep, with good water in it all the year round. At ten miles the track joined the Balor and Kej road, the latter going off in a westerly direction; and, one and a half miles on, passed some ruins and a well called Shah Batil, one hundred and thirty feet deep, filled with good water all the year round. Three miles farther it passed a well on the right, called Ghulam Chah, which was dry, and at five miles' distance a patch of cultivation watered from a dam. The road now turned south-east, and in three miles crossed a ravine two hundred feet broad with twenty-feet rounded banks. The edge of the hills bounding Kolwah on the south was now reached, and the road here entered them, and for half a mile ran south-west, then turning sharp round to the east went up a ravine between hills fifty to a hundred feet above the road for two miles, when it arrived at Balor.

This march was over black, stony ground with a gentle slope crossed by numerous shallow ravines, and up the Kolwah, running north to the Kej Khor valley, which is about eleven miles broad. The country the whole way is pretty thickly covered with kai trees from fifteen to twenty feet high, "pish," and tufts of grass. It had lately rained, and there was water in the beds of all the ravines crossed. Fuel and grass were everywhere plentiful.

Balor consists of seventy mat houses. A couple of miles inside the hills bounding the Kolwah plain on the south, water is procured from pools in the Balor ravine that drains to the Kolwah swamp.

On the 20th January he went from Balor to Nag, fifteen and three-quarter miles, in four hours and twelve minutes.

Leaving Balor, the road ran north by west for about two miles through low hills, when it issued into the Kolwah plain, which it crossed in a north-westerly direction. Four miles from Balor it passed a ruined fort, half a mile to the left; and at nine miles the old fort of Gat, to the right. Immediately afterwards it ascended the stony glacis on the south of the hills bounding the Kolwah plain on the north, and joined the Kaldan ravine, which it followed for four miles, winding between low hills; then leaving it, went nearly due west into Nag in one mile. A good deal of cultivation was crossed in the Kolwah plain, irrigated by water caught in dams.

Nag is a village of about one hundred and fifty houses, situated in a date grove, and watered by fourteen karez. The head men are Ganguzar and Abdurrahman, both of whom are related to Abdul Karim, the Naib of the Khan of Kalat, who lives at

Mashka. This village has about one hundred head of cattle, and is dependent for its supply of water in the hot weather on the holes dug in the bed of the ravines, as the karezes at that season dry up.

On the 21st January Captain Lockwood went to a halting-place on the Kil Khor, thirteen miles, in three hours twenty-five minutes.

The road left Nag, and taking a north-east direction, traversed a long slope for a little over one mile, when it crossed a small ravine which came from the hills to the left. Immediately afterwards it entered the Kaldan ravine, here one hundred and fifty yards broad, having a sandy bottom. The name Kaldan is taken from some date trees situated about a mile lower down the ravine, but the latter is also sometimes called the Kala Khor. The road then twisted up the bed of the ravine for some four miles, till it narrowed to not more than six yards in breadth, being shut in on both sides by rocky hills. A little running water was passed, but this dries up in the hot weather. The road then left this ravine, and ran up a smaller one to the right (which is in some places only three feet broad) for about a mile, when it arrived at the top of the Hotal pass. It then descended for a quarter of a mile down a very precipitous, narrow path, which became less steep on entering a stony watercourse, which it kept for about two and a half miles, when it emerged into an open valley running east and west, about two miles broad, which it crossed in a north-east direction, and passing some pools of water in a ravine, arrived in thirteen miles at the halting-place. Here at this time water was plentiful, but it was said to dry up in the hot season, when it has to be got from the same ravine a little further on. Grass and fuel were very abundant round this spot. Bar. 28·0.

On the 22nd January Captain Lockwood went from his halting-place on the Kil Khor to the Nafta Sham, eighteen and three-quarter miles, in five hours one minute, north by west.

The road started north by east, and wound for nearly three miles amongst low hills, when it crossed a low pass in the hills into an open plain, running, as all Makran plains do, nearly due east and west. Having crossed this in three miles, in a north-westerly direction, it then passed through an opening in another low range (some one hundred and fifty feet high above the level of the plain) into the Dashtak plain, which it traversed obliquely in a north-westerly direction. This was a flat plain covered with tufts of grass, and draining east to the Kil Khor. There was no ravine in it, but the ground was quite damp, though it had not rained for some time. Crossing another low range of hills running east and west, the road then traversed a narrow plain, called Sham, and then ran through a further low range of hills into a third plain, called Karpala, which it crossed to a gap in a low range, where there was a pool of water, called Mishkai-i-Kum. It is said never to be dry. The road then zigzagged through another range of hills running east and west for one mile, and then entered the Gumbak ravine, which was about thirty yards broad, with low hilly banks and rocky bottom, with a small stream of running water, seldom dry. Having followed this ravine for two miles, the road quitted it to the left, and crossing a stony valley, entered a ravine about six yards broad, in which it wound for three-quarters of a mile, and leaving it, entered another ravine, which it descended for half a mile to a spot where he found water and halted. The name of the place was Mala Sukandai or Nafta Sham.

The general direction of the march was north-west, and it crossed parallel ridges of hills, with valleys between them, gently ascending the whole way. The Karpala and Dashtak plains showed traces of former cultivation, though they are now quite bare. There was a small settlement of Baloches, one mile to the right of the road in the Karpala plain, but the grazing tribes who generally frequent these valleys had gone south from fear of Azad Khan, of Kharan, who was besieging Surdo. Guns, with a little labour in opening out the ravines, could be brought on this march. Grass and fuel were plentiful, and could be collected at any convenient halting-place.

On the 23rd January, 1877, Captain Lockwood marched from Nafta Sham to a halting-place on the Wash Jaorkhan ravine, nineteen and a quarter miles, in five hours seven minutes: north-west.

For the first mile the road ran to the west, over stony ravine ground, when it crossed a low stony kotal into a stony plain. Traversing this in a north-westerly direction, it entered the Zaham ravine at the second mile. This ravine was here sixty yards broad, with a rocky bottom, and had a stream of clear running water. The road then stretched up the bed of the ravine to the end of the Zaham hill, about one hundred and fifty feet above the ravine, which it passed immediately on the right. From this the road left the ravine, and turned more to the left, over broken stony ground between low bare hills for three and a half miles, when a road called the Rang went off to the left; the regular path, entering the Mantar ravine, wound its bed for four and a quarter miles between steep hills two hundred feet above it, which formed a formidable defile. There was a stream of water in places, which was never dry. Clearing this defile, the road ran nearly due west for two miles, when a track to Shahbaz branched off to the right, and in a mile further it crossed the watershed of the Kil Khor and Dasht drainage, and then passed for one and a half miles down the Kashi ravine, when it entered the Wash Jaorkhan ravine, where there was a perpetual pool of clear good water, and a cave capable of holding ten men. Descending this ravine for three-quarters of a mile, he halted. The road ran the whole way through bare rocky hills, which struck in ridges east and west. The gradient was everywhere easy; the road being nearly level the whole way, little labour would clear the Mantar defile. Grass of a coarse description, and water, were plentiful on the road.

On the 24th January, 1877, Captain Lockwood went to Kohban, in the Dasht plain, twelve miles.

At first the road ran north, and in about one mile passed down between two low hills by an easy gradient, which would, however, want making for vehicles. Then running over stony ground between low mounds, it passed at two and a half miles a track leading to Shahbaz. Immediately after this the road crossed the Tumpi ravine (one hundred and fifty yards broad, with shallow stony bed), which drains the foot of the hills to the Dasht plain. At three miles it got clear of the hills, and went over a stony slope running east and west. At five miles the Goran road joined from the left rear, and this path passed between a low row of isolated mounds that run east and west. One and a half miles further he passed the east end of an isolated hill, called Tumpi, and then went straight across the Dasht plain for five miles in a north-westerly direction to the mud fort and village of Kohban. Several large patches of cultivation, irrigated from "bunds," were passed between the Tumpi hill and Kohban. The Dasht plain is perfectly level, and covered with thin tamarisk jungle and camel thorn. Kohban consists of a contemptible mud fort, with eight feet walls, and a tower and some mat huts clustered round it. The population are Bar and Kashani Baloches. The head man, Muhammad Khan, had gone to Shahbaz to assist Azad Khan in besieging that fort. There are two wells in the village, thirty feet deep, of good water, and fuel and grass of a coarse description are plentiful in the neighbourhood.

On the 25th January, 1877, Captain Lockwood rode into Miri Isai, where I had arrived, as related above, eighteen miles, in four hours forty-nine minutes: north north-east.

Leaving Kohban the road went over the Dasht plain nearly due north for three-quarters of a mile, and then crossed the Gwarko ravine (draining from the right thirty yards broad, with high muddy banks and firm muddy bottom), leaving the fort and village of Sorai Dumb about one mile in the plain to the right. The road was through thin tamarisk jungle for a little over two miles from Kohban, when it arrived at the gravelly slope of the Kashani Koh. Ascending gently through some broken ground forming the west end of this ridge for two miles, it then for one mile turned due east, and subsequently north-east for a mile,

The Tanjgur Valley.

when it crossed the Nimcha ravine. A little more than two miles beyond this it passed over another ravine, draining from the Kashani Koh to the Rakshan. The road had now got quite clear of the Kashani Koh range, and out into the Sorwan plain, which it traversed for three miles, and then crossed the Rakshan ravine; returning to it, however, again in one and a half miles, it went up its bed for another mile and a half, and getting out of it, went round the east side of the Miri Isai date grove, and arrived at the Tul or fort of that place in ten miles from Kohban.

The portion of the Dasht plain thus crossed is level, with numerous dams scattered about, and covered with thin tamarisk jungle. The pass through the Kashani range is nearly level, nowhere rising more than two hundred feet above the plain. Very little work would make it quite practicable. The portion of the lower Panjgur, or Sorwan, plain was of the same nature.

CHAPTER V.

BALOCH POLITICS.

25th January.—Having slept over my determination of the night before to leave Miri Isai, I resolved to wait to see what Lockwood would say. In the course of the morning more men arrived from Azad Khan, evidently sent to see what I was up to. One of these, named Malih Shah, was more than usually inquisitive, but I managed to put him off by telling him about Kuhak.

I found I had not been able to procure enough camels, though Mahmud Shah had sworn by all his gods that all I required should be with me by the night before. And another more serious cause of detention was the non-arrival of my money. This, as I thought it would never do to travel with large sums of money in these parts, I had left with Major Mockler at Gwadur, to be sent on with some flour and other supplies by the direct road, and I had told him to pack the money inside the meal bags. But as it had not arrived, I sent off a Hindu with orders to bring in my flour sharp.

In the forenoon I was delighted to be told that a "sahib was coming," and on going outside my tent was intensely pleased to see old Lockwood journeying along in the distance. In a few minutes we had met, and we sat down to a breakfast that would not have disgraced more civilised regions. I had a first-rate cook with me, an individual I never omit to secure on these expeditions if I can help it, for though I am pretty strong, and as hard as my neighbours, I last much better by getting good food.

Three weeks is, after all, a considerable time to go without speaking your own language, and we had a tremendous talk over our hitherto respective routes, and over what was before us; and Lockwood agreed it would be better to wait till we had got our money and the remaining camels we wanted.

Next day was taken up in writing a letter to let people know how I was getting on. The following is a copy of the epistle in question:—

"The state of affairs in the Panjgur valley made it necessary for me to approach with the greatest caution, and so I made arrangements to keep myself well informed of the actual state of affairs from day to day. This course I have continued up till now. I marched by the road which passes Shahbaz, which is the regular caravan road. On arrival at this place late in the evening of the 20th, I heard that Azad Khan had sent an ultimatum to the Killadar to the effect that if he did not make his salaam he would come and attack him. Consequently, next morning I made a long detour round to the west in order to keep clear of any of Azad's people who might be prowling about, and I then turned towards Isai, the residence of the Khan's Naib. This place I reached without meeting many people, and those I did encounter, though most of them were sympathisers with Mir Isa, whom Azad had nominally come to help, were in every case most civil to me. I selected Thal as the most fitting place for my stay in Panjgur, as being the actual seat of the Khan's deputy; and events have proved that I was right in my choice. All the other villages are more or less mixed up in the quarrel that is going on, on one side or the other, and consequently to have gone to them and accepted the hospitality of their head men, which would have been inevitable, would have had the effect of making it seem that I was favourable to one side or the other. Whereas, with the Khan's Naib I have been able to maintain actual neutrality. I have received visits from no one but the Naib, and the only one I paid was to him. Of course several of the leading men have expressed their desire to come to see me, but I have thought it best always to have conveyed to them beforehand that under the present state of affairs I did not consider it advisable to receive any visitors at all. At the same time I offered to each such suitable expressions as were dictated by common courtesy.

"The actual state of affairs here is as follows: The invasion of Panjgur by Azad Khan, though undoubtedly it would be regarded in any other country as an act of hostility to the Khan, is not necessarily so here; and the avowed object, at least, is not an attack on the Khan's territory, but the prosecution of an old feud between Mir Gazian, the present, and Mir Isa, his uncle and former, ruler of Panjgur. The story of the feud is an old one, and goes back to the lifetime of Mir Gazian's father, who was the rival of his brother, Mir Isa, for the governorship of Panjgur. When I say this need not necessarily be considered a direct act of hostility to the Khan, I do not pretend to fathom the depths of Azad's mind. He may have other ulterior objects than merely replacing Gazian by Isa. But as far as Mir Isa is concerned, I understand he protests against its being thought for an instant that he wishes to rebel against the Khan. To show the probability of this assertion being true, it is necessary to give full weight to the actual state of affairs, both as regards the above-mentioned feud and the peculiar circumstances under which Panjgur is governed. There is, as I have said, a gentleman who is termed the Khan's Naib, but he is not the governor, and does not pretend to govern the country, or even to collect its revenue. He is, in fact, only the receiver of such revenue as the actual governor may have agreed to pay the Khan. The old agreement made between the Gichkis, the dominant family here, and Nasir Khan, was that the former were to be undisturbed in their possessions in every way, on condition of their paying over one-half of the revenues of the district to the Khan, and this arrangement still holds good. Consequently the government of Panjgur has always been allowed to remain in the hands of the Gichkis, the actual individual exercising the functions of governor being either he who was strongest, or he who agreed to pay most. Thus, in trying to oust Mir Gazian, Mir Isa does not necessarily throw off the authority of the Khan, but only wishes to make himself the actual governor of the district, and the payer of the Khan's half of the revenue.

"Azad Khan has made several attempts to open communication with me, and for me to have nothing really to do with him and yet not to irritate him has been very difficult. I have, however, I hope, fully succeeded. I have complete information brought to me of all he does and says, and there has been so far no sign of hostility on his part. While I have been getting this information I have not, of course, been ignorant of the fact that he has had his spies about me also, and so I have had to be very careful in speaking of current events before any of the people who surround me, and I have always alluded to them as matters in which I, as a simple traveller, have no concern whatever.

"Now I come to the arrangement for my onward journey, and first I would state that coming here was absolutely necessary to the success of my undertaking. For it is not only the only place where I could procure the supplies and transport necessary, but in no other spot could I have procured men to accompany me of sufficient knowledge and trustworthiness. And I have had to remain here some days both to permit of Captain Lockwood joining me and to make the necessary arrangements, which, inasmuch as they require much forethought, have had to be settled leisurely and with discrimination.

"Coming to a country like this, of which I was utterly ignorant, and of which the political agent could give me no information, the first difficulty I had was to find some really trustworthy and influential chief in whom I could confide. To this end I read all that officers who had visited the country had to say regarding the characters of the leading men, and I have made enquiries everywhere from the people I have met. From the information thus acquired I fixed on a man named Mir Kamálán, of Sami, an influential Gichki, as the most suitable person to accompany me.

"On arrival at Sami I had no difficulty in inducing him to come with me, but it was only after having been with him for five days, during which I took every opportunity of testing his character, that I ventured to impart to him a knowledge that the real object of my visit was to examine the country—swearing him to secrecy, a vow which I have every reason to believe he has faithfully kept. I then in the days that remained between us and Panjgur, passed in review every chief in that valley with sufficient influence to be of any service. It would be needless to inflict this list on any one; suffice it to say that some were found influential but not reliable, others trustworthy but not influential, while some had both these qualities, but had feuds which might interfere with the smooth conduct of my exploration. Thus after eliminating all these and re-enquiring into the merits of all the others, my choice at last fell on the son of one Muhammad Shah, formerly chief of Sib, but who had been ousted by Ibrahim Khan of Bampur. This man had property in Panjgur, in which he was then living. He was connected by marriage with both the Gichkis and Nowsherwanis, but he had no feuds with either of them, and his son was said to be acquainted with the country to be explored. On my arrival at Panjgur he fortunately with his father came to see me, and I was particularly civil to him, drew him out for two days, learnt all his hopes and fears and proved his character, and at last, being satisfied that he would prove faithful, I took him into the secret also. As he agreed to come, subsequent arrangements became easy, but still they required forethought and caution. I settled with him to supply me with an escort of twenty reliable matchlock-men, for it would be quite absurd to risk the success of difficult explorations to the mercy of a dozen stray robbers. Again, to take more men might suggest some other object, while to feed them would be extremely difficult. Twenty, then, being the number fixed on, I have arranged that each man shall be supplied with thirty days' food and fifty rounds of ammunition, and a water-skin and digging implement. As many of these as possible will be mounted on camels, but at present I have only got enough to mount some. All my things and Lockwood's also are carried on camels, and we have besides four guns apiece, which with the two chiefs make a total of thirty men armed with firearms. Provided in this way against all the ascertainable difficulties of our journey, we start to-morrow, prepared to meet and overcome the unknown difficulties which happen. We march in the direction of Kuhak at first, and then we turn towards the defile through which the Mashkel finds its way into the unknown deserts beyond. I have got with me two men who know the country, and we shall pick up others in Dehghwar. How far we shall be able to get is problematical, but most likely some marches beyond the latter locality; at present it is doubtful whether we can get further. Any way, the point we shall aim at will be about lat. 30, long. 62. As the last part of the road going out is the most difficult, so the first part of the road coming back is the hardest. I do not think there is any direct road from Seistan to Kharam, nor would it be advisable to place oneself so directly in Azad Khan's power as would be the case in a visit to his village of Sarawan. It also seems probable that no direct road across the desert exists, and therefore the most likely line we shall take will be to Nushki. I have telegraphed that we are just starting, and I send this off by the last opportunity I shall have of communicating with the outer world.

Thus hoping that we shall eventually turn up safe and sound, I take a header into the unknown."

I also wrote a long letter to Major Sandeman, telling him about the state of affairs in Panjgur.

About one p.m. Muhammad's brother arrived with three more camels, and shortly after I was delighted to see the man from Gwadur with my money arrive; but as I could not in the daytime ascertain if it was all right, I had it put down beside my tent, and took the opportunity of counting it after dark.

With some delay I got enough water-skins to give each man one, and managed to get some implements made for digging for water. The ironsmiths of Panjgur are not the most skilful I have seen, but still I managed to get them to make me some thirty iron scoops of this fashion:

Each of these had wooden handles about two feet long, and I afterwards found they worked very well in the soft sandy beds of ravines, where alone, of course, it was any use looking for water.

As I had not much to spare in the way of presents, I forwarded Muhammad Shah, father of Mahmud, who was to come with me, a horse; and that old gentleman showed his gratitude by sending back to say he had received an "animal," but it was no good to him unless I could give him a saddle and bridle also. I answered I was very sorry I had none to spare, but I would present him with a telescope: this he point-blank refused; so seeing that there was no satisfying the old man, I left him alone.

On the 27th January I quitted Isai, though not without some difficulty. Notwithstanding his promises, Mahmud did not turn up, but as I knew I should probably be served in the same way whatever day I settled to start, I determined to leave. What may be called an immense crowd assembled to witness my departure; that is to say, I suppose every man and boy in this place was present, while the scene was further graced by a bevy of the fair sex, who occupied reserved seats on the roofs of the houses to the rear. The whole of this morning must have been one round of amusement to these poor people, and they seemed to enjoy it most thoroughly in their own stolid, undemonstrative way. The first scene consisted of all the things of the Faringis spread out for inspection, and the pleasure being increased seeing that the aforesaid were in various stages of preparedness. What, however, seemed to cause the greatest interest was when the Faringis had their breakfast; then there was quite a hum of intense appreciation. Human nature is the same all the world over; at home there is no surer way of gaining the approbation of the "gods" at a theatre than to eat something in a grotesque manner, and so here, although I had no idea of conveying my humble fare to my mouth in a peculiar manner, it must have been that I did so, judging by the intensely pleased countenances of my audience. Nevertheless, it is, I venture to say, better fun reading or even writing about all this sort of thing, than enduring it; so we were very glad to mount our horses and get on our way. However, even at this last moment the amusement was not ended; for my horse then made an abortive attempt to mount Lockwood's. Shortly after leaving, a man came up on the horse I had given Muhammad Shah, bearing a message that the old gentleman in question had come to say good-bye; so I went back a little way, and he rode up, looking rather comical. The fact is he is very old, and, like many old men, did not like to show the proofs of his age afforded by his white hairs, so he had been in the habit of dyeing his locks. This morning, however, he must have been in a hurry, as the dye had only got as far as his eyebrows; these were deep black, the tip of his beard was blue, and this was gradually shaded off into purple and red, ultimately ending in pure white.

We made a short march of only five miles to Kalag, as I wanted to have everything quite complete before we got off finally. The road goes over a level plain, crossing many considerable drainage beds, one of which, the Rakshan, had close to Isai a stream of running water in it. Kalag is a wretched little place with a few mud hovels and the ruins of a fortalice situated in the midst of the usual accompaniment of a Mekran village, a dense date grove. The cultivation is irrigated by a karez which comes from the hills to the north.

The drainage of the whole of Panjgur seems to come from the Rakshan district, which is, they say, four days' journey off; and as far as one can be certain of anything from native information, it has no connection either with Pottinger's Budur, or the Budu of Kharan, the Sabz Koh range intervening between them.

The old ruined fort of Kalag was selected as the most suitable for our camp, and so we took possession. It was very evident it could not have been occupied by Baloches for many a long year, as it was almost clean inside.

Some time after our arrival, Mahmud appeared with the rest of the men and a new guide, in whose praise he was very loud, it being in his opinion a great sign of my luck that I had fallen in with such a man. I accordingly sat the latter down to question him and see what he knew. I am somewhat doubtful whether the cross-examination will be very interesting to my readers, but I have thought that a faithful account of the whole case is desirable. The reader who has followed me so far has come with me through a country with which the surveys of Major Lovett may have made him well acquainted, but beyond this was a tract which may be called absolutely unknown. In fact, I do not think that any part of the wide region which is contained within the political term Central Asia—that is, Asia between India and Russia—is more entirely unexplored. Regarding the Turkoman desert, far more information is open to the public, and the probability is that a plan of every fort is in the Russian archives of the region between Herat and Kabul; though very little is known, that little is sufficient to give a pretty fair idea of the nature of the country. Of the territory between Khokand and the Oxus we have quite recent Russian surveys, it having been lately visited by some Russian officers. But of the tract between the Helmand, Seistan, and the mountains of Panjgur and Sarhadd, one has only to look at a map to see how infinitesimal is our information regarding it. True, the daring traveller Pottinger, and the no less bold Christie, have skirted it on the north and on the south; true, Goldsmidt's party passed by it on the west, and St. John looked at it from Jalk; but on our maps, in all this tract, extending for two hundred miles from north to south, and the same distance from east to west, there are but two names—one Zirreh, in large letters, as if we knew all about it; the other, Piri Kaisar, in small. And if my readers will search all the works of those travellers who have approached this tract, they will be able to extract but small comfort from them. At least, I know I passed many an anxious hour turning and returning the pages of these books, in the hope that, like poor Marguerite's rose, they might tell me a tale in accordance with my hopes. In fact, it may almost be said, my reader knows as much of the tract as I did when I arrived in Panjgur, and will be therefore better able to appreciate the anxiety with which I pumped each man who could afford any information.

The guide whom Mahmud brought was named Nur Muhammad. He was an elderly man, with a long whitish beard and a very shrewd look, in which honesty and cunning seemed to be about equally mingled. He was a Roghi Baloch, and declared himself well acquainted with the whole tract about the Mashkel. From him I learnt that it was four or five marches to a place called Tankh-i-Zorati, the spot where the Mashkel goes through the hills into the unknown land beyond. This place, he said, was impassable, if there is much water in the river, but he held out hopes of being able to get round the bad point, which is termed an Abgir, a term which literally means water-locked, *i.e.*, the way is barred by water. Usually at these places the hills on each side come very close to each other, and between them is a pool, which is too deep to ford. Beyond this, he said it was two days to Dehghwar, whence, as well as I could make him

NUR MUHAMMAD.

out, a river comes in from the W.N.W., which drains a district called Ladiz. Three or four days beyond this the road, which has gone hitherto along the Mashkel, splits into three. The river goes off to the west, and ends two days off in a depression called the Hamun-i-Mashkel. When I asked him whether this was not the same as the Zirreh depression, or did not in some way communicate with it, old Nur Mahomed laughed scornfully, and yet pitifully, that I should for an instant imagine that Zirreh was so close. The next road was one that went to a district called Naru, which is so called from some hills named Koh-i-Naru. This region, he said, had in it some wandering tribes, who are rather a wild lot, but from whom, he hinted, I might get more information. Again, the road on the right of all goes north, to a place called Wad-i-Sultan, or Piri Kaisar, whence salt is collected; and there is a shrine to a saint of the last name. From it roads went to Rudbar and to Chageh, a district of Nushki. From this meagre information, which, though it only takes a few minutes to read, occupied me more than an hour to extract from the guide, one thing only was clear to me, viz., that as far as Tankh-i-Zorati I should be on the right track. Nur Muhammad also said there was a road to Seistan by Ladiz, but the old man said the manners of the inhabitants were a trifle rough, and he could not recommend a visit to them. At all events, the road to the Hamun-i-Mashkel seemed feasible, but beyond that appeared to be a plain, which may well be termed that of "No hope," for it has no inhabitants, and even Nur Muhammad said he knew nothing of it.

Naru was a totally new name to me; no one even hints at such a place, but Nur Muhammad said we should find people there who would be able to take us on. The road to the Piri Kaisar also puzzled me; it was like the "evasive bubble" in Captain Abney's excellent level. Walker puts it to the south of Bandar Kamal, and he draws a road right through it to Traku in a manner that made us long to place faith implicit in him; but according to St. John it is due south of Rudbar, while the guide's information seemed to make it not improbable that it was to the east of this again, and nearer Chageh. In this state of doubt I put out my light on the evening of the 27th January, and I dreamt all the night through of Narus, Hamuns, and Piri Kaisars. If I could only have remembered that dream I am sure it would have been amusing if not instructive.

On the 28th, Sunday, we halted; but it was by no means a day of rest to us, for we had to look at all the provisions of the men, inspect their powder and shot,—in fact, see that everything was ready. In a matter of this sort it is not the very smallest use trusting to a Baloch. Before there was any possibility of anything having been got ready, Mahmud had assured me in the most impressive manner that all was prepared according to my order; but when I came to see with my own eyes I found there was still much to be done. The arms were of a curious manufacture, and only fit for a museum. All the firearms were matchlocks of the most antiquated construction, their bullets were in no single case spherical, though attempts had evidently been made to produce this shape. The powder, too, was of the coarsest description, and never would go off without a prolonged preliminary phiz, that of itself would be fatal to any steadiness of firing. However, as the whole arrangements were of such a nature as to make accuracy impossible, this was of less consequence. After inspecting them all carefully, I next looked at their food arrangements, and these I found so unexpectedly complete that I took it as an omen that they did not expect to get much to eat where we were going.

I then had another long conversation with the guide, but elicited nothing more of importance, and it was clear we must wait till we got further on before we could hope to see our way clearly. In the evening I went round and looked at all the camels and their gear, and found them a very good lot, and all fit for immediate service. I had been lucky enough to get fifteen, and as two of the men and the leaders had camels of their own, and we could mount three more on our own camels, we were able to start with all mounted, and thus would not be delayed by footsore men.

The most intelligent man I had was one Mirza, a cousin of Mahmud's. He seemed naturally to take the lead, and was a very fine, soldierly-looking fellow, much more like a Sikh in appearance than a Baloch. He amused me much by appearing with a guard of four men at sundown, and asking for the ism-i-shab, or watchword. I told him it was not necessary to-night, at all events, but as he insisted on it, I gave him "Umid," *i.e.*, hope, as an appropriate one at the beginning of our trip.

CHAPTER VI.

PANJGUR TO BUDU.

MONDAY, the 29th January, found us fairly started on our journey. Instead of going west, as I thought we should, our guide led us north-west, but I soon found it was a plant on his part to induce us to halt at a camp of nomads; I, of course, would not permit of this, for though I had meant to make a short march, this was rather too short. Going on, we crossed the Soraf Khor, and then a stony plain much intersected by ravines and covered with "pish" bushes and "nadag" grass, and at ten miles came to another Soraf ravine. But as the water here was both salt and scarce, we went two miles on to a place called Guria Shep, situated a mile or so south of the west end of the range which bounds Panjgur on the north. Here is a pool of rain water, some ten or twelve yards in diameter, which they said never quite dried up, and as a sign of this a small pile of stones was erected to guide the traveller to the most probable find for water. We arrived a little after eleven, and had breakfast, but soon were put to flight by a swarm of loathsome-looking ticks, and had to leave the shade we had sought and take to the glaring open.

Koh-i-Sabz.

In the evening, after my now daily tussle with the guide, I went out and took a photograph of the hills from this, and then amused myself sketching some of our brave army. They were not a very presentable lot, but I hoped they were better than they looked. As a matter of course these savages regarded me with some awe when they saw my camera obscura, not being quite sure whether I was quite "canny."

30*th*, *Tuesday*.—Our march to-day lay for sixteen miles in a west-by-north direction, between two ridges running north-east and south-west, either over light sandy soil or small gravel; consequently we could see but little of the country. However, I took advantage of a halt to climb a neighbouring hill, and from there got a fair view. We seemed to be about the middle of a series of ridges, all running north-east and south-west, some only a few feet in height, others of considerable elevation. To the north lay the true range, called Koh-i-Sabz (green mountain), which extends from north-west to north-east, apparently about twenty miles off. This northern range may be connected to the east with the range which is seen fencing in Panjgur on the north, but no such connection is apparent, there being no hills far out to the north-east. Next to this range is the Panjgur ridge, which has been wrongly called Koh-i-Sabz. This decreases in height to the west till it ends at the junction of the Dashtak with the Rakshan. To the south there are numerous low ridges, then far off higher ones, called the Pimpishka and Sagarkand. Our camp was pitched at a place called Kachar, just below the junction of the Dashtak with the Draspara, two ravines which drain the tract between the above-mentioned ranges. These rivers join the Rakshan at an angle of about 60°, and that river here flowed in a direction 315°, whence it seemed to turn round gradually to the north towards the Tankh-i-Grawag, the gap of which is visible. The drainage on the west of the Rakshan also comes in from a westerly direction, and two ravines, the Ligork and Askan, here join it, the junction of the Mashkel being, according to the guide, beyond a low ridge to the north, called Dorud. The view from the hill above our camp at a place called Muli Gitan on the Draspara Khor, was very pretty. On the left was seen the Siahan ridge, dim in the far distance. Then there was apparently a gap, which is actually hidden by low hills, when the Koh-i-Sabz rises up on the right. Nearer than the other, and between both, are one or two low brown ridges, while the plain is studded with tamarisk trees, and here and there the glimmer of water in the pools of the river can be seen.

Fearing we might run short of supplies, we despatched a man this morning with a hundred rupees to Muhammad Shah to send us out twenty maunds of flour and ten of dates, which, with what we had, would serve to carry us on for fifty days. I was induced to this more by the great uncertainty which hangs over the country to be explored, than because I really thought we should require it all. I still hoped about thirty days would see us near Nushki, but we had to provide against all contingencies. I took three photographs this afternoon, one each of the Sabz Koh and Siahan Koh, and another of a curious hill called Daram, where the sand has been piled up against the south side of the hill, probably from the bed of the Rakshan. It looks very like

The Band-i-Tangzur.

Masson's description of the Rekh Ravan hill in Afghanistan. Our camp was pitched just north of the west end of the Band-i-Panjgur, at the junction of the Draspara and Dashtak ravines with the Rakshan. On the west was the Koh-Daram, and a little south of it the Ligork ravine came in from the west.

31*st*, *Wednesday*.—Our march on this day and that before elicited some new information regarding the country we had passed over. The fact is that no one has before visited the tract between the head of the Askan Khor, the easternmost point reached by St. John north of the range dividing the drainage of Mekran from that to the north, and Kalag, the westernmost point explored by Lovett. Therefore there are some errors in the drawing of the map here, errors which, considering the ignorance and stupidity of all Baloches, I do not wonder at. First of all, the latitude of Isai is placed too far to the north, and Kalag bears from Isai 263°—4¾ miles distant. The road to Kuhak is nearly rightly placed, but has a more north direction than is shown, going in fact in a line with the westernmost point of the range north of Panjgur, called the Band-i-Panjgur, which extends from 260° to 80°, and runs along the whole valley, on the north. This range has been named the Koh-i-Sabz, and so when I was in Panjgur it was called to me, but my guide, who comes from Grawag, a hamlet just by the defile (Tankh) of that name, assured me that this name is not rightly so applied, but is that of a range, the foot of which was still about twenty miles north. When I was coming over the Kashani Koh, I observed that the Panjgur range, at its extreme west end, seemed to be a double range, but that north of Isai it looked single; and so it proved. From the hill which I mentioned having climbed yesterday on the march, I first saw this range clearly, and at yesterday's camp, which was situated just north of the westernmost point of the Band-i-Panjgur, it appeared rising considerably higher, and still cutting off all views of the plains which we believed to exist beyond. To-day I got on a hill close to it, and found it to bear 110°, thus forming an acute angle with the Panjgur range, which bears 80°. The Dashtak ravine runs between these two ranges, and joins the Rakshan just north of the latter; from which point its head is said to be about fifty miles off, in a water parting called Sham Lundu, a road to Washak, which is about twenty to thirty miles further on, going along its bank. There appears to be no ravine called Grandas, shown in the map, but there is one called Draspara, which joins the Dashtak just above its own junction with the Rakshan.

The hills here, both on the east and west, seem to preserve the general south-east and north-west direction which all the ranges I have seen in Mekran have; and several ravines run in from the west. Among these is the Askan, which joins at a point where a low ridge on the right bank, called Koh-i-Sing, meets the river. St. John crossed the head of this ravine, and was doubtless informed that it ran into the Mashkel direct. The usual road leads along the bank of the Rakshan the whole way, but we had to turn away from that river, beyond the Sing ridge, to avoid a place where the water was too deep to admit of a passage; and we crossed a low ridge and then turned back to the river. The point where we

The Tankh-i-Grawag in the distance.

Siahan Koh from the East showing Glacis Slope.

Junction of Mashkel & Rakshan.

thus left the river was where the Kuhak road turns off. The Rakshan had now a great deal of water, which formed a running stream with many deep pools, and its bed was filled with "gaz" and "kowar" trees, affording abundance of camel forage. There is also plenty of grass and fuel. On arriving at the Mashkel we found that, for Mekran, it also had a considerable stream in its bed, and this made it doubtful whether we should be able to pass through the Tankh-i-Grawag defile. This was a great nuisance, as it would necessitate our making a long detour to the west to get round it, and thus delay us a day. I therefore halted in the bed of the Mashkel to gain further information, a proceeding which, according to Haji Abdun Nabbi, is the height of folly, for he says the Baloches have a saying that the Mashkel is so subject to sudden rises that any one who stops in its bed, even to tie his shoe, deserves to be a cuckold.

The bed of the Mashkel at the junction with the Rakshan is three hundred yards broad, with a pebbly bottom, scantily covered with tamarisk. Its northern bank is formed of a broken cliff of conglomerate, but the southern is low and sandy. It has a stream of running water, fifty yards broad and under a foot deep. Fuel, grass, and camel forage are very plentiful.

Immediately after arriving we climbed a hill above the left bank, and got a good view of the course of the two rivers, and also of the entrance to the Tankh-i-Grawag. Of these, and of the Siahan Koh, I took photographs, and in the evening I got a sketch of the latter from the bed of the river. This range does not differ from many I have seen in Persia;

viewed sideways, there is a glacis of stone and shingle running up at an easy slope to nearly the top, whence the ridge starts up abruptly into a thousand rugged peaks, making it absolutely impracticable along its whole length. It is also a peculiarity of the Mekran hills, that as long as you keep to the regular paths, the roads are quite easy, but the ridges themselves are everywhere else quite impracticable. From this point we got a view of the village of Grawag, which consists of a few huts and date trees, situated under precipitous cliffs, just at the entrance of the Tank, to which it gives its name.

My guide amused me much by his conversation to-day. Like all Baloches, he is deliciously simple in his ideas, and has none of the Eastern habit of putting things sweetly. When I was stooping down to get the slide for my camera, he looked at me and remarked, "Why do you have your trousers so tight?" I laughed, and said I thought they were very loose. "Loose!" he replied, "I thought they would split; mine are loose, if you like," holding out his to his side. Next thing he said was, "Now I have shown you my country, you must show me yours." "Very well," I replied; "but that would not be a fair exchange, there is nothing to see here, where there is nothing but stones; my country is one large garden." "Is it?" said he; and then turning to the men, he repeated, "His country is all a garden, date trees everywhere." I protested that there were no date trees. "No date trees! whew!" and he looked as if he thought a country without date trees could not be much worth seeing.

Coming along to-day I noticed that many of the

Tankh . i . Grawag .

"pish" bushes had a stalk growing out of their centre, on which were a number of round black berries. These are called Kunar, and are eaten by the Baloches. They have a large stone in them, and taste very insipid, but something like a date.

In the evening I had my usual innings with the guide, and settled that as the road through the Tankh-i-Grawag was not practicable for camels, Lockwood should take all these and the baggage round by a route which turns the defile, while I went with a few men on foot and climbed the hills by a break-neck path. This would enable me to see whether a road could not be made through the defile, above the high water line. As some of my brave army had "friends" beyond the Persian border, which was close at hand, I was to take these with me in order to prevent the possibility of their falling in with their enemies. Lockwood was rather apprehensive that this would leave me at their mercy; but a calm view showed me that I need fear nothing, as it could not be their interest to harm me; "besides," I said, "my boy, I shall have my claymore and revolver, and unless I am taken unawares, I think a Macgregor on the hillside ought to make something of four or five Baloches."

I gradually took sketches of each of my brave army, most of which I have since lost. This is a pity, as they made very queer pictures. Some really were quite ruffians, and others looked it. Their habits were anything but soldierly, and they thought nothing of firing off their matchlocks at any moment; but I tried to put a stop to this. To-day, just as we were bathing, we heard a shot fired, and then shrieks as if a man was being murdered; as soon as I could get on some clothes I went out, only to see a hare running for its life with half-a-dozen wild Baloches shrieking after it. Lockwood thought we were attacked, and had run out with his rifle regardless of appearances. Certainly one trait of the Baloches is their intense avariciousness. If you give them anything, they unblushingly ask for something more. The fate of my present to Muhammad Shah has already been mentioned. Again, some days ago, I gave Muhammad my gun, and he came to Lockwood to-day to ask what it was worth; and lastly, I gave the guide a capital clasp knife; he took it, never said thank you, but remarked to his "rafik" (companion), "It has neither got a sheath nor a sling." Whenever you ask a Baloch to do anything for you, he invariably says, "What will you give me?" The other day one of my paid escort wanted payment for coming to the top of a hill with me!

1*st February*, *Thursday*.—Having seen Lockwood start, I departed for the Tankh. We first had to round the low ridge which I climbed yesterday, and then we entered the defile. At the point where it makes its first turn is a small patch of cultivation with a few date trees, which gives its name, "Grawag," to the defile. This is simply composed of the bed of the Mashkel river, which twists and turns about to find itself a way through the Sabz Koh. As the water was very high, the road was in many places nearly impracticable, from the river having to be frequently forded; but when the water is low the roadway must be good. The surrounding heights are very steep and impracticable, and no doubt an intelligent enemy could render a very efficient opposition to a force threading this defile; but though an advance might of course be delayed, it could not be stayed, as there are several paths by which the various positions taken up

View from hill above Tankh-i-Grawdg.

Sakhta Koh in the Grawag Defile.

The Siahan Koh.

could be turned, and also a road by which the same result could be achieved as regards the whole defile. I took two sketches on the defile, one near the south entrance, which gives a good idea of how the hills interlace and dovetail into each other; the other of a very curious hill called Supta or Sukhta Koh, met with near the north entrance, where the strata are upheaved so as to be standing end on, each little peak of the hill being actually the end of a stratum. The defile is about six miles long, and water is probably always abundant throughout its whole length. While we were in the defile, I once saw two men perched on a hill just above us, and as I thought that might mean mischief, I made the guide call and find out who they were; but they proved to be two of our own men who had preceded us out shooting. They came into camp soon after us, and said they had fired two shots at an oorial, but had missed.

On emerging from the defile, the Siahan Koh burst upon us, the whole extent of the ridge being visible. It is higher than the other ridges, but is in no other respect different, presenting the same bare, uninviting appearance, and the same impracticability. From west to east there appear to be only two paths over it, one called the Rag, where a curious vein of white clay runs up the hill side, which, however, is passable for footmen; and the other to the east, which is just practicable for camels. There are no signs of habitations along its foot from one end to the other, though it is said there are about one hundred families of Baloches who take from it their names of Siahaniss. Between the Sabz Koh and Siahan, there is a long stretch of high ground, which slopes rapidly to the Mashkel, and three miles to the left are trees which mark the site of a deserted hamlet called Tump, which had some cultivation watered by karez. Looking at the Siahan from the south, below the rugged summit of the range is a slope which ends in a scarp. This is composed of white clay with a layer of brown sandstone on the top, and it has been much cut up by water, so that at a distance the dark lines of the stone, broken at intervals by ravines, have exactly the appearance presented by the caves of the houses of one of the villages on the hill sides in Kurdistan. This stretched for several miles, and looked just as if there were an enormous cave village extending along the base of the hill.

From the defile our path took us over a stony plain. At three miles we passed a road from Kuhak to Kharan, and at four reached the bank of the Mashkel, which had been running close to the right. On arrival the guide pointed out a snug bit of high ground with many tamarisk trees, affording a grateful shade, and suggested it as a camping-ground, adding in peculiar idiom, "If you will be friends with it." I arrived at 1.30, though I had stopped for nearly an hour and a half on the defile to sketch; but no signs of Lockwood were apparent.

After, therefore, making sure from Mirza that there was no chance of any hostile individuals being about, I caused several of the trees to be set ablaze to guide him to us. After waiting in vain for five hours, and thinking he must have halted somewhere else, he appeared just as it was getting dark, having made a march of thirty miles to come to the same spot I had reached in eleven. He had been, moreover, much delayed by the necessity of keeping his people together, a necessity which they did not appreciate, and after all managed to evade, as it was found that an African servant of mine, called Doshamba, *i.e.*, "Monday," had been lost, and Mir Mahmud and his brother had gone in search of him. On the way, when near my bivouac, he noticed some men skulking along on the flank, and on pointing them out, some of our men went in pursuit, and succeeded ere long in bringing four individuals, who, however, proved to be friends, three being Siahanis, and one, their leader, a Reki and a relation of our guide. They said they were going to join Azad Khan, it being no use to continue enemies with him, as he had destroyed so many of them. However, they were advised by the guide not to trust themselves to his mercy, and the following morning they went back to their hills, promising to bring us some sheep at our next camp.

Lockwood's road, for the first eight and a half miles, went in a westerly direction, four miles of it up the bed of the Mashkel, and then between low hills. At eight and a half miles it entered the Gazinda ravine, and turned north-west, winding through it for five and a half miles, when it left it and entered another watercourse amongst low hills, in which it wound about for some two miles, when it issued on a high plateau, sloping to the south at the foot of the Siahan Koh, and between them and the hills round the Tankh defile. It then entered the Tump ravine, which runs west by north, and continuing in it for four miles, got out on to the open plain which slopes down to the Mashkel. The Gazinda ravine mentioned above was in places only three yards broad at the bottom, and had perpendicular sides of conglomerate fifty feet high. The whole of this road was over stone and gravel; the hills and surrounding country were perfectly desolate, with no inhabitants, and there was no water after leaving the Mashkel.

As the missing Doshamba had not arrived late last night, I sent some of the men after him with food, and we lit fires to show them the way to our bivouac.

On the morning of the 2nd none of the absent ones had arrived, and though I got up and prepared for the march, I had to abandon the intention. The upshot was that they put in an appearance about two or three in the afternoon, Mr. Monday having been found wandering listlessly in an aimless manner. He was discovered by the Mula, and from what I heard, I made out that Mir Mahmud had quietly gone off and passed the night at Kuhak, though he declared he did not. Certainly he had no signs of having spent the evening in the open, and I was really very angry at the loss of a whole day which had been caused. I, however, dissembled, and gave Mahmud to understand I had passed sleepless hours thinking of him. The fact was he had already shown signs of a mulish disposition, but as we were actually more or less in his power, we had to try and keep him contented. Not that he was of much use, but as his was the influence which brought the men together, without him they would probably not come on at all. In fact, he was the string with which I had to keep my bundle of faggots together. The best man we had got apparently was Mirza Khan, who was not only very intelligent, but always ready to do anything, even to shoeing one's horses. The men also seemed very quiet, willing, and ready to help.

We spent about the most miserable day we have had, the wind blowing the light, impalpable dust into clouds, and covering everything an inch thick. And to add to the enjoyment of the scene, I had a return of fever. In the afternoon, as there were signs of rain, we changed our camp to some higher ground, and we had hardly done so when it came on to pour.

I had time to get my things and the servants' bedding into the tent, but they, poor devils, got a drenching. The wind blew cold and piercing all the night, and so I made my servants come and sleep in my tent, a boon which their sonorous snores showed they fully appreciated.

In the evening, I had my usual talk with the guide. I had by this time gone over the routes to the north so often with him that I had a fair idea now of the relative position of places, though it was difficult to get more than a very approximate notion of their actual site. The reason of this was because the Baloch has no measure of distance except a day's march, and as this is very expansive, varying from twelve to forty miles, it is difficult to form any satisfactory idea of distances. I, however, discovered that they do make some difference in their marches, and reckon that three laden camel marches equal one riding camel march. The rain last night made it doubtful whether we should be able to get through the Tankh-i-Zorati, which was said to be much more difficult than that of Grawag. I, however, determined to go through it myself on foot, as it was necessary for me to see it in order to judge how far it would be possible to make a road that would be above the water line.

As the place on which we spent this most delightful day did not rejoice in a name, we set ourselves to invent one. I suggested it should be called "Doshamba

Gum" (Lost Monday), but Lockwood improved on this by proposing its name should be Bad-i-Shaitan (Satanic Wind), both of which conveyed impressions of our feelings on the day in question, Lockwood being the more annoyed by the wind, I by the delay caused by the loss of Monday. However, we finally rejected the latter as calculated, if translated, to shock polite ears, and adopted the first; but any future explorer in these parts need not, of course, expect to find his guide knows the name of Doshamba Gum.

3rd February.—To-day was our second day without any meat. I do not record this fact as the commencement of a pile of agony to enlist the reader's sympathies,—after the fashion of gentlemen lost on a desert island: "To-day we eat our last biscuit,"—but simply as an interesting fact; unless in the course of our explorations we discovered some oasis, it did not seem likely we should get any more meat for a month at least.

The march to-day lay first over a hard stony plain, and then through ridges of clay hillocks. The plain all drained north to the Mashkel, and was quite bare, except where some trees marked the site of a deserted village called Gariok. The clay ridges we passed through are offshoots of the Sabz Koh, and, from the constant action of water, have assumed the most fantastic shapes imaginable, some resembling a mushroom, others a roof, a hat, a tower, etc. The accompanying sketch gives a fair idea of them, and, strange as they appear, they are really exact copies of one part of a ravine we passed. I fancy that formerly there was a long slope of clay from the Koh-i-Sabz to the river, both of which were probably at a much higher level than they

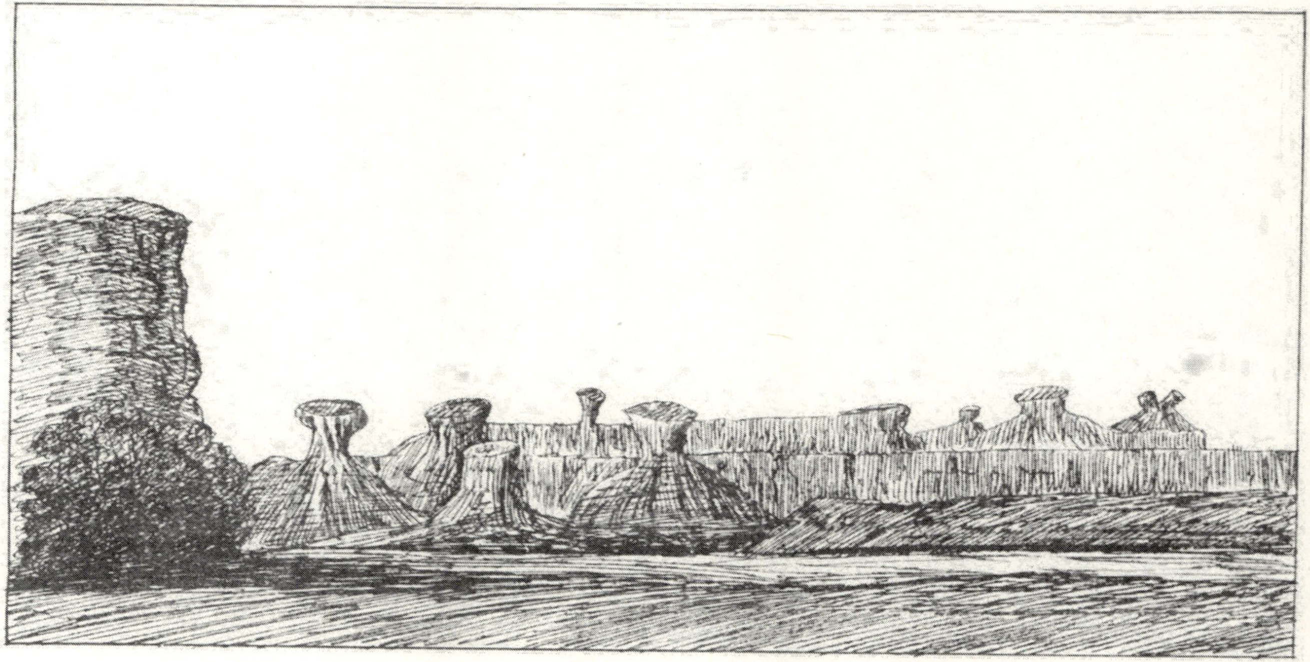

Water-worn formations of white clay on the bank of the Mashkel.

are now, and the drainage has gradually cut deep beds for itself, which form the present ravines, while the water, acting on the dissoluble clay, has cut all this away in parts, leaving hills of the above fastastic shapes standing on some harder stratum. The wind continued to blow all day, and as the whole plain and river-bed is covered with a light soil, which forms into an impalpable dust, the air became quite loaded with it, carrying a haze, through which the country we were traversing was only dimly visible. We made seventeen miles to-day, and pulled up on the bank of the river Mashkel, as the guide said there was no more water for many miles. We got a nice high place for our tents, which raised us above the ravine; but the men did not appreciate the position, and said it was too cold, so they ensconced themselves in a deep ravinelet close by, where the wind blew harmlessly over their heads; and, as they had an unlimited supply of firewood, they were pretty comfortable.

They were very nasty fellows to manage, and often said and performed most impertinent things; but as long as they did what I wanted, *i.e.*, gave me the moral advantage derived from their presence, I was satisfied. Besides, with such savages it was not always easy to see whether they meant rudeness, or were only ignorant.

Our march to-day took us very much east, and as the Tankh-i-Zorati, the defile by which the Mashkel leaves the hills, is still some miles off, this will make a difference in the delineation of this river from that shown on the maps. Our bivouac had no name, but it was situated close to the Mashkel, which here had

9

a stream twenty yards broad and about one foot deep. There was an abundance of grass, fuel, and camel forage about.

4th, Sunday.—From our camp of yesterday, which has no name, our road to-day first went a little way up a considerable ravine, called Buzurg Gaz, and then, crossing a low ridge of clay, we regained the river by another ravine, called Zani. From this we kept to the river, crossing from side to side very often, till about three hours after we started we reached the entrance of the defile, called Tankh-i-Zorati. Of this time we halted twenty-five minutes to let the baggage close up, the boulders on the bed of the river making it very difficult travelling for camels, so that the distance was not more than eight and a half miles. In the defile the road winds about with the turnings of the river, which it crosses and recrosses several times, and when the river is low the roadway must be quite easy, though very stony. When, however, the river is up, the fords become quite impracticable, and it would be difficult even for a foot-man to get along by keeping to one bank. The heights on both sides are very steep and rugged, and are composed of sandstone rock, the strata of which is upheaved straight on end. The defile is of course eminently defensible; in fact, it is of that nature that it would be described by a non-military traveller as a place where a few men could stay thousands. But the fact is that, like most defiles through rugged hills, while it would present an almost unforcible obstacle to a front attack, yet it is very open to be turned both as a whole and in detail; so that, unless defended by an intelligent enemy, it would not detain

Tankh-i-Zorati.

well-commanded troops a single day. A road could no doubt be made along the foot of the hills, above the water-line, but it would have to be almost entirely over rock,—of easy fracture, however. I should be inclined to doubt its ever being really impracticable except during floods, and these always run off pretty quick. One of the difficulties of the road is the presence of quicksands, and therefore every crossing would have to be carefully examined before animals were committed to it. Just at the exit of the pass there is a long deep pool, which stays the direct road along the bank of the river; but there is an easy path leading up a little gully, west by north, to the left from this spot, which avoids it. The defile is shut in by hills the whole way, which rise in perpendicular cliffs of some two hundred feet in height on either side. The breadth is nowhere very confined, being generally about one hundred and fifty yards, and not going lower than eighty yards. There are no indications of any very high rise of the water, but if this were to happen to the extent of twenty feet it would be quite sufficient to block the defile altogether. Coming into the bed again, we saw that it still had a considerable jungle of "gaz" and "kowar,"—a welcome sign to us, who could not have gone on if camel forage had failed.

After we had got in, I put my rug under the shade of a "kowar" tree, and several men of my brave army presently came round me. Among them their lackadaisical chief, who is a character, though an utterly imbecile one, who said he wished to speak to me, and he began without further ado. What followed is a specimen of what I had often to listen to as patiently as if I was catching pearls of wisdom.

"Sahib," began Mahmud, in a drawling lackadaisical voice, "I am a Baloch, and though I am no one, my father was some one. He was chief of his own country till the Kajars took it, and now we are not much. This is what is called fate. Now, Sahib, give me your ear, remember what I say." "I am all attention," said I meekly. "Well, this." he continued, bending over to me confidentially, and assuming a mysterious air, "this is perhaps the most dangerous country in Iran or in Turan, nay, more, in the world. I am a Baloch, and I say it." "Never mind," replied I, smiling, "I will take care of you; as long as you are with me no harm shall come to you." This rather took him aback; he evidently thought to frighten me, in order to make his services appear of more value. However, he said, "Truly your luck is great." "Yes," I rejoined, "my luck is good." "Or else," put in the guide, in his quaint, shrewd manner, "we should not have got through the Tankh-i-Zorati as easily as we have." "Yes," I said, "you see what it is to be with me; everything has gone right, and you will find everything will do so till I dismiss you all with a present." I trust the reader will not put these remarks down to swagger on my part. I am very fortunate as a rule, and a great believer in luck, but, of course, except with these people I would not talk in this way. With them, however, it was different; they were very ignorant, and easily moved by signs of good luck or bad, and I thought it sound policy to impress on them that I was born under an auspicious star.

I can't say I think there is anything very likeable about these people. Some savages are possessed of fine qualities, but I could discover none among them. Perhaps it is that their ignorant and insolent avarice prejudices me, but it certainly is a fact they were the most greedy wretches I had ever met.

We were now north of the range which bounds the desert on the south, but we could as yet get no view to the north. The day was very hazy, and beyond us all the country was shut off by more of the above-described clay ridges. We were now very near Pottinger's road, as he must have crossed our line about lat. 27′ 40″. The interesting question at that time for us was, Where is Pottinger's Budur? We had, of course, finally settled that it does not run through the "Tankh" to the Dasht, as he supposed. But where does it go? He says he came to a river bed, called the Budur, at least a quarter of a mile wide, which he supposed forced its way south through a "Tankh," which must be the one we came through to-day. He asserts, moreover, he went up its bed for five miles, and that he was told it went to Garmsel, —two courses which are clearly irreconcilable. Our supposition was that the river he calls Budur is the Mashkel, and that he really went down its bed. It may seem difficult to understand how one could go down the bed of a river for five miles and think he was going up it, but to those who have seen the drainage beds of these countries it will not appear in the least improbable, especially when it is remembered that Pottinger must have been ignorant of the geography of the country through which he was going; and our view was strengthened into a conviction from the guide having told us, without any questioning on my part, of a place called Budur on the bed of the river. The Mashkel at the point where we halted was from a quarter to half a mile broad, with a pebbly bed covered with thin tamarisk jungle. The latter is shut in on both sides by high cliffs of conglomerate, which diminished in height towards the end of our march. The country above was quite flat, with a gentle northerly slope, and covered with small black gravel. The whole bed showed signs of having been recently covered with water. During the first part of the march there was a rivulet some twenty yards broad by one foot deep, but towards the end the stream got much smaller, and at our halting-place there was only a large pool.

5th, Monday.—Our march to-day was nearly all on the bed of the Mashkel, which continued to run between cliffs, fifty to one hundred feet high, of conglomerate. The distance was seventeen miles, and it was with difficulty we induced the guide to come on so far. The cliffs form the edge of the desert, which is at a much higher level than the bed. This difference in level, however, decreased rapidly towards the end of the march, when it was not more than forty feet. At about the twelfth mile, the water in the bed ceased to flow above, though the pools were evidently replenished from below, and trees began very sensibly to thin, till, when we reached our stage, a dozen tamarisk was all that remained of the usual dense verdure we had been accustomed to find in the Mekran ravines. Here there is very little camel forage, but there is abundance of fuel in the bed of the river. We were now well out into the desert. On either hand, as far as the eye could see, was a dreary stony plain, without a leaf or a sign of life. I took bearings from this point to the Tankh, 195°; to the Tankh-i-Lori, 155°; to the furthest visible

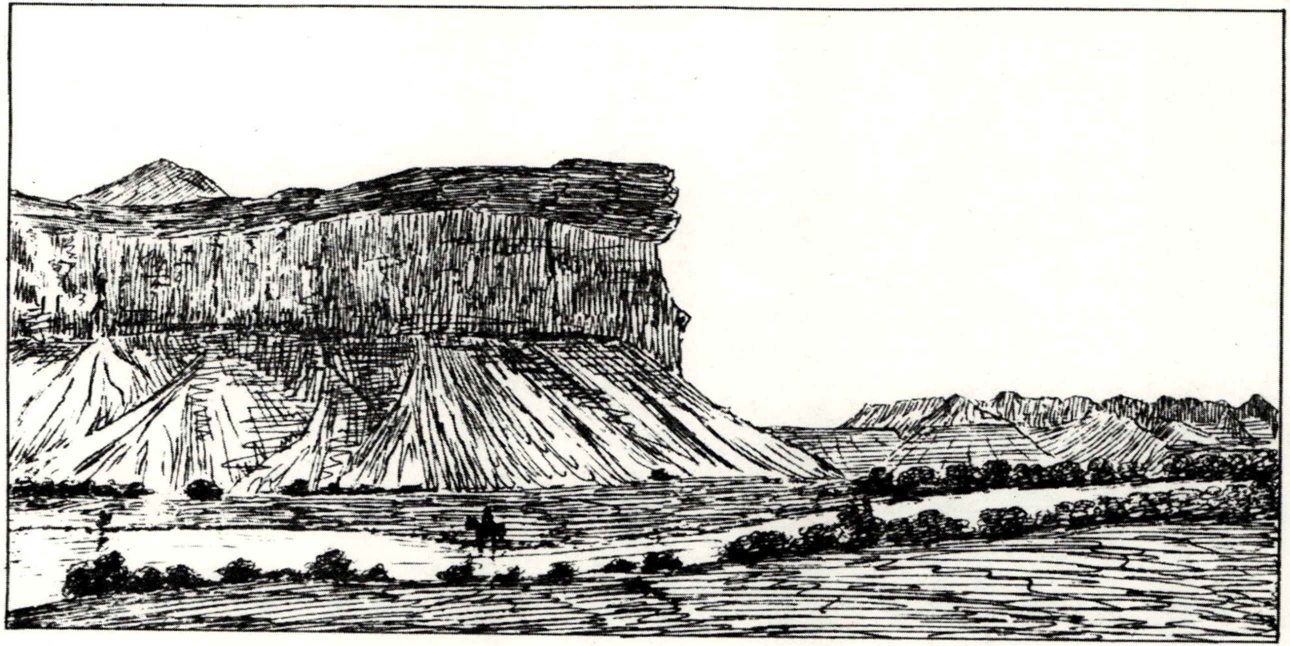

Hill on the Bank of the Mashkel.

point of the Siahan ridge, 122°; whilst the river now turned decidedly north. The Tankh-i-Lori is a point where a stream called the Bibi Lori, which rises north of the Band-i-Panjgur, breaks through the hills into the desert, when it runs probably nearly parallel with the Mashkel, till, gradually nearing it, it joins a few miles ahead of our camp to-day. This was formed at a point on the river called Mian Rud, a name given to an island of conglomerate, which, rising on the bed, causes the river to divide into branches to pass the obstacle.

6*th*, *Tuesday*.—Crossing the dry river bed below the junction of the two arms which form the island called Mian Rud, we ascended on to the high land above the river, and went over small black gravel for an hour and a quarter. We then descended over heavy sand, into the bed of the river, and, passing an old camp of that determined raider, Azad Khan, came in one and a half miles to the junction of the Bibi Lori ravine. This, which has a bed some four hundred yards broad, takes its rise in the north face of the Band-i-Panjgur, and is the only stream the waters of which ever reach the Mashkel. Along its bank there is a road to Panjgur, which is practicable for camels, and which is shorter than the one by which we had come. I regret I did not know this before, or I would have sent Captain Lockwood by it to meet me at this spot; but of course, as it happened, this was impossible. A mile or so beyond this we came to a sand ridge, called Budu, whence there is a road to Kharan. This place must undoubtedly be that which led Pottinger to call the river Budur, as, according to our reckoning, he must have crossed the river just at this point. If he had crossed to the south, he would have seen the bed of the Bibi Lori, which he does not mention, while the heavy ridges of sand make it very improbable that he could have gone to the north. The river at this point answers very much to the description Pottinger gave of it, and, putting myself in his place almost on the same spot he must have recorded the observation, I came to the conclusion that his mistake about the course of the river was not only possible, but a very natural one under the circumstances, and if due weight is given to the fact that he knew nothing of the geography of the country beforehand.

From this we went over ridges of heavy sand above the river-bed for three miles, when we again descended into the bed, and the baggage and army being now very much behind, I halted for it to come up. After waiting half an hour, all had arrived but Mahmud and a Sowar or two, so, getting on my horse, I told the guide to go on. There were now signs of incipient mutiny. I heard a voice say, "Don't go." But as I did not see who it was I thought it better not to notice it. The guide, however, went on, but most of the men remained, and I found the leader of this mutiny was Gholam Rasul, Mahmud's brother. This want of all hold over my men was one of my principal difficulties, and I had to be very careful in managing them, not to give in to them too much, yet not to be too exacting. My system was always to think very carefully before giving any order, to give up wishing for, and consequently ordering, any matter of small consequence, because the effect of a trifling command being disobeyed would be as bad as if the matter were important. But when necessary, I gave my orders to Mahmud or

Mirza, and they had them carried out. Thus, though every minute of the day these men were doing things which jarred on my military feelings, I took no notice. I left them to themselves as far as possible. This system had succeeded so far, but now it seemed as if a storm was about to burst. After our arrival in camp, Mahmud came into my tent. He was evidently very angry, and entered in the most ceremonious manner, as if he had a painful duty to perform. I therefore quickly motioned him to a place. He then began talking in a wild, rambling way of the services he had performed, as a preliminary to what was to follow. As, however, I did not know what he was likely to say, I thought it best to make no remark, but to watch him and think what had best be replied as he went on. He evidently did not like the operation, and as I answered nothing, but kept my eye steadily on him, he began to quail and wander, till at last, when he fairly got off the rails, I seized the opportunity to turn the drift of the conversation altogether. He had remarked something about not knowing where we were going, so I said, "I know you don't know where we are going; but that is only because I don't know. I told you that all this country was totally unknown to me. It is because I really am not certain of the direction of places that I have not been able to settle where to go to. But now you are here, I am very glad, as I shall be able to have your advice. You see, Nur Muhammad says Naru is to the north-north west, and Zirreh to north-west, while the Hamun of the Mashkel is to the west," and so on, till Mr. Mahmud was plunging into the middle of a quagmire of geographical supposition, quite pleased with his own intelligence, and the rising storm was averted. Our camp to-day was at a place called Nallaf, where there was abundance of water, fuel, and a sufficiency of camel forage. The river bed, which, from Chekulu to the Lori, had been stony and very thinly sprinkled with trees, now became again sandy and densely wooded. The high cliffs of conglomerate also had entirely ceased, and their place was now taken by ridges of sandhills, which stretched as far as the eye could reach.

Bed of the Mashkel.

Balsch Desert.

CHAPTER VII.

REKH BOREDA TO SHANDAK.

7th, Wednesday.—The road to-day went for five miles along the left bank, keeping between the bed, which is here fully half a mile broad, and the sandhills, and winding through pretty thick tamarisk jungle, which made it difficult to see where we were going, and necessitated our scrambling on to the top of the sandhills from time to time to get bearings. We then arrived at a place called Rekh Boreda, where the sand had encroached on the river-bed, and had obliterated all trace of a road. The guide, therefore, took to the sandhills on the left, and we floundered about among them for an hour, not making more than two miles in that time. Nur Muhammad gave as his reason for not keeping below, that the bed where wet formed dangerous quicksands, which made it impossible to cross to the right bank. However, we then got down below, after I had taken a couple of photographs, one of the sandy desert, another of the bed of the Mashkel at this point. I only hope they will convey some idea to the reader, as no description of mine could do justice to the scene of utter desolation presented by the miles of thirsty sand heaps which stretched before us.

The road after this led through the same sort of ground as the first part of the march; we had to keep the left bank of the river, just along the edge of the sand, and in nine miles we reached a halting-place called Rekh Farang, because, said Nur Mahomed, some Faringi had once halted there. Who this Faringi could have been I could not conceive, but it was curious to find a tradition to this effect. It was not improbably some reminiscence of Pottinger's visit.

The behaviour of Mahmud was much improved to-day. He smirked encouragingly to me, and took notice of Lockwood in a kind manner; but he smiled, I think, most at himself. The fact was he was pleased with himself; he had come into my tent yesterday like a lion and gone out like a lamb, and he attributed this to his own cleverness. The total distance we got over to-day was about sixteen miles. At Rekh Farang we found plenty of water in pools in the river bed, and abundance of grass, fuel, and camel forage everywhere. On the sandhills passed there grew a species of tamarisk which they called "Ta Gaz," and which the camels eat greedily, and our horses did not at all disdain.

Our next stage was to a place Nur Muhammad called Mairum, from which he said two roads go to the point which we marked on our maps F. P., or furthest point, and which we proposed to name Ja-i-Maksud, *i.e.*, the place of our hope. One of these roads was said to go by Gorani and Talab to Zirreh, and to be twelve long marches, at all of which, except three, there was water, but in most cases it was said to be salt; forage for camels was pronounced to be scarce.

This route goes for a considerable distance west

before it turns north, and it was said to be somewhat dangerous, being exposed to the raids of the Sarhaddis, and it had also to go through Persian territory. The other road was said to be in every respect better, leading in five stages to Naru, a district where water and camel forage was plentiful, and where some supplies could be procured. The guide also considered it best because it was safer, and we could leave some of the camels there to recruit, while we went on with the best with light loads; and finally there was no doubt about its being on Kalat territory, to which we had hitherto confined ourselves. Still I much wished to go by both routes. This, however, was quite impossible, as we had only one guide, and it seemed to me to start a party in such a desert to find its way even for three days, would simply be to condemn it to death. One might steer by the compass, and I should have had no fear of not turning up somewhere near the right point; but to do this we should have to carry water for the whole distance, an undertaking which was simply out of the question with our present animals, one of which, as if to warn me not to demand too much from the rest, had just had to be abandoned, being unable to move another step.

In the evening Nur Muhammad came to have the terms on which he was to proceed with me settled. I had not done so before, as I understood from Mahmud that he had arranged everything with him; but now I found that, like most other statements of this "truth-loving" Baloch, this was untrue. I had no wish to quarrel with the guide; to do so would have been more idiotic than to have quarrelled with your *chef* on the eve of a grand entertainment; and therefore Mr. Muhammad found me very willing to listen to his requests. At the same time I had to be careful not to seem to yield too readily, as the old fox would very soon have understood, and doubled his demands. Finally, we came to terms, and I agreed to give him three rupees a day for the trip, except the bit to Zirreh, which was to be four rupees. These terms are high, certainly, but considering nearly the whole success of the expedition depended on this man remaining faithful, I thought the money would be well expended.

After he had gone, I spent half an hour in keeping Mahmud in a good temper, by making a show of asking his advice. He was much pleased, and drawled on for a quarter of an hour some twaddle about what he thought we should do. As I did not listen, I cannot give the reader the benefit of his sage remarks. To have seriously appealed to Mahmud for advice would have been absurd, and whenever I really wanted an intelligent opinion I asked Mirza, the only truly sharp fellow in the batch. During the conversation, another difficulty, which threatened to be serious, cropped up. I mentioned that I proposed to return by Chageh and Nushki, when Mahmud informed me he would not go there, as he had a blood feud with Sarfaraz Khan, the chief of the former village. It appears that long ago Sarfaraz's ancestor made a raid on Sib, and killed some of Mahmud's progenitors. On this the latter retaliated and killed Pasand Khan, Sarfaraz's grandfather, and sixteen of his people. Consequently it was Sarfaraz's turn now, and Mirza thought that he would not let such a chance slip; he confessed he would not himself lose such an opportunity, and he saw no reason why Sarfaraz should be more merciful. This was really very serious, as it might have caused Mahmud to leave me at a critical part of the route, and before I could get arrangements made with any other responsible party to take me on. I, however, told them that I would think the matter over, and they agreed with me, there was no immediate necessity to come to any resolution, which could be better done when we reached Naru, where we should learn how the wind lay; and if the worst came to the worst, I hoped to be able to induce some of the men who had no feud with Sarfaraz to go on through Chageh, while another party travelled south-east before getting there, and made for Sarawan, thus avoiding it altogether. I foresaw that in one respect the contretemps might turn out fortunate, as it would afford a very sufficient reason for our wishing to go in two different directions.

To-day, we were lucky enough to get a couple of teal, which were a great addition to our meal, we having been now for some days without meat. Lockwood told me that when he shot the teal a scene something like that depicted in *Punch* occurred; both he and Mahmud fired simultaneously, and one said, "My bird I think, sir," the other, "Mine I fancy, sir." The point of honour was never settled, but we eat it—a far more important matter.

8*th*, *Thursday*.—Last night was very cold; the thermometer went down to 18°, and all the water in our skin bags was frozen; but, thanks to my plenteous wraps, I did not feel or even know how cold it had got, till the morning. Luckily there was any amount of fuel, and so the men kept up roaring fires all night, and did not complain of the frost. The cold made us later in getting off, as it would have been cruel, not to say useless, to have expected them to leave their fires till the sun had risen high enough to warm them a bit. The road went all the way for sixteen miles over sand, which was at times extremely heavy going for the horses, though it suited the camels exactly. The bed of the river was now entirely sand, and so I was not surprised to find that very little water remained in its bed beyond our last night's camp, though abundance could be procured almost anywhere by digging. At three miles we came to seven curious pillars of mud, erected on the left bank of the river, to the memory of some heroes who had been killed many years ago in a raid on the Naruis. It speaks volumes for the dryness of this climate that these structures, which very little rain would wash away, are still standing. The place which is called Nilan marks the point where roads go to Jalk and to Chageh.

Not long after our arrival in camp, and just as I was bathing, a false alarm occurred. Mirza, jumping on to his horse with great alacrity, galloped to the front, and certainly the way the men swarmed out to his support was a good omen of what they would do if we had been unfortunate enough to have to sustain a real attack. I hoped, however, that this would not happen, as whichever way a fight went would be bad for us. Whether we won or lost, our road onward would probably be blocked, and if we should happen to kill one of the enemy we should have the whole tribe down on us. Therefore, while there was yet time, I

Nilan.

warned the men as to what must be their line of conduct if attacked. I sent a party out in the evening with Mirza, to get on to the surrounding hillocks, and search the country round with the telescope I gave him, for signs of lurking foes; but none were reported. We reached a point at twelve miles where the river divides into two branches, one of which, running in a direction of 280°, is called Ragab, the other, from 335°, being known as the Mairum. Both these go on separately for two days' further on, when they are lost in the Hamun to the west. We went between these ravines, but, inclining towards the former, ended our march of sixteen miles near a pool on its bank. Here we found a snug spot, where some sandhills cut off our tents and fires from all probability of being seen to the front, while they formed excellent points of observation. The day was extremely hot, and this, after the great cold last night, knocked my man Muhammad over with fever. From this point we saw the Naru hills, bearing 336°, and about seventy or eighty miles distant apparently. To the south there is one unbroken range, extending from the Tankh-i-Zorati, whence we had còme, to the Koh-i-Safid to the west. There was abundance of fuel and coarse grass at this place, and water was easily procurable by digging.

9*th*, *Friday*.—To-day the road lay entirely along the course of the Mairum, and was generally not so heavy as on the former days, owing to there being less sand. Some parts of the bed presented a curious appearance, just as smooth, hard, and black as a regular road, and it is difficult to imagine how this could have been formed. Another feature of to-day's march was the continuation of the thick tamarisk jungle, which, except near Mian Rud has accompanied us all the way. Though we were now in the midst of a desert country, there was no sign from the road that such was the case, for wherever the eye turned it rested on green, or at least shrubs that had been green. The soil, too, to-day, became much less sandy, and there is little doubt that it could be made to yield fair crops of wheat and barley. It was not, in fact, worse than many parts of the Derajat, or even of the Punjab itself. The distance we came was only twelve and a half miles, but we were obliged to halt at this place, Gudar, as it was the last water for many miles, and it was necessary we should start fair from this on the next day's march. At about nine miles we passed a road leading to the Wad-i-Sultan Pir Kaisar, and also to Chageh. While we were approaching the end of the march, I noticed the marks of camel feet straying about all over the jungle, as if a large number of these animals had been feeding there, and when we got in I sent out parties in every direction to examine the marks and trace whence they came and whither they went. On the ground where we pitched our camp, the marks of feet were numerous, and there were traces of camels' feet at the water, while the camel dung was still moist. Gradually some of the parties arrived, and each as he came had a long face, each had an alarming surmise to make; nearly thirty camp fires had been found, therefore it was evidently a very large force, and could not be a Kafila, as there were no signs of anything but camels' feet, and a Kafila would have had sheep with it. The more knowing ones were appealed to, and they came to the conclusion that the party was a very large one, from five hundred to one thousand men, probably composed of Sarhaddis, who, hearing Azad was at Panjgur, had seized the opportunity for raiding Kharan. The thing was as clear as day; the only question left to be settled was—What road would they come back? If there was another road, they would probably come by it, in preference to returning by the same road, and as they would not like to go nearer Azad than they could help, they would in all probability take a direction which led them further round to the north. In short, it was agreed that we were in for it; our only hope was to stay where we were on the chance that they would not come here again. Mirza was the most hopeful, and said that they were probably Yar Muhammadzais, and if so, would not attack us if we could get speech of them before they began. On hearing this, Gholam Rasul, who had been in a green funk, gave his moustache an extra twirl, and informed the company he was not a woman. Still even these grains of comfort were not in sufficiently large doses to soothe the fears of many of the men, and while some of them turned philosophically and practically to look up the priming of their matchlocks, I noticed a considerable number praying, and over the faces of many came that sickly green, alternating with yellow, which the old soldier learns to know so well.

I confess I myself did not half like the prospect; to be attacked, and get some of my men wounded, would be a complete stopper to the expedition, to say nothing of worse consequences. However, I said very little, but tried to raise a laugh whenever

I saw the opportunity, always adding that till Nur Muhammad came back it was no use talking, as he was the only one who knew the country. As that worthy did not appear, I took the opportunity of going round to look at our position, in case we had to fight: we did not want a very large space, and I was pleased, on scanning it over again, to see that the ground we had first taken up was as good as the vicinity offered. To the rear, where the river had steep banks, below being a deep pool, which extended for fifty yards, we were evidently safe; no Baloch would assault that bank in the face of two Winchester rifles; next, extending from the bank obliquely, was a low sandbank, which seemed made for a breastwork, only requiring a little fashioning to render it all right. On it and in front of it tamarisk grew thickly, and these I settled to have cut down at once, and formed into an abatis to cover that part. There therefore only remained one point, the gorge of the salient thus described; and this I determined to close by forming a breastwork of the baggage, aided by the saddle-bags filled with earth. I had ordered the camels not to be taken away, and these, the most difficult part of our party for whom to arrange, I determined to take inside and make them sit down as closely as possible; for though running over these preliminaries for a fight, I was not unmindful of the means of securing my retreat.

I was just finishing this survey when Nur Muhammad returned, and I called to him to come and sit down, and the men crowded eagerly round. Nur Muhammad was a character—a bad character, perhaps, according to our notions; that is to say, he would plunder, and perhaps murder, you or me, gentle reader, without any sort of compunction, for it is the fashion of the times he lives in.

Sitting down, with a twinkle in his eye, this worthy gave his turban a cock till it became near falling off, and then quietly began filling his pipe in the most *nonchalant* manner, not deigning to utter a word the while. "Well," I said, "what have you seen? The men are dying to hear that it is a Sarhaddi army, and I hope you won't disappoint them." "What did I see?" said Nur Muhammad, emitting a puff of smoke, "I saw a lot of marks of"—and he paused a while—"camel feet." At this confirmation of their worst fears I saw Fateh Muhammad and some of the others change from green to white. "Camel feet!" they all exclaimed. "Then it must be Sarhaddis!" "Must it?" said Nur Muhammad; "I daresay you know better, but I say it isn't." "Then what is it?" "A Kafila, of course!" "A Kafila," said Mirza, who felt bound to speak up for his own theory that it was Sarhaddis. "If it was a Kafila, there would be marks of sheep, and here there are nothing but camel feet, and the Sarhaddis have only camels. It must be a lashkar," *i.e.*, army. "I have seen a good many Kafilas," said old Nur Muhammad, with a twinkle, "and a good many lashkars, and I say it is the former." Though much relieved, the others did not like to give in, so they still held out for their pet theory of the marks being those of a Sarhaddi army. Nur Muhammad was evidently making fun of them, and would not for some time let out his reasons for being so sure of his view of the case. But at last he said, "Of course it's a Kafila. Look here!" holding up a stick he had in his hand; "that stick came from the Helmand. It is what the Helmand camel drivers use to urge forward their beasts. Wuggo! wuggo!" And the old man put on his most knowing look. "Oh, yes; trust me, it's a Kafila. Haven't I marred enough of them? Wuggo! wuggo!" and he sang the tune of the Helmand camel drivers. "Yes, they have come from the Helmand, and they are going to Jalk for dates. Why, if it had been Sarhaddis, the whole ground would have been covered with date stones, and there are none there." This was conclusive, and it immediately became evident to the others that it could not be Sarhaddis, as they would not dare to attack Kharan with old Azad on their flank at Panjgur, and Gholam Rasul assumed an air as if he was annoyed at the luck of the Sarhaddis in escaping him.

Close to the north-east of our present camp was a large salt-bed, called Wad-i-Sultan Pir Kaisar. It was on the road to Chageh, which branches off from here, and the place was resorted to by people from Garmsel, Nushki, and Jalk. The salt is described as lying in a layer a foot and more thick, and it is dug out into blocks and carried off. There is said to be an inexhaustible supply of the condiment, and it is, of course, to be had for the carrying.

We were also near the point where the two branches of the Mashkel run into the Hamun-i-Mashkel. This, it now became evident, was clearly quite a distinct depression from that of Zirreh, which was still a very long way to the north-north-west; and when I hinted at the possibility, Nur Muhammad scorned the idea of there ever having been any sort of connection between them. Further, he said there is another depression between the two, called Talab, which receives the drainage of Sarhadd. And he added, moreover, that the Zirreh depression was on the north side of the Band-i-Naru range. The tract of country about here was called Chitar, and it certainly had no appearance whatever of desert. The soil is light and sandy, but quite arable in places, and water being close to the surface, there seems no reason why this tract should not be cultivated. That the country has a value may be gathered from the fact that Azad Khan built a fort called Gulugah, a few miles from our camp, on the Ragab, and raised crops off the same sort of ground; but Dilaor, Khan of Jalk, not liking his proximity, sent a force to destroy it. The country between here and Jalk is described as all cultivable, except where there are patches of sand. It is worthy of note that Azad Khan claims the tract as belonging to Kandahar, stating that the Affghan boundary in the palmy days of Ahmad Shah reached to Jalk. Dilaor Khan, however, also claims it for the Kajars, but it seems doubtful on what they rest their right, as no boundary in this direction has ever actually been laid down. Whosesoever the left bank of the Mashkel and Ragab may be, there can be no doubt that beyond to the east is not Persian. Clearly it belongs to Azad Khan, and through him to Kandahar, if the plea of allegiance to the Affghans is allowed to hold good, in face of the fact that not only this, but the whole of his territories are politically, geographically, and ethnographically in Balochistan. Were this country settled,—and there is not much reason to doubt that it might easily be so,—this tract might be populated and cultivated, and thus form a convenient half-way place to the Helmand. At present the whole region is exposed to the raids of the

Kharanis, Naruis, and Sarhaddis, whose roads to each others' territories all lie through it. But if we aided the Khan to control the two first, and put pressure in Persia to curb the latter, there is no reason why it should not soon be as safe as any other part of Balochistan. Indeed, even now, with all the risks of passing through it, caravans come every year from Seistan and the Helmand for dates to Jalk.

It is, perhaps, somewhat early to speak of the limits of the desert which is marked in our maps as that of Kharan, but there seems little doubt that though its boundaries may be approximately stated with correctness, its impassable nature has been exaggerated. It is, in fact, intersected in almost every direction by roads which have a more or less plentiful water supply, and the fact of its being cut in two by such a fine natural highway as the bed of the Mashkel at once disposes of its terrors.

10th February, Saturday.—To-day our road, about a mile after leaving Gudar, entered a plain covered with salt efflorescence, a veritable Kavir, and over this we marched for fourteen miles. To the east the plain was continuous with the salt-bed called Wad-i-Sultan, and stretched beyond it as far as could be seen; but to the west it was limited by the Mairum ravine, which runs parallel with our road, to its junction with the Hamun of the Mashkel. At about ten miles we came abreast of a low sand ridge which runs pretty nearly east and west, gradually lessening in height till it crossed our road, and died into a slightly elevated plain at Gaz-i-Dauran at the fifteenth mile. From this, where there are some bushes for fuel and camel forage, the road goes over a flat plain of sand, covered with very minute black

Gat . i . Barot

gravel. On the right the view was cut off by the sand ridge above mentioned, but on the left the bed of the Hamun was distinctly visible, though, owing to the intense mirage, it was not easy to say whether there was water in it. There did not appear to be any reeds on it as in the Seistan Lake, but the edges had a thin sprinkling of the variety of tamarisk called "Ta-gaz." Half a mile before reaching our camp, at a spot called Meski, we descended a few feet into another depression or lake bed, which Nur Muhammad informed me was called the God-i-Morjin, which is at times filled by flood-water from ravines coming from the direction of a hill called Gat-i-Barot, which was dimly visible bearing 31°. Where the water is high this depression is connected with that of the Mashkel and the west. From this point there was a pretty extensive view, and something of the boundaries of the plain could be gathered from the fact that nearly all round hills could be seen. Thus from due south to due west was one continuous range; at 290° and 300° isolated hills appeared an immense distance off, and then came the Koh-i-Amir bearing 320°, which appeared continuous with the Koh-i-Sultan, bearing 335°. Then no hills were visible to 10°, where there was a hill which Nur Muhammad said was called Bulu. More south again there were several hills, as the Gat-i-Barot, bearing 31°; Nohli, 43°; Koh-i-Sohraf, 81°; the two last probably form another continuous ridge, and the latter was moreover said to continue to Kharan. Therefore, as we knew there were hills from the latter right across to due south, it followed that the desert was quite surrounded by mountains. As there was no water at this place (Meski) we carried with us in water-skins sufficient for the day's consumption, and on arrival I served all the servants out about a gallon apiece, and keeping my share, gave some to my horse and kept the rest for his morning drink. Although there was no water, it is probable that a very deep well would not have to be sunk to reach it, the depression in which we bivouacked being some fifty feet below the ground round it. At all events it would be easy to dig here a tank or series of tanks, which would contain a supply for any number of people. There is also here fuel and camel forage, but no grass for horses.

11*th*, *Sunday*.—For half an hour or two miles after starting, we went over the bed of the depression in which we were yesterday camped, when we camo to the dry bed of the Morjin torrent, which is said to be the only other river draining into the Mashkel Hamun. In one and a half miles further we came to the edge of the terrace surrounding the depression, which we then left and got on to a plain of sand covered with minute black gravel, and reached a little hollow in one and a half miles further, called Jai. Here there was a collection of rain water, and as the ground is admirably suited as a site for a tank, there would be little difficulty in arranging that there should be always a supply of water at this place, and of course it might be as abundant as was required. If this were done, it would reduce the distance without water to less than twenty-five miles, which at this season is within the limits of a forced march.

Continuing over the same sort of plain, we arrived in two miles at the Kalandi ravine, which, though of considerable breadth at this point, has no great length, as it rises on the plain beyond Paniham. Crossing

Lanihan.

this river bed obliquely, we got on to high ground on its left bank, and in three miles came to it again, and descending reached our camp at Paniham in a mile. We were obliged to make this short stage, as the guide declared there was no water for two long stages beyond. Paniham is a site on the bed of the Kalandi ravine, where there are some date trees and a good supply of water in the bed of the ravine. There is very little camel forage here, but a fair supply of grass, and the water is very abundant and good, being taken from wells on the bed of the river about three feet deep. This plenteous supply of water in a tract which is desert in every direction round it makes Paniham much resorted to by caravans, travellers, and, as Nur Muhammad grimly added, "chapaos," and many a fight has taken place here for the possession of the draught of life, a fact which is sufficiently attested by the number of graves round. This made it a rather dangerous spot, as, being right on the track of all the raiding parties, it was not unlikely one might turn up while we were here. I therefore put out videttes all round, and sent the old fox Nur Muhammad to have a look at the country in front for any signs of man. However none were discovered, and the night passed off quietly. The date trees here were growing in huge dense clumps, and not in the separate manner I had hitherto seen. These clumps were of all sizes, the biggest having a diameter of about one hundred feet and a height of fifty, and inside there was a snug little retreat, which with very little ingenuity and trouble might be converted into a very fair dwelling-place.

Talking as usual to the guide about the road, he amused me much by saying, "What on earth do you want to go to Zirreh for? there is nothing to see, and what there is I will tell you all about. You had much better not go, but just write down what I tell you, and I shall put my seal to it and there you are. You give me one hundred rupees, and you will save yourself a great deal of trouble, besides two thousand rupees." I said, "I don't much believe in hearsay evidence of a country; why you know Pottinger Sahib, that came from Nushki to Jalk, put down what he heard, and he made the Mashkel go into the Zirreh." "Oh yes," said Nur Muhammad, "but he was told lies; all I say may be taken as Gospel."

12*th*, *Monday*.—Leaving Paniham, the road went up the ravine to a place called Paniham Nowar, where there is plenty of grass, forage, and fuel, and water can be had for the digging. The word "Nowar" signifies a place where there is water, and appears after the names of many places in Balochistan. Ascending out of this on to higher ground, we then went over a bare plain, which extended in unvaried desolation right up to the Naru Band, nearly forty miles off. The plain was entirely composed of sand, mixed with gravel and stones, the latter of every colour, a beautiful jet black and a deep maroon red predominating, though many were of various shades of green. We went on over this, till the continued hints of the guide and Mahmud warned me the party had had enough of it, and as there was evidently no chance of reaching water that night we bivouacked on the bare plain. One advantage of this very uninviting spot was the abundance of camel scrub, and as we had brought on our water, and found a little grass for the horses, we got on pretty well.

13*th*, *Tuesday*.—Continuing over the same plain

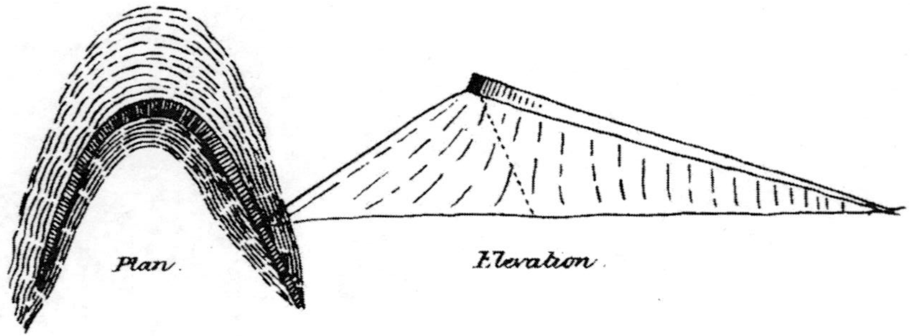

SAND CRESCENTS.

next morning for eighteen miles, we reached the Shandak ravine, which Nur Muhammad informed me drained to the Talab depression, and finding no water there, we went on through heavy sandhills to some wells.

On the way we passed through a great number of sand hillocks, shaped like crescents or horseshoes. As I have never before seen anything like these, nor have I heard of them, it may be well to give some description of these curious formations. This I have attempted in the accompanying sketch. All are shaped alike, and, as I have said, are of the form of a crescent, the horns being to the south, and the toe to the north. They vary a good deal in height, the top of the largest ones being about sixty feet above the plain, and sloping down gradually to the horns, where they mingle with the sand. The outer slope is at an angle of about 30°, bulging a little in the centre; and the inner at about 45°, or as steep as sand will stand. At the top of the outer slope and at the toe of the crescent is a steeper slope about three feet in depth, and this gradually disappears at the horns, where the whole outer slope is uniform. It is difficult to imagine how these sand crescents can have been formed on a perfectly level plain, but I imagine that in the first instance the sand blown from the north has met some obstruction, such as a bush, which has had sufficient strength to withstand the weight, till a bank of sand has been formed at the toe, and then the horns have been formed by the sand being blown from the toe towards the south. Each of these crescents—and there are hundreds of them—would afford cover enough for a regiment or two.

It had been evident to me since leaving Meski that our road should have turned off north-west from that place, but I was obliged to come on so far north for several reasons. First, our guide was, I think, about pumped dry, and he did not seem to know the road beyond, and it was therefore necessary to replace him; and, secondly, many of the camels were knocking up from the hard work, and it was necessary, if possible, to make some arrangement to leave them behind to recruit, while we went on with the ones still having a little go in them. Now the only place where there was any hope of accomplishing these necessities was Naru, near which we had now arrived.

I therefore determined to halt at Shandak, while Nur Muhammad went on to find guides and some responsible person to take charge of our camels. This plan would, of course, delay us considerably, but there was no help for it, and I meant to try and have the direct route from Meski to Amalof examined on our way back.

On nearing our camp to-day we came on numerous marks of sheep and their shepherds, and it was therefore probable they were not far off. Meanwhile we took up a position under a commanding sandhill close to the water, from which there was a good view round, while our camp was hidden by lesser hillocks. I placed a picket on the crest of the hill, and had everything ready to take up our position directly any hostile party should appear, and I had little doubt we could hold out there till they were brought to their senses, either by blarney or bullets.

For the last three or four days we had frequently come on the marks of the wild ass, but as yet had found none. I have seen this pretty animal both in the Lower Derajat and Upper Sind and in Persia, and always, as in this case, in plains of the most desolate nature, far from water. So much is this the case that when one is told that wild asses are found on a certain tract, one forms an immediate idea of the utter desolation of the locality. The name for this animal in these parts is "Gur," and in Persia "Gur Khar," which some ingenious individuals in India derive from the two words, "ghora," a horse, and "khar," a donkey; forgetting that in the countries where the wild ass is known as the "gor khar" the word ghora is unknown. This is very much on a par with the derivation of the name for the bustard, "obara," from the "ahu," a deer, and "bara," a something else. While on the subject of names, I may mention that Major St. John is not right in correcting the usual spelling and meaning of the word which appears on our maps of these parts in very various positions as Piri Kaisar to Pir Kasr, an old fort. There are two places to which this name is applied, one the salt-bed which we passed the other day, which is called Wad-i-Sultan Pir Kaisar; the other the hill which is close to us now, and which is termed Koh-i-Sultan Pir Kaisar. The fact is that this Sultan Pir Kaisar is one of the many saints who appear to have once flourished in this heaven-forsaken country, and he is the special patron of Baloch robbers and Baloch camels,—two animals who are very aptly classed together. Again, though I am no great authority on the Persian language, it seems to me that the coupling of the two words, "pir," old, and "kasr," a fort, is a very improbable combination to suggest itself to these people. In the first place, though "pir" does mean old, I have never found it applied to inanimate objects, and then the word is used in a religious sense to denote "a venerable saint." In the second place, the word "kasr" is a Turki word.

Regarding another explanation afforded in the same place by the same officer, I most readily concur. "Lut" certainly indicates a waterless tract, and in one of the notebooks I used in Persia there is a memorandum to exactly the same effect regarding the meaning of the word. Indeed, I cannot imagine, notwithstanding the derivation of the Russian authority who takes on himself to sneer at English officers, how any one who passed through the tract he did could have concocted the fanciful derivation he has given to the world in translating "lut" as "lot."

The 14th and 15th February were blank days, for we had to halt to wait for the result of Nur Muhammud's mission in search of inhabitants, and as the spot was not the most delectable in the world, and I had to forbid any shooting, we had not much to do to while away the time. To me, however, the occasion was by no means without its anxiety; in the first place we knew nothing of the people, or the manner in which they were likely to receive the news that a Faringi had arrived among them. They are generally supposed to be the greatest robbers on earth, and it was doubtful whether they would let such an opportunity slip, and so any moment we might be fighting for our lives. And even if the dulcet tongue of the old fox Nur Muhammad should induce them to forego any such disagreeable intentions till his return, it was doubtful whether they would produce guides and supplies, of both of which we were sorely in need. Of the second we had enough to carry us on till those for which I sent back came up, but the time of their arrival was uncertain, and it was therefore necessary to practise economy till they appeared. As we had now been for thirteen days living on "chupattees" (unleavened cakes), dates, and bad water, a little meat for ourselves also would not come amiss, but that of course was a very minor consideration to the others; man *can* live on bread alone for some considerable time, and we hoped to make that time stretch till the objects of our expedition were accomplished. The want of guides was the most serious obstacle to our onward progress, and though I could have procured men at Panjgur who knew this part of the country, it did not make the difficulty any the less a cause of anxiety. To go on without a guide to show us the watering-places at least, would be a most serious danger, and though to form a heap of bones, as the nucleus of a sand crescent in the middle of the desert, would doubtless be a very glorious ending to one's career, it would fail in attaining the practical objects of our journey. Still, as we set out with the determination to reach the furthest point attainable to the north-west without going into Affghan territory,—which, as before stated, we wished to avoid,—that point I was still resolved to reach, in spite of all difficulties, obstacles, or dangers. I could not have it said that one of my name failed from want of determination.

In the afternoon of the 15th Nur Muhammad returned with an individual named Zangi, the chief of the Naruies, who inhabit the district known as Koh-i-Sunt, or the end of the hills. After they had had a little preliminary talk among themselves, the whole posse came up to make their salaam, and then I heard the entire course of events since Nur Muhammad left yesterday. He had gone off to a place in the hills to the north, called Dewanak, or Lal Khan Chah. On seeing him appear, Zangi, who recognized him, immediately got his men together, feeling sure that where Nur Muhammad was there would be mischief; but getting speech of him he asked him how he had come. Now the latter was always boasting of his truthful nature, and he perpetually assumed an air as like injured innocence as he could get his villainous old face to twist itself into, if I ever asked a question which expressed a doubt as to any of his statements. Yet with the obtuse perverseness of a Baloch, he must needs on this occasion tell a lie. If he had said at once he had come with a Sahib, all would have been well; but he replied, "I have come with a Kafila," and this statement nearly brought a volley into him; the Naruis received it with derision. "You are not a Kafila man," they said; "you have come with a 'chapao,' but we are ready for you; be off, you dog, and son of a burnt father." Then he told the truth, and after he had sworn to it on a Koran, they let him enter in, and on his disclosing everything Zangi readily agreed to come and do anything I ordered. He was a gentlemanly, quiet-looking man, and I became prepossessed in his favour at once; though the chief of such a clan of ruffians, and though his dress was but mean, there were very evident signs of the chief in him. Now my plan with all such individuals is to address them as if I took it for granted that they would not only obey, but be willing to carry out any of my orders, and so after the usual salutations were over, I began. It really was a very extraordinary thing for one Englishman to appear in the midst of the fastnesses of one of the most notoriously lawless clans of all the lawless Baloch race (of whom Pottinger has recorded: "Bound by no laws, and restrained by no feelings of humanity, the Naruis are the most savage and predatory of Baloches")—to send for their chief and then proceed to dictate orders to him. But it was clearly my *rôle* not to appear to think there was anything unusual in my coming, or anything unreasonable in my expecting to be obeyed; so I addressed Zangi thus, watching him narrowly the while: "I have sent for you as your name is well known to me, and I wish you to do some work for me." "Whatever you order will be done," he replied. I bowed,—as much as to say, "Of course, I never doubted that." I then told him I should be very much obliged if he would send me some sheep, and supply me with a guide for Zirreh. Both of these he agreed to furnish me with at once.

This was very lucky, and I took occasion to remark to Mirza, how I had told him all would go right as long as he was with me. He laughed and said, "Your luck is indeed great." Zangi informed me that Zirreh was still five days' journey, four of which were very long; and that Bandar Kamal was two days' beyond. Thus it was evident it would take six days altogether for us to reach the point which we had marked in our maps as F. P., or furthest point, and which I used to call Ja-i-Maksud to the men.

CHAPTER VIII.

ZIRREH.

Friday, 16th February.—Accordingly, having arranged matters the night before with Zangi, such of the camels as were knocked up were left behind, with all the extra and less useful mouths and a guard of ten men, and we only took on with us as many persons as the camels would carry. It was arranged that all the others were to go to Lal Khan Chah, and there wait our return. Though this reduced our party a good deal, and was doubtless a great risk, it was the best thing that could have been done, as only as many men as the camels would carry could go with us, it being quite impossible for us to be detained by men on foot, wading through the heavy sand. Thus as the choice of evils, I trusted Zangi unreservedly, and if he had any thoughts of playing false, and stealing some of our things, this must have taken the wind completely out of his sails. I went on the excellent principle that if you must trust a person, you had better do so without any reserve. Having said good-bye to Zangi, whom I initiated on this occasion into the fashion of shaking hands, explaining to him the cause of the custom, I said, "I give you my hand thus in token that my heart is as free from guile as my hand is open, and I take yours believing the same of you." When he understood, he brightened, and said excitedly, "God knows there is no deceit in my heart; I am your servant, and will do what you wish."

The road to-day was most uninteresting, leading all the way over confused heaps of sand which shut out the view in every direction. After going about fifteen miles, we arrived at a place called Manzil, where was one of the shrines to that famous saint Sultan Pir Kaisar. This was erected on a hillock above a depression in the sand, where, by digging, some salt and filthy water is to be found. It is evident that the admirers of the saint are of opinion that the best monument to a man's name is the fame of his good deeds; perishable monuments of stone and brick crumble away, but these remain ever green. Anyhow, all that had been erected here was a few sticks rudely put together in the form of a hut, and ornamented by the heads of some mountain sheep, ibex, etc. The guide, who was a Narui, evidently had a great respect for the saint, as he took a small piece of bread,—a very small piece, by the way,—and put it respectfully down at the door, and then standing with his hands clasped reverently, he called on the saint to help him; what he said I, of course, did not know, but though his words may have been simple, they were evidently earnest. "O Saint, O Sultan!" we may imagine him saying, "if a Kafila shall come our way, let me have early intelligence thereof. O Pir! if the Sarhaddis or other vile scum should wish to attack thy servant, confound them utterly. O Sultan, my father's blood still cries out unrevenged;

deliver thou the murderer into my hands; and finally, revered prophet, my camel is sick,—make it well, O Saint!"

Mazar the guide was so pleased with the result of his devotions, that he proposed our staying here. I said, "But the water is very bad: is there none other?" "The water is not very good, certainly" (it was black and stinking), "but it is the water the Pir drank, and can't do *you* any harm." "No doubt," I answered, "but not being a Narui or a camel I think sweet water, if it can be found, would suit my constitution better." "Oh!" said Mazar contemptuously, "if you want sweet water, there is some close by;" and off he led in a huff to a spring of good water.

On the road to-day the only things noticeable in the generally unvaried monotony presented by the sand-waste we were passing through, were several low hills, half of which were formed of a white stone, almost like limestone, and the other half of a perfectly black shining stone, which had the appearance of coal; but my ignorance of geology prevented my hazarding a guess as to what they really were. It was also somewhat interesting to notice the gradual process by which all the low hills are being converted into sand-heaps. The sand is blown against their feet on one side, and gradually rises higher and higher until it reaches the top, when it rushes over and forms a heap on the other side, which increases till the sand on both sides meets, and the hill disappears. To the north-east of us there was a long ridge, which stretched north as far as could be seen, towards the Helmand, from the Malik Naru range, which I have no doubt whatever was originally part of the same range, but is now divided by sand-heaps.

We had not yet, I am sorry to say, got to the end of the camels who knocked up, for to-day another of Captain Lockwood's gave in, and so I arranged to send it back with one of the men to Zangi's place. As this was the last spot from which we could do this, any that break down hereafter will just have to be left, as of course no one can remain behind to look after them. Though this place produced some ta-gaz and a little grass for horses—and it was a very heaven-forsaken spot — yet it possessed one great advantage to a wayworn traveller, in a supply of the most beautiful water. This was got by digging in certain spots where the dampness of the sand directed the search, and it certainly was very curious to get water from the midst of such a waste of sand as was here to be seen. Assuredly no one would look for water in such a locality, especially as it was quite off the roads, and without a guide it could not be discovered. Generally speaking, in a sandy desert water will be found only where there are hills, or in the bed of a river. But here there were no rivers, though it was a short distance from the hills, whence the drainage beds all originate; even these had given up the hopeless task of trying to flow on through the mass of sand by which they are surrounded in every direction, and which itself never ceases to blow about. Thus the fact is that nearly all the drainage of these hills is sooner or later arrested by the sand. And I imagine it is to this cause that we owe our plentiful and delicious supply to-day, as the water probably found a way under the sand to this spot.

17*th*, *Saturday*.—The march to-day was more interesting, though it still lay over the same interminable sand waste. After going for nine miles in a west-north-west direction, to our dismay we found the road actually running south by west; thus we had the misery of feeling that, so to speak, for every two steps we took forward we were going one back. The direction of the point which figured in all our conversations as F.P., furthest point, was north-west, and it was hard indeed to find, just as we thought we might count the hours which would take us there, that we were journeying in another direction, which made the accomplishment of our desires indefinitely postponed. However, on these occasions it is never good to be sanguine; far better is it to school oneself to a sort of dull, leaden feeling, that nothing matters—miles of sand, a glaring sun, salt water to drink, chupattees to eat; every day, every hour, some mulishness of the Baloch army to overcome—what does it matter? it must end some time, and meanwhile it is all in the way of trade.

The Koh-i-Sultan, as seen from here, was certainly one of the oddest-looking mountain masses I had ever seen. It gives you the idea that long ago it may have been a rather good-looking mountain, but the wind and the rain, the sand and the sun, have all been doing their best to disfigure it, and what they have left undone has been effected by earthquakes. So now it seems to bear but a quaint resemblance to its former outline; all the earth that no doubt once gave a symmetrical roundness to its contours has been washed off it, and now forms a long glacis at its foot; its face has been disfigured by the heaps of sand which now rest high upon

Koh-i-Sultan.

it, while it is broken up by its spasms into a number of separate peaks and masses, whose only recommendation is, that they are fantastic in shape.

However, like very many plain people, the Koh-i-Sultan has more than good qualities enough to make up for its ugliness. It produces, so Mazar, the new guide, told us, sulphur, with which they make gunpowder for the destruction of their enemies; and "mak," an earth, with which they dye the trousers of their loved ones a beautiful red; assafetida, which they use for a relish—Heaven help them!—and as a medicine, and lastly, there are many springs of water in its recesses.

It is much frequented by Babars and Kakars, who come from Kandahar to take away the assafetida; after going about twelve miles we came across the road by which they arrive from the Malik Dokand direction, carefully marked by heaps of stones. They come in parties of twenty and thirty, about the end of March, and stay for three months or so, sending away the proceeds of their labour on camels. This fact is interesting and noteworthy, both as showing that there is a supply of water in these months, and that the heat, though doubtless very great, is not so bad but that these people can work and travel in it. The names of the principal places where there is water in the Koh-i-Sultan ridge, are Washaf, Kundi, Chakul, Padagi, Soru, and Gamichah; I cannot give the positions of these localities, as I utterly failed to make out from the descriptions afforded me where they were.

The whole ground on the march was strewed with a stone something like a pumice stone, and called Sang-i-Purpok. It is used, so Mirza informed me, for washing, and is very effective in getting the dirt off. But judging from all the Baloches I have seen, I should say either that its qualities have been too highly vaunted, or that the evidence is hearsay.

One of the peaks of the Sultan range is very remarkable as seen from the east, about twelve miles off. It is called Koh-i-Kansuri, and bears a resemblance to the Sphinx, at least close enough to seem as though a very little chiselling and touching up would make it exact. On approaching it, however, this illusion disappears, as we found the figure of the Sphinx was formed of two different hills of totally opposite shape, which had at a distance seemed to be one.

There is another really wonderful peak in the same range, which came into view on the road, consisting of what looked exactly like a huge pillar erected on the west of one of its spurs; we passed it about ten miles off, and so of course had not a sufficient opportunity for giving a very exact description of it, but I had scanned it very carefully through a powerful telescope, and it looked as if it was the ruin of one of the towers which are seen in various parts of Persia.

Yet of course I knew it could not be one of these, as it was of too enormous dimensions to be the work of man. I regretted much I could not spare the time to have a close examination of it, as it was the one really curious thing I had yet seen in this journey. I have, however, tried in the accompanying careful sketch to give the reader an idea of its outline. It is of course connected in the traditions of the wild inhabitants with the wonderful Pir Kaisar, and is called Niza-i-Sultan.

Koh-i-Kansuir.

Koh-i-Sultan from the E.

The last part of the march was over heavier sand than usual, and after going on till past four, we stopped in a hollow amongst sandheaps, having done about twenty-four miles. There was no water here, but we brought some on with us from Manzil. There was plenty of "ta-gaz" about, and this did for camel forage and fuel. The Koh-i-Malik Dokand was visible in the latter portion of the march, bearing 148°.

Next morning was Sunday the 18th, but to us it was no day of rest, and we were yet far from ceasing to flounder among the sand-ridges. So we got off a little earlier, and in three miles came to the end of the Sultan range, or rather of its north ridge, for on reaching this we found another spur extending as far as could be seen to the west, parallel with our road on the left, while on the right there stretched a waste for seventy miles to the Helmand, all sand, without a drop of water. We got one peep of the top of the Niza-i-Sultan, but did not see it properly again, and at the ninth mile the Koh-i-Dalil came into view, bearing 225°. This was said by the Narui guide to be the boundary of the Khan of Kalat's territory in this direction. Going on for four miles, we were startled by seeing the perfectly new footmarks of one camel, and so we got every one together and kept a sharp look-out ahead. Not that we did not do this always, as we had been kept on the *qui vive* in this way for upwards of a month; but now we had to give our attention an extra twist. Many were the surmises. It might be the marks of a man sent to look for us, and his party might be in front. If this were the case, he had probably seen us, and was hiding, or returning with his report. I therefore caused the marks to be carefully examined, and sent men to the tops of the neighbouring sand-hills, to see if any signs of movement could be found. At last it was ascertained that the marks went off sharp towards the Helmand, and Nur Muhammad at once said, "Oh then, it is a thief; he has stolen a camel, has probably watered at Kundi,"—a place close by to the south,—"and now he is off." Then he showed that the marks were not so fresh as I thought, for on one of them he had seen the traces of a hare. "A hare," he said, "does not go about in the day, and so the man must have passed yesterday." Shortly after this we got into a very bad bit, the sand having obliterated all semblance of a path, and the guide was evidently out about the road; we soon found ourselves floundering about trying to get over a very massive sand ridge, which was such heavy going that the camels sunk to their knees at nearly every step. I accordingly got off my camel and made every one else do so also, and then we had a very trying trudge of two miles through the heaviest sand. Luckily the day was cool and we did not mind it so much. There was a strong wind blowing, and this produced an effect on the sand-heaps I had noticed before. It blew the sand out from their edges, for a foot or so, just as if fired out of a number of squirts; and the whole of the sand-heaps seemed to be in constant motion.

Surmounting this really formidable obstacle, we descended into the bed of a Khor or ravine, which evidently had met the fate of all drainage beds in this country, that of being stopped by the sand a short distance to the north. Crossing this we ascended and traversed a low pass over a spur from the main ridge, and then wound round the face of the hill for an hour, when we began to descend to another drainage bed, down which our course then lay for two miles, when we went through a gap in low gloomy black hills, and found ourselves at Amir Chah, having come a distance of twenty miles from our last stage. Here we met with a well in the bed of the ravine, about twenty feet deep, which produced an unfailing supply of very nasty fetid water. The camel forage at this spot was very good, and Nur Muhammad recommended a halt before we braved the desert between us and Zirreh. This was perhaps not altogether necessary, but the distance was so uncertain that we thought it as well not to neglect anything that would increase our chances of success. I therefore gave the order for a halt, and we passed a most miserable day, owing to the great heat, in this little basin surrounded by sand-heaps and bare black rocks. We passed many camel tracks on this march, and in some places the road was well marked, but Nur Muhammad said they were the tracks of the parties who come for assafetida. This we found growing on the bare rocky sides of the hills. The young shoots were just appearing, and had been protected to a certain extent from the sun by little coverings of stones, erected, the guides told us, by the parties of last year.

19*th*.—A difficulty now cropped up which was the most serious we had yet had to face. The guide, whom we got at Naru, and who there declared that if you blinded his eyes he could take you by the road to Zirreh, now said he had never been by this path at all, and had only received instructions from a man who had followed it. The fact therefore was, that we should have to attempt the desert without a guide, and though we had the advantage of the local experience and the wit of the old fox Nur Muhammad, I liked the idea so little that I tried to see what else might be done. I learnt that from this there were two roads by which you could get to Zirreh, one the one direct above alluded to, the other by Amalaf. But Amalaf, on careful enquiry, proved to be fifty miles south-west of the point we wished to make, and therefore entirely out of our line. It was not, therefore, to be thought of for a moment. The only other thing to do, it seemed, was to rest satisfied with what we had seen, and go back. But to this view, which was advanced by Captain Lockwood, I was entirely averse, as it would have left the work most incomplete. We were now apparently not more than eighty-five miles as the crow flies from Bandar, and of this about fifty miles were said to remain between us and Zirreh. Therefore to go back now and leave it still an open question whether these sixty miles were practicable or not was what I could not bring myself to contemplate for an instant; I therefore determined that we must get to Zirreh or perish in the attempt, and I arranged that every single thing that was not absolutely necessary for our preservation should be left at Amir Chah and buried in the sand, while we went on, carrying everything with us that would hold it full of water.

I determined next day before starting that every one should take a good draught of water, and then we would go as far as possible that day, drinking as little as we could, and this the next day, and the next, till either Zirreh appeared or our water failed. Then, if we could not get there on foot, we must just perish. There would be no help for it. It was therefore a very great responsibility for me to take on myself, but I had, I thought, very fair grounds for hoping for success. First, I knew that Zirreh was a long depression, which it would be nearly impossible to miss, and if we hit it anywhere it was probable we should get some water, not very good, perhaps, but still water. Second, the distance, apparently, could not be more than seventy miles, and we could go thirty miles each day, and ten on the third day. Besides, I believed the distance had been done frequently by Kafilas, and the desert was often crossed at points that were clearly broader than what we had to face. Still, it was a responsibility, and what made it harder was the attitude all the men took up in recommending me not to try it. But after I had talked to them for some time, I am glad to record that they eventually agreed, saying, "We will go now. We came here to go there, and we can never go back and say we have not been." So it was settled that we should start on the morrow.

Early next morning, on the 20th February, I sent and had the things buried, and then we got off. Our direction led us across a very heavy ridge of sand, which we got over about an hour after starting, and then we reached a plain of sand, covered with fine black gravel, which we kept to the end of the day. As there was nothing to see on such a march, there is little to record. Immediately on our left was a sand ridge, which kept with us the whole journey, and which, indeed, was the guide by which we were to find our way. The only remarkable thing on the ridge was that at about every four miles it rose with great regularity into a peak, and then died away gradually to the next peak. We were, of course, dependent on what we carried for our water, but this was getting quite a common occurrence, so we felt no inconvenience from it; but I am free to confess that this night was one of some anxiety to me. We were now fairly embarked in our venture, and on me rested the whole responsibility. Luckily, responsibility is not a thing that weighs very heavily on my soul. We made thirty-eight miles, and bivouacked in the open.

Next day, the 21st, we got off again, and kept the same description of country with us for some twenty miles. Here the sand-ridge ended, but four miles off was another parallel range of exactly the same description. As long as the ridge was on our left, and the going was good, we got on very well; but then our guide began to show signs of wavering, and looked about him in a helpless manner, till I thought it was time to appeal to Nur Muhammad, whose sagacity came to our assistance. He had never come this way before, but he had a general idea of the locale of Zirreh, and he knew he could not be far wrong if he kept the salt, which now began to appear, on his right. And so on we went, now floundering in a sand-ridge, now going over a bit of "pat." At last the soil began to improve, and though it never got better than the poorest, still, compared to the sand, it was rich. Trees also began to appear, though they looked very dry and thirsty. Still we proceeded. Not a sign of water had we found, and I would fain have gone on till we came to it. But the camels now began to give in one by one, and warned me that it was time to stop. So, after making thirty-four miles, the second day and night passed without water; but as for this every one was prepared, it did not tell on the spirits of our party, who, sitting round their fires, seemed very jolly.

22*nd*.—The third day was now to come, and it broke in a manner sufficiently alarming to be a very bad omen of what was before us. I have before alluded to the hopelessness of getting my Baloch allies to carry out any order, however reasonable, and how they perpetually were doing things which gave my military feelings a jar. Among these "decrees" was one about which I was most particular, that every night all the camels should be brought in and tied up in a circle all together. This command had hitherto been fairly carried out, and I was solemnly assured that to-night this had been the case also. That the camels were all there before I went to sleep I had seen myself, but they could not have been all tied, for it now appeared that seven of them were missing! This certainly was enough to try the temper of a saint, and damp the hopefulness of the most sanguine. But it is one of my peculiarities that, though small things irritate me, real serious crosses cool me, and my nature, being sufficiently elastic, rebounds, as it were, after even such a blow. So having ascertained the extent of our loss, and that steps had been taken to repair it, I at once began to think what had best be done now. Half our camels were gone, and we were forty-eight hours from the last water, and an uncertain distance from the next. I therefore determined the only course practicable was for some of us to go on and find the water and send it back to the others; so I called for the guide. "The guide has gone for the camels," was the answer. Blow number two! The problem now stood—Forty-eight hours without water, half camels lost, position of next water unknown, and no guide. What is to be done? Some considered the best thing was to sit where we were and wait for the camels. I thought quite otherwise. Camels were not our first necessity, but rather water. If we could get the latter we could still carry on, despite the want of the former; but put *vice versâ*, all the camels in creation would not save us from dying of thirst. I therefore sat down, lit a cigar, and proceeded to look this new bogy calmly in the face; and after a while his features, which had had a most lowering expression, began to assume a semblance of benignity, nay, even of hope. After all, things were far from hopeless. If we did not know where water was, we knew where we were. That is, not far from the right bank of the "Shela," or old waterway of the Helmand, and therefore, if we made for that we should *probably* find water in its bed; and besides, Nur Muhammad had been to Shah Godar on this waterway, where he had met with water. I say probably, because I knew the Helmand had not been down now for many years, and, therefore, finding the precious liquid was by no means a certainty. However, to go on was clearly the only thing to be done, and we started, leaving Mahmud behind to wait for the camels and water which we would send back. I told him if we were successful we would send some back at once; if we were not, we would wait for him.

On leaving, we went away for four or five miles pretty smartly, Nur Muhammad, with his turban cocked, appearing as if he knew all about it. But now and again a perplexed expression began to steal over his features, and he looked about from side to side, till at last it was clear he was out. We were now in the midst of a waste of sand hillocks, and there was no sign of a road. All I knew was that the "Shela" must still be to the north, and so I told Nur Muhammad to press on for it. We were just going on again when a man appeared on a camel in the distance, and waiting for him, we found it was the guide. This was the first glimmer of hope we had experienced this day, but it was not destined to be of long duration, for after going about four miles more he also seemed to be out, and after a while he, with a sickly smile, acknowledged his head was "turning," and he did not know where he was. This gave the hope that had been springing up in my breast a sad *douche*, and I looked about in a listless manner, when my eye rested on a black object in the far distance. It was not a tree. What was it? "Nur Muhammad," I asked, "what is that?" "I don't know," replied that worthy, and he did not, for he was not far-sighted. "Look through your telescope," he added. I looked, and said, "It is some sort of a building." "A what?" said Nur Muhammad, quite excitedly, "a gumbaz?"* "I don't know whether it is a gumbaz; it is a building of some sort." "Then it's Shah Godar," and he laughed sardonically. However, Captain Lockwood, looking through the telescope, declared there were trees, but no building could he trace. Mirza confirmed my view of the case, as he naturally would, and to show his confidence said, "If that is not a building, you may give me four stripes." If he had been more liberal in the allowance of the proposed stripes, it might have occasioned us more cause for hope. However, I looked again, and the result was that though I did not offer to permit any one to stripe me, or even substitute

* A dome.

the English equivalent of proposing to eat my hat, yet I said, "It is a building!" So off we went towards it, keeping our course pretty decidedly. Nur Muhammad got on ahead of me. I suddenly saw him stop, and turn sharp off to the right, and down went my hopes to below zero. He is now sure it is not the gumbaz, and he is going to try the "Shela," and before I could get up to him, we had arrived at it. "Stop!" said Mirza, beaming. "This is your Ja-i-Maksud. All our troubles are over." I looked, and the "Shela" was before me; and a more unpromising-looking find for water it would be hard to conceive. There was a sort of waterway, certainly, but most of it was level with the bank, and all was deeply covered with sand. Nowhere was there the slightest sign of dampness. Then we sat down and waited while Nur Muhammad and Mazar went one up and the other down the bed to look for water; Mirza, with a touching hopefulness, proceeded to select a place for my bivouac. Presently a voice was heard calling us, and Mirza said, "There, they have found water. Let us come." We got up, and walked up the bed. Everywhere it was the same; nothing but sand, and all the vegetation as dry as bones, crumbling into dust at the least touch. There seemed no reason why we should find water, or why we should not go up its bed for hours without success. I knew from Goldsmid's book the Helmand could not have been down for more than eight years, and in this thirsty soil what hope was there water would be retained so long? For a mile and a half this went on. This mile and a half seemed to me like twenty. I was almost giving up all hope of water here, and was thinking what should be done next; for I will do myself the

On the road to Amalaf.

justice to say I had no idea as yet of giving up the game.

At this moment, Mirza, suddenly awaking to the hopelessness of the situation, said, "If we do not find water now we must just die." But I was by no means disposed to acquiesce that the time for dying had arrived. Water would certainly be found either at the Helmand or in the Kacha Hills, both of which were not more than forty miles off; and the question to me, therefore, was not of dying, but of reaching one or the other. I had about made up my mind to try for the latter spot, when I saw Mazar down on his knees, scraping the sand away excitedly, just like a terrier after a rat. I got down and watched him. The sand was evidently getting damper and damper, till at last water appeared. Now the question was, would it be drinkable? I knew that water in the "Shela" was good enough if taken out soon after the Helmand had been down, but now the Helmand had not visited it for a very lengthened period. Gradually it trickled into the hole, till enough had collected to fill my little cup, and they gave it me. It was quite brown, and of the consistency of pea soup, so putting my handkerchief over the lip of the cup to form a strainer, I tasted it. Mazar, poor devil, watched me with the most intense anxiety; to continue my former simile, still just like a terrier looks when a rat is held aloft, nervously expectant, hopeful, yet fearful. And as I drank and did not make a very bad face, he burst out delightedly in a short, sharp yelp with the words, "Wash! wash! wash!" *i.e.*, drinkable. Yes, it was drinkable,—very salt, very nasty, but still no doubt drinkable. So I set all the men to work to make wells.

All this time I had not seen Nur Muhammad. I fancied he had gone on ahead to look for water, and would be sure to come back to us on hearing we had found some; so I sat down by the hole Mazar was digging, quite contentedly, thinking, "Well, at last it is all over; here is water, and the end of our outward journey;" and I indulged in sweet reflections, in which there figured a day when there should be no more sand, and no more Baloches, and sweet water to drink. In the midst of these castles in the air, one of my men came up from the rear and called out, "Nur Muhammad says there are men coming." I jumped up, called out "Where?" and ran to the bank and looked through my telescope in the direction indicated. Before I had time to make out anything for certain, the individual in question came running up breathless, saying, "I have seen some men." At this confirmation of the report, I felt extremely riled, and calling for my rifle, and getting all the men up to the high ground, we stood for an instant like a herd of bulls at bay; I indeed felt at bay, and very vicious. After all our troubles to be driven off our water, ere we had tasted a drop, was too much, and in that short moment I determined that all Balochistan would not make me leave that water without a fight. So we stood to wait the result of a man who had been sent out to see and report who the strangers might be. Before he had gone far, he met two individuals, who seemed to have matchlocks in their hands, but who really had only sicks, and who made peaceable gestures; and it turned out that the enemy were a party of peaceable "Makkis," or men who go to the hills for the yellow earth they called "mak;" and so we had not to die, but got our water after all.

And such water it was. Ugh! the remembrance of it will stick to me till I die. There are certain things I never forget; one is a particular powder an aunt used to give me at Portobello, when a child, and I am sure another will be this water. It might have some recommendation to people who are suffering, for I am sure it would cure as many things as Hunyadi Janos is said to be good for, and I am sure constipation, singing in the head, indigestion, heartburn, etc., etc., would not have a chance against it. An enterprising chemist who introduced "Zirreh Water," with a recommendation from some eminent physician, would soon realize ample returns, and the villa and one-horse chaise would no longer be castles in the air for his imagination. If any should wish to save themselves the trouble of going to Zirreh to fetch it, I think I could give a recipe which would taste something like it. Take, then, the first nasty-looking water you can find, mix salt with it till you make it taste as nasty as it looks, then impregnate it with gas from a London street lamp, and add a little bilge water; shake vigorously, and it is ready for use. N.B.—The test of its being sufficiently nauseous is, that after drinking you cannot even speak for a second or two.

Anyhow, although thus inexpressibly nasty, the camels appreciated it and drank greedily of it. The supposed enemies we had seen proved real friends, for they guided us to a place where the water, if not better, was infinitely more plentiful, than any we had yet found.

Thus passed one of the most anxious days I have had in my career.

23rd February.—As the lost camels did not return till after dark, it was impossible to march to-day. In fact, I had no intention of doing so in any case. All our animals had had enough of it, and if we were to continue our journey at all, it was necessary to rest them. I gave rewards to the men who brought back the camels, and to the guide who found the water, as well as a rupee or two to the Makkis, who supplied us with a little flour. The latter were much astonished at receiving anything, having given up their flour with a very bad grace; but on my explaining to them that I was an Englishman, and it was our custom always to pay for everything, I found our friends, ever ready to take advantage of the new turn of events, became quite as grasping in their demands as our other Baloches. As we had no tents, and I wanted to have a bath, I made my lazy followers rig me up a sort of screen out of my blankets, and behind this I enjoyed what must have appeared to them a very uncalled-for luxury, to wit, a wash.

The day was unfortunately very hazy, and we could not get a good view of the Lar Koh and Kacha Koh. This was a nuisance, as we were the first Europeans who had seen them from so near. They appear to form one range, which is continued right up to Seistan; and they must have been crossed by Goldsmid's party on their road to that province. I cannot make out whether they have any connection with ranges further back, but most probably such is the case.

In the afternoon we went over some heavy sand

to a ridge on which were situated the ruins called Gumbaz-i-Ṣhah, and found them to consist of six buildings, built in a line north-west to south-east, along the top of the ridge, and about fifty yards apart, facing south-west. Each had been a square-domed building, about forty feet square, and the same height, all but the dome being of unburnt brick. They had no pretensions whatever to architectural beauty, or even quaintness, and were quite of the commonest kind of structure. There was no writing upon them anywhere, and all the people knew was, that they were called Gumbaz-i-Shah Maksud. Apparently they must have been tombs, as there were other graves scattered about on the ridge. The fort, which is named Kala-i-Shah Maksud, also calls for no remark, being but a heap of rubbish.

It is a very curious coincidence, that long before I heard of there being any such place as Kala-i-Maksud, I had laughingly determined to call the furthest point we reached Ja-i-Maksud, or the place of desire, the object of the journey; and now to find such a name applied to the spot I had all along meant to reach was at least curious and strange. Beyond this place, to which the waters of the Helmand had in former years evidently come down, there was no other halting-place, till that river was reached some forty miles off. To have gone on would, however, have taken me to Bandar Kamal Khan, which is in Affghan territory; and I was quite satisfied with the information given me by the Makkis, who had just come across, that it was all sand with no water anywhere; so I determined to go no further. Having reached the point we started from Gwadur to find, we both, after our frugal dinner of dates and chupattees, polished off pint bottles of champagne, with which Major Mockler had provided us, drinking to his health and our own safe return.

The day cleared up before the evening, and we were enabled to get some bearings as follows:—Malik Siah Koh, 271°; Kacha Koh, 212°; Lashlak Hill, 245°; Trahu, said to be 45°; Bandar Kamal Khan, 56°; Darwaza, 305°; Balochaf, 296°; Hurmak, 280°; Koh-i- Khoja, in Seistan, 322°.

CHAPTER IX.

HOMEWARDS.

24th February.—We now turned our heads homewards, with what pleasure the reader can imagine. We still had before us miles of sand, long hot days, with salt water and bad food; but we could see in the dim distance the end of it all. The road first went over the sand-ridge called Siah Rekh for some five miles. This ridge is so called from the sand being sprinkled with a black gravel. Leaving the tombs on our right, we took a direction south-east, and after crossing the ridge we went over a stony plain cut up by innumerable ravinelets, all draining to a depression under the sand-ridge called Nowar Siah Rekh. The distance accomplished was twenty-three miles, and there is nothing to record, except the great heat and glare over these burnt-up plains. The fort of the Kacha Koh range was not more than some five miles distant to the south, while to the north stretched a sand-ridge some thirty feet high, which completely shut out all view of the road by which we had reached these delectable parts. There was no water at our bivouac, but we had brought with us enough of that delicious liquid from Zirreh. While on the road to-day we met one of the camels which had bolted on the night of the 21st, and as we had left Amir Chah early on the morning of the 20th, this poor beast could have had no water for five days. I was going to shoot him, but one of the Makkis who was with us begged it might be given to him, and as the Zirreh water was only a few miles off, I complied, and hope the poor beast got a drink before it was too late. Strange to say, he was not looking much done up, so, as there was abundance of camel forage, it is possible he may have got some moisture out of the bushes he eat.

25th.—The name of the place we halted at was Gorakgori; there was, as I have said, no water, and hardly any fuel or forage for the camels, and no grass whatever.

On Sunday the 25th we got off about eight in a direction south-east, over the same sort of plain as the day before; after going for an hour we passed the end of the Nowar Siah Rekh, a small depression where probably water might be found at times, certainly after rain. Crossing this plain for twenty miles, which all drains to this Nowar, we came to an opening in the Kacha Koh hills, at a spot called Syndak, where there was a little water; and then we went up the bed of a ravine covered with salt efflorescence, and with low difficult hills on either hand, for another five and a half miles, till we reached a place in it called Amalaf: here a supply of filthy water was to be got by digging in the bed, and there was some "ta-gaz" for forage for the camels, as well as some long coarse grass and plenty of fuel. The Kachaband range is said to be inhabited, and as the denizens therein bore the repute of being always on the look-out for a chance of robbing somehow, Nur Muhammad felt convinced they would kill us if they caught us, and he significantly added, "Amalaf is a very favourite resort of theirs." Accordingly I thought it advisable to put out some look-out men in the neighbouring hills. Our supply of food was now running very low, and it was necessary to put every one on an allowance. Mine consisted of four small chupattees for breakfast, and four more for dinner, and these washed down by stinking water cannot be considered a luxurious feast. All our dates were gone, and we had not had meat since the day after we left Naru, viz. the 16th. Notwithstanding Muhammad's forebodings, the night passed quietly, except for considerable annoyance I received from Mahmud, who kept grumbling at the top of his voice nearly all the night through.

26*th February.*—Starting at 8.35, the road from Amalaf went for some four miles south-east, on the western slopes of the hills, and then turned north to get through them, afterwards for four miles crossing obliquely a continuation of the same plain we had passed over the day before, which is here called the Dasht-i-Gholaman. It then gently ascended in a direction nearly due east for five miles, till it got into a low watershed, when in two miles further it descended again at an almost imperceptible gradient across a plain called the Dasht-i-Digar Chapri, where a peculiar isolated hill is passed called Trashta Kurik, and from this another ridge, a few miles off, forming an excellent landmark, and called Koh-i-Dalil, bore 106°; this latter was said to mark the boundary of the Khan of Kalat's dominions. The track then went over a low ridge, which was succeeded by a second about two miles further on the road; it then wound over a plain, latterly covered with heavy sand, for some twelve or thirteen miles, when we thought it was about time to stop; so we got down into a hollow between two hills of sand, and halted for the night, having done about thirty miles. There was no water here, but abundance of camel forage and fuel. On the road about three to four miles from Amalaf, we got a peep of a snow-capped peak, which bore from us 223°, and which the guide said was called Daptan,—the same as the Koh Taftan seen, I believe, by Goldsmidt's mission on their way to Seistan. The whole of the country to the west of us as far as Nurmashir, and to the south as far as Bampur, is as yet quite unexplored, and we could learn but little of it, except that it was called Sarhadd, owing to the men who were with us being all enemies of its inhabitants. I was sorry I had not time to turn south and thoroughly examine this tract, as I think it is not at all impossible that a practicable road could be found running right through it, from Jalk up to Goldsmidt's route to Seistan.

Tuesday, 27th February.—We got off this morning about 7.40, in a direction nearly due east. The Sarhadd hills were visible almost due south of us, and after going about three miles we passed the Koh-i-Dalil, one mile off, and again saw the Koh-i-Daptan. The road for the first nine miles was pretty good, going over a gently ascending plain covered with sand and gravel; but the rest of the way there were heavy sand-ridges, over which our poor worn-out camels floundered most painfully. At about six miles we passed a road which was said to go from Talab to Zirreh. On our left were some low isolated hills partially buried in sand, and on the right was

Miza-i Sultan.

a high spur of the Sultan Koh, some four or five miles distant. At 3 p.m. we arrived at our old halting-place Amir Chah, and found the men we had left there all quietly snoozing near the well, without a single person on the watch. I rode in and told them if we had been Sarhaddis they would have all been murdered; to which they replied philosophically, no doubt they would if such had been their "kismat" (fate). Even the stinking water of this well was welcome after our twenty-three mile ride. Here we dug out the few things we had left, and I sent men on the hills to look out. There was a very strong little position on the hill to the right of the well, and I determined before dark, in case of an alarm, to get on to it. My friend Mahmud continued his grumbling all the march; in fact he became quite mutinous, but it was pleasant to think that in a couple of days or so we should get rid of him.

On the 28th we got off at 8.20, and gradually for some four miles ascended the path by which we had come, with hills all round us. Then instead of going over the low Kotal on the old road, we continued up the ravine for two miles, when we crossed a low ridge into a level plain, making straight for the Niza Sultan, of which we had now a better view. After going about seven miles we crossed a track said to come from a place called Kunri, with rather fresh footprints on it; so we proceeded after this very carefully. Over the above plain the road continued for about ten miles, and then crossed a frightful mass of sand for four miles, when we descended into a ravine, and continued up its bed for a couple of miles to its head, just under the Koh-i-Kansuri. From the sand-ridge we had a capital view of the salt waste to the east of Zirreh, and of the sand-ridges to the north, between it and the Helmand. White, silent, lifeless, it had quite a depressing effect on us. Our halting-place, called Chakol, was at a pool of sweet water in the ravine, the first we had found since the 17th. There was no forage and scarcely any fuel here, so we had difficulty in collecting enough roots to cook the few chupattees we could afford to eat. We were now in the heart of the Sultan Koh, the principal peak of which bore 125°. The halting-places of Gamichah and Washaf were a few miles to the south; at the latter the water was said to be sweet.

On the 1st March the road ascended steeply for one mile over a Kotal which connects the Koh-i-Kansuri with the Sultan Koh range. From the summit we got a view of the Koh-i-Malik Dokand, bearing about 59°. We then descended into a ravine, and followed its dry bed for ten miles, when we left it, and for five miles went over the eastern face of the Sultan Koh, which here descends in a long glacis slope covered with gravel. We then got once more amongst very heavy sand-hills, and blundered about over them for the rest of the distance, some eight miles, to our old halting-place near the shrine of Pir Kaisar, where again we found beautiful sweet water by digging in the depressions between the sand-hills. From the top of one of the sand ridges we got a view of the Naru range, end on, and saw a ridge which seemed to run out from it to the north and gradually to become covered with sand till it disappeared in a waste of sand near the Helmand. There was very good camel grazing here, but no grass, and so Lockwood's horse, which he had brought on with him, now gave it up, and as he could not move further a bullet put an end to his sufferings. I had left my horse at Naru, and had wished Lockwood to have done the same, but he thought he would get it through. At this halting-place there were a number of circular spaces as perfectly clear of sand as if they had all been carefully swept. I suppose the wind had somehow blown in eddies and cleared these spots, just as we sometimes see bare places round trees otherwise enveloped with dead leaves.

On the 2nd March we marched some eighteen miles in a direction east by south. Fifteen miles of the journey was over heavy sand mounds covered with "ta-gaz," and then we entered the stony bed of a ravine coming from the Naru range, and in three miles further arrived in the Diwanak Khor at Lal Khan Chah. As we were riding up we saw the camp of our friend Zangi in the distance, and after a bit could make out a lot of people and cattle making off to the hills as fast as they could, and when we got in they told us that, though they thought it was us, it was just as well to make sure of their safety. Here I found my servant Muhammad, who had come all the way from Baghdad with me. He had my little tent ready pitched and cleaned out, and within an hour after we had got in had made us a breakfast which we thought perhaps the very best we had ever tasted; but then we had not seen any meat since the 17th, and for the last five days had not had more than one pound of flour per diem to eat. Take it all round, this was the nastiest bit of work, with the shortest commons, I had ever yet experienced. From the 17th to the 2nd, fourteen days, we had twice had drinkable water; for nine days we had lived on two pounds of flour and a handful of dates, and for five days on one pound of flour only. We had no covering night or day, and had only managed one really good wash the whole time. If it be remembered that before this for fifteen days we had also lived only on flour and dates, I think the reader will be able to realize that our system seemed to outdo Mr. Banting's altogether. Yet we were both very well. At least, I never felt better in my life, and I am sure at this time Lockwood looked the picture of health; in fact, I remember our having an argument as to who was the most fit.

3rd March.—We enjoyed what I hope the reader will consider a well-deserved halt. We had besides a good deal to talk about and arrange, as we had determined to separate from this point and return to India by separate routes. We settled that Lockwood should go by the most direct and practicable route he could find from Lal Khan Chah viâ Chageh and Nushki. This line would take him on to that followed by Christie in 1810, after he had parted from Pottinger at Nushki. At Bulu, or some other convenient spot, he was to make very careful enquiries and notes of every road he could hear of that led to the Helmand between Naru and Nushki. From the latter place he settled to go viâ Mastung, by the most direct route practicable for camels, to Bibi Naru in the Bolan, and thence to Jacobabad as fast as possible. Lockwood was to take with him three of the men under Mula Abdul Rahim, who was one of the best of the lot, he having on all occasions proved himself most willing, intelligent, and reliable. Whether danger threatened or hardship had to be undergone, he was always foremost, quiet, trustworthy, and indefatigable. We both had the very highest opinion of him. Lockwood took with him also his own servant, a Kaldani Christian whom he had brought from Baghdad, one of the best and staunchest servants I ever met. We had seen several of these people serving as sailors on the Resident's steamer at Baghdad, and were much struck with their splendid physique. If the Kaldanis are all like these, it is no wonder they have held their own against Turk, Kurd, and Persian to the present day. I was to take with me old Nur Muhammad, who had particular objections to going to Nushki, owing to his having more than once raided the people of that district; also Mirza, to whom I had taken a great liking, and who wished to come on with me, and two others. All the rest of the crew, with their worthy leader Mahmud, were to go back by the Mashkel to Panjgur. Short as was the time this creature had been with us, it was more than enough to show how utterly unworthy of any sort of confidence he was. Shameless in his greed, without honour in his dealings, he was as uniformly insolent in his address to us as he was without power over his men. Though what I had agreed to pay him was far above his deserts, he lost no opportunity of swindling or wheedling me out of more, and though he was on all occasions treated with every consideration, he never returned our kindness by one hour's honest service. His character seemed to me to be a concentrated essence of all that was bad in Baloch nature. His brother Gholam Rasul was a fitting relative for such a man. The greed, absolute dishonesty, and insolence of Mahmud were in his case rather intensified by his superior intelligence.

In the evening I sent for Mahmud and his brother, in fact for all of them, and I first expressed my pleasure with the conduct of Mirza, Nur Muhammad, Mula Abdul Rahim and some others, and then paid them their wages. Turning to Zangi I said, as he had proved himself so faithful though we had no claim on him and had trusted entirely to his honour, I would double the recompense I had promised him. All the above were intensely pleased. I had spoken to them and rewarded them first, because as I had a rather nasty business before me I wished to have some one on my side.

I then turned to Mahmud and Gholam Rasul, and said, "And now for you and your people: I have been extremely dissatisfied with you all from beginning to end. You came to me full of high promises of service, and you have not fulfilled one of them, and therefore all I shall do for you is to give you the wages I promised;" and I handed him over a bag of rupees. He took them very quietly and counted them, and said in a sneering tone, "They *are* all right," adding, "Where are the guns, et cetera, you promised us." I said, "I promised you them if you behaved properly, but as you have not I shall not give you one." He glared at me and said, "You must." I replied, "I shall *not*." "We will make you," said Mahmud. "By God, will you!" said I, jumping up and pulling out my revolver. On this they all followed suit and seized their arms, and it looked rather as if there was going to be some fighting; but I never thought so. I knew the crew too well. Mahmud was plucky, I believed, but Gholam Rasul was a skunk; and though the rest of them were more numerous than we were, and I could not expect much assistance from those who were so far with us, still I thought Lockwood and I, his servant and mine, and the Mula, were enough to cow them. Here Mirza came out and caught hold of Mahmud. Old Nur Muhammad sneered out, "You had better keep your courage for the road back." Gholam Rasul had turned a whitish-green, and there was not much very formidable in the looks of the others, so they all walked off, Mahmud saying, "If you do not give those guns to us before morning we'll take them." I thought it better to say no more, but drawing my men together we went off to a little distance to talk the matter over. Old Nur Muhammad said, "It is all wind; Mahmud is plucky enough, and mad; but the others are only Panjguris."

Still, though I had partially shut up Mahmud, I by no means thought the matter finally arranged. It had been my intention at the commencement of the journey to have rewarded every one most liberally, should their conduct have warranted it, and I was quite prepared to part with all the arms that could be spared, as well as the other presents I had, and anything of my own which I thought might be useful or acceptable to them. I am always a great advocate for rewarding honest service liberally, but it must be real. I have no idea of the justice of recompensing all men alike, whether they have worked well or not. I think, perhaps, there are some who may be of opinion that I should have given Mahmud and his brother their presents and let them go. No doubt, by so doing, I should have earned an easy reputation for liberality, and he and the whole of his dirty crew would have gone away rejoicing, doubtless, but not grateful.

They would have been pleased, but would have laughed in their sleeves at the ease with which the Faringis had been frightened into parting with their goods, and, conscious of their own demerits, they could not but have attributed the giving of the presents to fear of withholding them. The result of this would have been present freedom from care for me, but a crop of insolence and bad service for any who came after me. The word would have gone round that the English reward whether they are served well or badly, or not at all, but I had no wish to leave this legacy behind me, but rather to produce a conviction that only good service would meet with reward. Thus it was that thinking all this over, I had a somewhat anxious night; I was determined not to yield in the matter of presents, and though I was not afraid of actual violence, I anticipated insolence. I had met with specimens of it before, but all had, doubtless, been tempered by the hope that they might receive some reward; but now they knew there was no such prospect before them it was impossible to foresee what length their insolence might reach, and certainly hard to determine how far it should be allowed to go without being resented. Mahmud and his brother had frequently insulted me personally, and I had passed it over as the vapourings of a half-wit; but if he should insult my Government or my country, I felt that the matter could not be overlooked. But what notice could I take that would in any way adequately avenge the insult? I had already felt it necessary to inform him that I considered his conduct so bad that I was not going to give him anything more than the pay I had agreed on, so that my last card was played. Having deprived him of hope, I had no further hold over him; sense of honour the man had none; though, as he often boasted, descended from ancient kings, his meanness was such that the lowest slave would have been ashamed to have imitated him. Then he was quite irresponsible; an exile from his own country, he, of course, acknowledged none other, and the authority of the Khan, generally rather hazy, I fancy, is but a shadow in Panjgur. It would not do to engage in any war of words with an insolent man, still less would it be wise to deal out to him the swift retribution of a blow, for that might lead to the drawing of cold steel, and then, having not a soul beyond our own selves upon whom to rely, all of us might have been massacred; or if, as was by no means improbable, the whole took to their heels at the sight of two wrathful Britons, with their swords drawn, a far worse fate might befall me, and I might be told by some young secretary, the most agitating circumstance of whose life, perhaps, had been a fly in his tea, that he was astonished and grieved to find that I had so little control over my temper. Oh, I thought, if I could only take the whole crew, one down and the other come on, I am sure my good claymore would not fail me, and I do not think my right hand would play me false! Then I laughed at myself at being thus reduced to that great solution of difficulties, the cutting of the Gordian knot. Ah! how easy everything would be if we could all thus get out of our responsibilities. And so I went to sleep, and dreamt of happier times.

Next morning, the 14th, I was up early, and soon the men began to move about, while I was happy to find that Mahmud and his brother sat silent, rather with the gloom of despair on their faces, than with the mien of any stern resolve. Could it be, I thought, that in the calm stillness of the night they had talked it all over, and thinking it out had arrived at the conclusion which comes to all of us at some time or other, "we have made fools of ourselves," and that now they had not sufficient life in them but just to sit and look at the things that might have been theirs being packed up? Any way, I lost no time in bringing matters to a head; it was better, I felt, to have done with it. So I sent them all the flour I could spare for their return journey, on which, "more Balochi," they sent and asked for grain for their camels also. I then picked out the camels I meant to give them for the road, and sent them. Still no sign was made, still Mahmud sat looking at Gholam Rasul, and becoming, as people do when both are in the wrong, mutually snappish. Still, the preparations went on, each of the three parties that were to separate this day gradually getting everything ready, till at last Mahmud got up, and with the whole body of his dirty "gholams," as he called them, came up. I was in a very good temper, and prepared to hear myself reviled with due submission, and to avoid any row, if it could be done with honour. He came straight up to me, and holding out his hand, said, "I have come to ask forgiveness, I was wrong to speak like I did yesterday; do not bear it in your heart against me." This disarmed me at once; for everything but a frank avowal of error like this I was prepared, and if he had continued this line of attack, I should, I think, have given way. However, my displeasure at his conduct was founded on no imaginary grounds, and so I said, "Mahmud Khan, I do forgive you; God knows I will bear you no ill in my heart; I am very sorry indeed that you should have behaved in a manner which makes it impossible for me to give you those presents, which I brought all the way from London to distribute to those who served me well; I regret I cannot think you have done so, and I hope it will be a lesson to you, that though the English are ready to reward well, they never do so without adequate service." He replied, "It is my loss, but do not let me go from you angry." "No," I answered, "I am not angry; good-bye," and I gave him my hand. He left, and in two minutes more he was on the camel I had given him, and *en route.* After all, though he had got much less than I had hoped to give him, he had not done badly. He had received three hundred and sixty rupees in pay, six camels as a present, and a gun, and he had probably made not less than two hundred and forty rupees out of the camels he had bought for me. I then turned to the few who had done well; to Mirza, the ever cheerful, ever ready, ever obedient; to the Mula, one of the most quiet, willing, indefatigable men I have seen; and to old Nur Muhammad, the shrewd, greedy, but faithful guide, and said, "He has been his own enemy; you have seen that he has gone empty-handed, because I am not pleased with his service; you, who have done well, I will treat quite differently."

The things were all ready now, so I said good-bye to Lockwood, and we parted, to meet, we hoped, again at Jacobabad. The day was very hot; I was suffering great pain from a boil, which made riding very painful, and the march was intensely uninteresting, among low black hills, from which I could get no view, yet I had not felt so light-hearted for a long time. My face was turned homewards, and I had got rid of Mahmud. The march was a short one, fifteen miles, and we halted in the Juli ravine, where there was a pool of brackish water. In the evening I climbed the highest hill near, and got bearings to the Koh-i-Sultan and Malik Naru, while in the far distance were the peaks Koh-i-Safid, Morpish, and Dokand, which we fixed on the way up; I was disappointed, however, in not seeing the Gat-i-Barot, which formed such a capital landmark.

5th.—Since we left Panjgur, we had been marching after breakfast,—not because I in any way approved of the system, but because my escort appreciated it a little at first, and Captain Lockwood all through. I myself never liked the idea; I never expected any more comfort from it, or any more efficiency, and I think the result showed that I was correct. We used generally to get off by nine, and having thus lost three good hours, we had, of course, to carry on for more than that time longer in the afternoon. And the result was we were always going in the hottest part of the day, an arrangement which cannot by any possibility be good for the animals, especially when water is scarce. Then we always arrived too late to let the camels have a proper graze. Indeed, the only advantage the system had was to allow of a couple of hours longer in bed. However, now I was alone I changed all this. We got up at 3.30, and off at 4.30, just before daybreak, and by 8.30 we had done fourteen miles. I wished to go on after watering the animals, but there was no water for fifteen miles further, so we halted till the afternoon, and then did nine and a half miles more. In this way the camels got a good long graze and a rest during the heat of the day. The road left the hills, and kept outside them all day, going over high stony plateaux, divided by broad ravines. To the left was a spur of the Naru range called Karzak, which is also the name of one of the ravines we crossed. We halted in the bed of the Dahna ravine, the head of which is far off, close to the Naru peak. There is a good deal of water in its bed, in pools, but it is unfortunately brackish, though not so much so as to be undrinkable. There is also plenty of fuel, forage, and some grass, so it is well suited for a camp. Leaving the Dahna ravine at three, we very soon got into a still larger one, called the Amuri, whose source is on the opposite side of a spur to the Dahna, and as far north. It is very broad, and its bed is covered pretty thickly with tamarisk. After following it for about five miles, the path goes on east, and leaves the ravine which comes from a gorge to the north, and, crossing a couple of low watersheds, enters a narrow gully, down which is a small ravine called Wadi, which runs south; after getting clear of the hills we halted in its bed. This is one of those things which are supposed to be very foolish to do, but, like everything else, it depends entirely on circumstances;—the country, the nature of the ravine, the time of the year, the state of the weather. And so, having taken all these into consideration, and found it was about a thousand to one against the ravine coming down, and ten thousand to one against its catching us if it did, I did that foolish thing, and camped right in the waterway.

On the 6th March we got off early, and, going over the same stony ravine-cut plateaux as yesterday, arrived in a couple of hours at a well called Nilagan, where the water was pretty good. I meant to have watered the animals and gone on to the next water without stopping long. But we had to wait an hour for a man who had forgotten and gone back for something. Here we got a view of the Malik Siah Koh, and could see another highish range joining it from the west. At last, however, we got off, and passing a road coming from Jalk, reached a place called Girom in two and a half hours. Here we were lucky enough to find excellent water and good grazing. On the road to-day we passed pretty close to the Gat-i-Barot, which we had first seen from Meski, and which proved to be much further to the east than we then thought it. It is an isolated rock, after the manner of the Droogs in India, which rises abruptly out of the plain and forms an excellent landmark. It probably was once connected with the Nohli range, which runs not far to the south of it, but now it stands quite apart. I was unable to procure a good guide at Naru, and the one I got spoilt this day's work altogether. We reached the Girom ravine at 10.20, and I wanted to go on to another water-spot, called Jaori Chah, which he had told me was near. But now it was evident he did not wish to proceed, so he swore it was very far, and would take half a day longer. I felt almost certain this was untrue, but was obliged to halt at this water, and let the camels graze a bit. In the afternoon we resumed our march, meaning to go as far as we could towards the next water, and then bivouac for the night. But we had only been travelling an hour when the guide stopped suddenly and said, "This is the well Jaori Chah." This was too bad. He had positively sworn it was not under half a day's journey in the morning, when it would have been as easy, in fact better, to have come on here as to stay at Girom. But now it was difficult to know what to do. In these countries it is very hard to leave water when once you have got it, and as Mahmud had taken all my " mussucks " (water-skins) we were hard up for things in which to carry any of the precious commodity. However, we had made so little way to-day that I determined on attempting a further push. So I watered the horses and camels, and, carrying as much as we could, we hastened on our way. But the fates were against us. The road soon became very bad, descending and ascending out of very steep ravines by stony, difficult tracks, which made the travelling very bad. So after an hour, when we got into the Ghedan-pasti ravine by a break-neck slide rather than path over sheet rock, I thought it best to stop. The halting-place was called Lagujgarh, and the ravine in which it is situated is very narrow and stony. It has plenty of water, but very salt, though the camels and horses seemed to drink it all right. There is also abundance of " pish " for fuel, but very little forage at all.

The pish which we left at the Tankh-i-Zorati, and had not seen since, had now come back to us, this ravine being the first place in which we found it again. I cannot say I cared much to see it, though its verdancy did help to relieve the monotonous brown of the Mekran hills and ravines. But some of the men were quite delighted, and they immediately picked enough to fit themselves out each with a bran-new pair of sandals.

Our camp was again in the bed of the ravine. Indeed, I have a fancy for such localities, especially when, as in this case, all the ground around is stony. A soft spot can generally be found in them, and on this night I selected a bit of salt efflorescence as the best place available.

7th March.—Our road led us up and down a succession of ravines divided by little ridges, till we emerged into a plain close to the Gat-i-Hamun, an isolated ridge of low but steep hills, and after crossing a considerable ravine called Mehrui, which has its source from the Malik Siah, and eventually drains into the Morjin depression, we came to a ravine called the Hamun Khor. Here we found abundance of excellent water by scraping a few inches anywhere in the bed, and there was also plenty of fuel and forage, and a little grass. So far we got on very well, but nine miles was of course too little for a day's work, and it proved quite impossible to make out from the guide what was the distance to the next water. So after feeding the animals and ourselves we got off again about twelve. Luckily the day was very cool, the sun being quite obscured by the clouds. After crossing several ravines and going over the same stony intervening plains, we, at fifteen miles, came to the Sorgil ravine, in the bed of which there was abundance of water, at this time quite sweet, probably being the proceeds of recent rain; but there was every sign that it would soon turn brackish, and the guide said that it was seldom drinkable. Unfortunately here there was no forage for the camels, and as this was not less necessary for them than water is for man, we were obliged to resume our journey. We went down the bed of the Sorgil for a mile, and then scrambled over a most interminable and provoking set of low hills covered with stones, which were very trying to the camels. For three miles we plodded on manfully, and then emerged into the Dasht-i-Golab, which is continuous with the Dalbandin plain; but we still had a couple of miles to accomplish before we came to sufficiently good grazing ground. This we reached at five, having made thirty miles in the day.

There was a great deal too much southing in our route, but the guide and Nur Muhammad assured me there was no other practicable road, the most direct line to Dalbandin being stayed by the ridge we crossed at an easier point. In front of our bivouac, stretching to the east and west as far as could be seen, was a very heavy ridge of sand, which runs parallel with the Soraf range. This was about twelve miles off to the south, and consists of two distinct and parallel ridges, the further one being of a considerable height. To the west the sand range did not continue very far, but to the east it went on as far as could be seen.

8th March.—It proved as I expected,—we had journeyed a great deal too far south yesterday; so we had now the mortification of going back north by east to get into our right line again. I had all along an uncomfortable feeling we must be off the right road, though the guide and Nur Muhammad both said it was not so. For ten miles we went across the open plain in a direction of 60° to a camp of nomads.

Here we halted and breakfasted, after which we sent off some of the men for water. This place is called Lagdund, and it boasts a considerable lot of cultivation, the first we had seen for over forty days. In the after noon we went on still in a more northerly direction, and after twelve miles reached Lyada Dalbandin, the end of the day's march. As it was dark before we got in I sent Nur Muhammad on ahead to warn the people we were friends, while we stopped a bit. After a while he called to us to come on, and as we were reaching the camp they signed to us to turn to the left and go on to the water. This I considered a great piece of impertinence, though I was not sure whether it proceeded from this cause, or from ignorance or suspicion, or both; any way, as these gentlemen have earned for themselves the reputation of being the greatest thieves in Naru land, I thought it as well to tell my men to keep a brighter lookout at night than usual. Morning, however, arrived without anything occurring.

9th.—In the morning Khan Jahan Sanjarani, the chief of this part of the world, came to see me. He was a very gentlemanly-looking man, with clear-cut features. He brought his two sons and a brother, all of whom were the image of himself. After the usual salutations the customary enquiry elicited the rather startling information that the Khan had returned to Kachi, and was soon coming up to Kalat, when he was going to bring with him twenty thousand English troops; an estimate which must have been formed from an exaggerated idea of the Khan's importance, combined with a small opinion of the value of British soldiers. I asked what they supposed twenty thousand men were going to do? "We don't know, but we suppose you do," was the laconic reply. The fact is, recent interference in Kalat affairs, however beneficial it may have been in other respects, was having the effect of unsettling men's minds in these parts. It was quite within their understanding that we should want to settle terms between the Khan and his chiefs for some ulterior object of our own, but that we should do so merely for the sake of peace on our border, they would not swallow. Consequently they had a story that we had made the Khan a prisoner, and were going to have a cantonment at Panjgur. I said of course I did not believe any force was coming, and certainly not such a large one; but it was evident they did not believe a single word I spoke. Twenty thousand English troops! why, there is nothing in the whole of Balochistan to withstand two thousand. Khan Jahan informed me that the district or province of Chageh included the whole of the country to the north-west of Nushki, all being under the orders of Sarfaraz Khan, who is also chief of the Sanjarani tribe, by whom it is inhabited. It consists of the following subdivisions: Chageh proper, Koh-i-Pusht, Koh-i-Sunt, and Dalbandin.

While on the subject of boundaries, I may as well record what Nur Muhammad considered those of Kharan. These are Kala Nimroz, above Azad Gaz, on the Budu; Gwarjak, Rakshan, Rageh, beyond Rakshan towards the Mashkel; Panjgur Band to Bibi Lori; thence to west foot of Sohraf range; thence along east foot of Kala Nimroz.

The Rekis, to which tribe Nur Muhammad belonged, say their boundaries extend from Bibi Lori, along the foot of the Siahan, to Tankh-i-Zorati; all

Dehghwar, from five miles north of Jalk; thence to Mir Hop, north of Ladiz, six miles; Mir Janm, Jujak, Talab, Paniham, Wakab, and Bibi Lori. Their chiefs are Sakh and Kadir Bakhsh, who live in Jalk. Formerly they were under the Khan of Kalat, but not since Mahmud Khan's time, during which Azad Khan had some sort of command over them, till about seven years ago he built the fort of Golugah, with the intention of bringing them more under subjection; thereupon they fled to the Kajars, who sent a force under Ibrahim Khan, and destroyed this fort. Since this time they have been in a way tributary or under the protection of Persia, that is, they pay nothing, but give "Kamar bandi." Azad Khan has some seventy of them with him, and he raids the others whenever he takes a fancy that way, and from this cause he is now looked on as their greatest enemy.

I halted this morning to give the camels a little rest, and make arrangements about another guide. It was arranged that Nur Muhammad and all the men except Mirza were to leave me here and go by Kharan back to their homes. The former old gentleman for the last forty days had been the central figure in all our explorations, and on the whole he served me right well. He had, I believe, told me all he knew about the country, and this was probably more than any one else, and he was a great success as a guide, seldom making any mistake in places he had visited, and ferreting out the road with great shrewdness or "dalil," as he called it himself, in parts with which he had not been previously acquainted. He *possessed* in an eminent degree the greediness which is so prominent a feature in the

Baloch character, but as he did the work well, I never grudged giving in to his unconscionable demands, and now in addition to the pay I agreed on, I made over to him a couple of camels, these being, as he informed me, the greatest friends he possessed, more so than any of his wives, of whom he had three, all "Kittle Cattle," he said. I think on the whole he was pleased with the treatment he had received, but he could not resist the temptation to get something more out of me, and though he had just received one hundred and sixty rupees,—more than he ever before possessed (honestly, at least) in his life,—he came up, and twisting his rugged and villainous features into the nearest approach to an insinuating smile he could, begged for some more rupees to buy a water-skin. He was one of the Rekis who had separated from their tribe, and who are now living under Azad Khan. He led me by the very road I was in quest of, and laid bare all the secrets of the great silent desert, in which he had been my companion for forty days, and so I was satisfied. The key to the whole of this tract lies in an accurate knowledge of the watering-places, and I think he told me of every one that exists, together with their Baloch classification of "Shirin," "Wash," "Waragi," and "Talkh," which mean respectively, sweet, good, drinkable, and bitter. There are seldom any tracks left in the ocean of shifting sand of which the desert we had passed through is composed, but there are no difficulties of roadway to encounter; so if one knows where to look for the water, one can steer by compass just as if on board ship.

CHAPTER X.

BRAHUI LAND.

HAVING paid every one up, I arranged to go on with only Mirza and my servants to Sohraf. This was said to be six good days off, and we made a short march this afternoon to a camp of Brahuis, where it was said guides and camels would be forthcoming.

Accordingly we moved off, and going over a similar sort of plain, bounded on the north by the same low stony ridge, and still limited by the sand ridge on the south, we arrived, after twelve miles, at a Brahui camp, near a watering-place to the north, called Pishak. As we were going along, an elderly gentleman rushed out with a small carpet, and called out, "Hi! where are you going? Stop here." And when he saw we still kept on our way, for I wanted to be near the water, he said, "Hi! stop here, you are my guest, don't blacken my face. Agha (Sir), do stop; for God's sake be my guest," and so on. I was so amused that I halted; then he came up, and seized hold of my leg, and said, "Then now you are going to stop." But I protested that I wanted to go on to be near the water. "Water! I will give you water, and meat, and milk, and bread—whatever you want." So I said, "I am very much obliged, and since you are so kind I will stay here." "Kind," he called out, laughing, "wait till you see. Now what do you want? A little milk? Nothing else? Have some bread." "No, I have bread; but if you get us a little wood——" "Of course; and you'll have some meat? I have lots of meat." "Thanks," I said, "I have meat; could you get some grass for the horse?" Before the words were out of my mouth, he shouted, "Hi, Shahu! ho, Mehrula! run and get some grass for the Agha's horse.—Now what else do you want?" "Nothing more," I replied; but he went on pressing me for a long time to have this and that. This, as a specimen, and a first specimen of the Brahuis, was certainly a great improvement; I was more than a month among the Baloches, and no man ever offered me a glass of water, and the last Baloch I met, Khan Jahan, when I arrived at his camp told me to go on. The benevolent old gentleman, who was called Shah Dost, continued his attentions late in the night, and in the morning it was just the same; I feel sure there was no *arriere pensée*, for he never asked for any payment, and when I gave his little daughter a couple of rupees, as a delicate way of returning his kindness, he wanted to return them; at which the young lady pouted, and was going off into a "Boo! hoo!" I said, "Let her take them on my account; your kindness cannot be paid for by money." How different from the Baloch, who, if he does anything for you, always precedes it by an enquiry what his "hakk" is to be.

As the guide I expected was not here, I sent for him.

10th March.—In the morning he arrived, and with him Mahmud Shah Khan Sanjarani, son of Sarfaraz Khan, the chief of Chageh. This young man was an uncommonly good-looking fellow, and he was quite civil enough. His manners savoured rather of the camp than the salon, but I believe he was sincere in his offer of service. He did not seem to know anything about Mirza, and perhaps it was as well, as their respective grandfathers had quarrelled many years ago, and the blood still remained unremitted. After some talk it was arranged we should go on to the camp of the guide, Sumar, at a place called Istun, about five miles off, and there breakfast, while he got ready to start with us; so taking leave of Mahmud Shah, Khan Jahan, and, least though he was in rank, and last though I mention him, certainly first in my regard, old Shah Dost Khan, whom I told, if I ever had an opportunity of serving, I would, we started on our way.

On the road to Sumar's camp we reached a depression evidently subject to inundation after much rain, but there were no signs of salt anywhere. We passed two or three of these yesterday, and the plain was gradually being more encroached upon by the sand, and though what remained seemed equally good soil, it was losing its uniform character. From the greenness of the grass round about, and the frequent occurrence of these depressions, I should argue that water was not very far off, and that the cultivation of this tract might be extended to any limit, if irrigated from wells. There seems to me, in fact, very little doubt that this plain of Dalbandin, or whatever be the name for the whole of it, might with very little management support twenty to thirty times its present population, and in fact there might be several large villages here, each with its cultivation, the waste bits being kept for the sheep and goats, and the sandy bits for camel grazing.

When we arrived at Sumar's camp, I sat down and began peacefully to reflect over the five miles we had come. Soon I heard a female voice, of not the most musical description, making a great row; but having become quite callous to horrid sounds and fearful smells, I took no notice. The accents, however, got louder, and so I looked up, and to my astonishment found an old lady whose grey hairs should have taught her better manners, talking at me and gesticulating violently. They say that in moments of supreme danger, the most nervous often become quite cool, and in this case it certainly proved true. Generally, I am rather afraid of the fair sex, and have often entered fully into the feelings of the young gentleman who said he would rather meet a lion than face a ladies' school; but now I was perfectly and unaccountably cool, and I think, having stood the trial of being slanged in Brahui, by an aged and excited old lady, I shall have more confidence with the fair sex in future. I turned for an explanation, and was told she was imploring me not to take her Sumar away. I told the interpreter to say I only wanted a guide; if I could get any one else Sumar might stay. But Sumar did not like this at all; he had got the "kulladar" * itch too, and did not admire having to give up this chance of making a little money; so he told his mamma in the most unfilial manner to hold her tongue. Luckily

* The "kulladar" is the name by which the rupee with the head of the Sovereign stamped thereon is known throughout Central Asia.

she then turned on him, and said, all being interpreted to me as she went on: "Don't go, Sumar; don't go! Who knows who this Faringi is?" Then, after using all the arguments she could think of, she added, "Don't go, Sumar,—he may kill you!" At this every one burst out laughing, and Sumar said: "No, he is a Sahib, he won't be treacherous," and the others called out to her, "Never mind, if he kills Sumar, we'll kill him." "No, you won't kill him," screamed the old girl; "he'll have gone away, and Sumar too; if you want to kill him, why don't you do so now?" Dear old lady, how kind of you! but when it came to talk of killing, I thought it was time to put a stop to the little entertainment, so laughingly I told the interpreter to say, "Killing an Englishman is rather an expensive amusement, both at the time and afterwards. You see, dear Madam, I have got here a rifle that goes off sixteen times before one of your men could get his off once, and here I have a pistol that goes off six times; so if Sumar's men tried to kill me"—"God forbid!" broke in Sumar—"I shall probably kill about twenty of them before they kill me; therefore don't you think it would be better to let Sumar come with me and get a few rupees?" On the failure of all her efforts she went away yelping to her tent, and after this amusing little contretemps we got off, and made nearly eighteen miles more before halting. The road went through a succession of the depressions I mentioned above, divided by sand hillocks. After journeying about six miles we passed a road going to Nushki. The sand now became more and more abundant, proving, as it always does, more than an equal antagonist for the good soil. The sand hitherto had been confined to one long ridge on the south, but now isolated hillocks began to appear, and these were evidently increasing in size. We passed three or four places where rain water was still remaining, one, called Namrekh, being over a hundred yards long; and at last we halted at a spot called Konarak, having done nearly twenty-three miles, which was as much as I expected after the delay caused by Sumar's mamma. From Namrekh there is a road which goes over the range to the south between the Kamburan and Charian peaks by the Rahio pass in three days to Kharan. It is, however, very difficult, and is not practicable for camels. On the left of the road, bearing 41°, is a hill which the guide called Pulchota, but which is the same as is shown on the maps as Mekh-i-Rustam, and away to the east is a lake-basin or Hamun, which receives the waters of the Nushki river.

On the 11th we got off at 5.25 a.m., and went over an easy sand-ridge, and then over a long narrow plain between sand-ridges, with the Kamburan range on the right. In two miles we reached a halting-place with no water, called Pul-i-lob, and, continuing on the same plain, at the sixth mile, crossed a ravine lower down, on which was a watering-place called Ghazl, and on our right the Seh Saman hill, over which there is a road to Besamar. At the eighth mile the Chah Sar hill was passed about two miles to the left, and at the eleventh mile we came to a place called Meski, where I halted for a time. Going on again, we crossed a ravine, and then the country became very stony; at the fourteenth mile we reached a well, situated in a ravine, called Khushki. The well is very deep, but the water is good, and there is plenty of fuel, camel forage, and grass about. Here I halted to have breakfast, and went on again at 2 40 p.m., and in four miles came to Chandran, another well, also deep, with plenty of fuel and forage round about. Going on again, after five miles we came to a place called Padag Kiri, situated at the south end of the plain known as the Dasht-i-Padag. The Kamburan range seemed to end just beyond the Koh-i-Shaikh Husain peak, which bore 70° from our bivouac. But I afterwards found the range took a turn to the east from this point.

On the 12th we did not get off till near six a.m. The road went nearly east, over a very stony glacis at the foot of the Raskoh range, gradually ascending by a very stony, but not difficult, path to the Ali Sahak pass, which we reached in about ten miles. Below us, to the north we saw a Hamun, called Wad-i-Sultan, which covered the whole ground between the range on which we stood and the low Pulchota ridge. This receives the drainage of the Meshki river, but at the time it was nearly dry, and covered with thick salt efflorescence. Only to the south on the Dasht-i-Padag there was a quantity of coarse grass and reeds and a little water. Descending from this we went down a narrow ravine bed at an easy gradient, to its junction with a larger one called the Ghani Khor, which drains south, and lower down is named the Maralkan, joining the Budu river near Kala Nimroz. Here water was abundant and good, but there was no fuel, and forage was very scarce. Having halted to have breakfast and let the camels pick up what they could, we went on again at 2.40 p.m., going up the Gani Khor, with the Dras Koh ridge on our right, and in about a mile came to its head, and crossed a low pass over a ridge which connects the Dras Koh—itself a continuation of the Gwash Koh spur, which comes from the main range called Raskoh—with the Koh-i-Shaikh Husain. Descending in an easterly direction, we got into the Chasi ravine, which also forms the Budu, and arrived at the Chasi shrine at five. Here there was plenty of water, but little fuel and forage. To the south lay a large stony plain, all draining to the south. From this a road goes from Nushki to Kharan, along the southern slopes of the Koh-i-Shaikh Husain ridge.

On the 13th I got off at 5.40 a.m., starting in a direction a little south by east. We first ascended to an almost imperceptible watershed, and then descended into a ravine joining the Seham Khor, which we reached in eight miles. From this we saw a hill, which bore nearly due south, said by the guide to be just above Kala Nimroz. The bed of the Seham Khor was very stony, and had a good deal of water in it in pools, and also much jungle. We then crossed several deep ravines, which all come from the Koh-i-Shaikh Husain, and in three miles further, arrived at another largish one, called Adari Khor, where there was a little forage, so I halted to let the camels graze. Going on from this, in a mile we reached a broad, well-defined track, leading from Nushki to Kharan, which, I think, is certainly the road by which Pottinger passed these parts. A mile further there was a large stream, called the Gwaragan, with running water in it, and abundance of fuel and forage. Letting the camels get a mouthful or two, and cutting some of the tamarisk to take on with us, we crossed this stream, and almost immediately got into low, easy hills, which we ascended, winding about very much for the next three and a half miles, to a pass over a range connected evidently with the Shaikh Husain ridge. Descending from this by an easy road, we journeyed to the Sikkin Khor in two miles, where again was running water. We then crossed another low pass over a spur of the above range, and got down into the large river-bed of the Budu. There was, however, no water in it at the part we crossed, but the guide declared it was the largest of the river-beds which go to form the Budu, and that there was running water a little lower down. Here was another road leading from Nushki to Kharan. The whole bed was covered with bushes, but unfortunately there was no forage for the camels. We now entered the Tazinan ravine, which joins the Budu at this point, and went along its left bank generally, but sometimes descending into its bed. To the north the view was entirely blocked off by hills, which rather surprised me, as I thought the Budu seemed to come from much further off. But on asking the guide, he said that the river, though sweeping round to the east, really came from the south, and that we should again cross its head on our onward journey. Going up the Tazinan Khor for some seven miles, we came to a shrine where there was plenty of running water, and so we halted. Of fuel there was plenty, also some coarse grass, but very little forage, which was unfortunate, as my few remaining camels were fast giving in. Here our guide left us, and we got a new one from some shepherds we passed on the road.

14*th March.*—The new guide unfortunately could not talk any language known to any of my party. His tongue was Brahui, which no ordinary individual can be supposed to know. Pottinger says the Brahui race is of Tartar origin, while Latham describes their language as Tamil,—a wide difference, truly! It was very difficult to get on without some sort of an interpreter. I only knew one word of Brahui, and I am sure Zaman, the guide, did not know one of Baloch, yet I managed to pick up scraps of information from him by dint of signs. In this way I learnt that some curious-looking heaps of stone on the road were meant to indicate the road. These people seem rather good at marking their roads, as one generally finds little piles of two, three, or four stones stuck about in conspicuous parts, and I have frequently got back into the right track by looking out for one of these "sign posts." One day when we were halting, we saw old Nur Muhammad prowling about the hills, looking shrewdly round him. "Well, Nur Muhammad, what are you doing?" said I. "I am just taking a look round," he replied, "and putting up a few stones here and there, in case I want to come here again on a chapao, or with a kafila. Who knows which it will be?" The fact is, unless some trace is thus left of the road, passers-by are so infrequent that their track is soon obliterated. This reminds me that I have several times seen our troops at fault through the road not being properly marked, and I am sure some such system is necessary in wild countries. The Baloch method of putting stones up would take too much time, and besides, it is neither distinctive nor plain enough, and therefore I think a very good plan was the one we adopted in Abyssinia. A trooper rode on ahead with the guide, with a pot of paint attached to his stirrup-iron. The paint may be any colour, as long as the pot has a hole in it, so that a drop may ooze out at regular intervals. These little drops, falling on to the stony ground, remain a long time visible.

The road led up the bed of the Tazinan ravine the whole way, and was generally most execrable, going over the stones without any intermission. There was, however, plenty of water in the bed, and also a quantity of fuel and coarse grass. Parts of the banks were strewn with a very pretty plant something like the crocus, here called "trishiko" by the natives.

Zaman pointed out one spot strewn with graves, which I made out to have been the site of a fight in days gone by between his tribe, the Mahmasenis, and the Nowsherwanis. This last tribe is included in Pottinger's list of Brahuis, but there appears little doubt that they were originally Lurs belonging to the tribe of the same name to the north-west of Shiraz. They now reside about Nal, and also, I believe, in Kolwah, their chief being a certain individual of the name of "Goony."

On the road we passed two or three delightful little peaceful dells, quite enclosed by the surrounding cliffs, and shaded by unusually large trees for this country, while a stream of clear water ran past banks of bright green grass. No doubt the scene appeared to me much nicer than it really was, for after wandering about salt and sandy deserts for forty days, the sight and sound of running water is very pleasing. I noticed, too, that these secluded spots had not been without their inhabitants, for there were the remains of some huts in them.

In this defile there was one of those natural barriers which they call "Gat," but it had partially fallen away. There, however, remained a wall or sheet rock on either bank, and a sort of island of the same in the middle.

For some ten miles we went up this ravine, and then we had to leave to cross a spur. The ascent was very gradual for two miles, but the last bit at the top was frightfully steep. The Tazinan goes round the foot of this spur by a defile which is said to be impracticable even for foot men, owing to the deep pool of water in the middle. This pass forms one of the strongest positions I have seen; below to the west there is a perfectly clear line of fire for two miles, and the heights above it on either side are very precipitous, and would be almost impossible to storm.

From this pass we descended again to the Tazinan, which still had water in its bed, and then we kept ascending and descending numerous spurs for another six miles, when we got to a main spur cutting off the Tazinan from the other affluents of the Budu. Here, as the animals were scarcely able to move, we halted for a time; after which we again descended numerous small spurs, and I found that all the rivers drained to the north, and the guide said they all went to the Budu. After going about three miles further I was obliged to halt in the bed of a small ravine with a "pipal" tree in it. Here there was water and plenty of fuel, but no grass or forage. This very nearly did for the rest of our camels; how the poor brutes lived I don't know. It seems to me a camel can go a long time without much food as well as without water, and that they have wonderful pluck. As it was, one had to be left behind.

15*th March.*—The morning broke very bleak and

cold, and consequently there was a natural disinclination on the part of everybody, myself included, to turn out. It was, in fact, the coldest morning, except that in the Mashkel, we had experienced since starting, and of course this was owing to the considerable elevation on which we were perched. The first news that greeted me on turning out was, that the camel which had been left behind last night could not come on, and that they proposed to abandon it altogether. Not quite believing this story, I went back to the other side of the pass where they had left the poor brute, to see for myself, and found it true enough; all we could do to get it to move had no effect, it only moaned in a pitiful manner; so I ordered it to be shot, staying by till the order was executed, as my companions were quite capable of leaving the wretched creature there on the chance of finding it alive when they came back.

Our road led us up and down a lot of spurs in a most worrying manner, never for long following any ravine, but going down it for a bit, then out of it, and over a spur to another. As I expected that now we had got over the range we should find the drainage going south and east, while as a fact all the ravines seemed to be draining in the opposite direction, I asked Zaman the meaning of this, and he said, "It all goes north-east, and then into the Budu." "To the Budu!" I exclaimed with astonishment, for I thought we had quite done with that river; but, as he was very positive in sticking to his assertion, I was forced to wait and see what I could make of it when we should get to some sufficiently high hill. We proceeded very slowly; the truth was all the camels had had enough of it; one, we have seen, had quite broken down, another was dragging its long legs painfully along, and I momentarily expected to hear it had "sat down," so that everything had to be put on to the other camels while we all walked. Since crossing the Tazinan pass they had scarcely got a stick, and though I gave them all the flour I could spare this was not enough, and the guide remarked in a cheerful manner, "There is not a blade of fodder till Sohraf." "Then what are the camels to do?" asked I. "God knows better what they will do!" said he. "They will die if they get no food!" I said. "Yes, I suppose so," was the laconic reply. After going ten miles we halted to give the camels a rest and what little grass there was, and after three or four hours we resumed our somewhat melancholy procession, I debating the while what was to be done. We stopped at about fifteen miles from Sohraf, utterly unable to get any further, and I determined to push on in the morning and send back fresh camels. Luckily, owing to the rest he had been given at Naru, my horse still held out, and I did not doubt that camels would be procurable in abundance at Sohraf, which had for so long been my Will-o'-the-wisp. The guide was loud in the praise of this said locality, which according to him possessed cities, gardens, cultivation, population, in fact everything. Getting out of the hills soon after leaving our resting-place in the Samri ravine, we plodded over a plain called Tatakar, to the north of the road, and to the left of it Siah Kumb, the centre of which had a considerable patch of cultivation belonging to the Mahmasenis. We then crossed a ridge which looked more formidable than it proved, called the Siah Kumb, and descending a ravine filled with shrubs poisonous for camels, we came to a ravine known as Dragi, where there was a little water and plenty of fuel and some patches of "shis" grass suitable for the horses, but for the camels there was again not a blade.

From the hills to the west of the Siah Kumb plain I got a view to the north which convinced me that the guide was right about the drainage to the Budu. It was quite clear it did not go south, for we crossed a distinct water-parting which would prevent any such course, and to the north the appearance of the hills justified the guide's theory.

This is certainly a discovery in regard to the topography of these parts. Though very little was known of this region, such information as I had managed to collect had led me to suppose that the Budu rose to the west of some ridge to the south of Nushki, which then bounded its basin on the east, and when I saw the Tazinan, I thought this must be the range in question; but it seems I was mistaken, and the real source of the Budu was much farther off and nearer the east and south.

16*th March.*—Next morning, directly the things were loaded, mounting my horse I went on as fast as I could to Sohraf, the goal of my hopes for so many days past. Immediately on arrival I sent for the gentleman who rejoiced in the vague distinction of Ja-Nishin (literally, sitter in the place), and I soon found that the title, in this case at least, had not been misapplied. In the first instance an individual appeared who informed me he was the brother of that important official. Mentally breathing a prayer that his brother was not like himself, I requested the latter to send for him. After several hours' delay the worthy arrived, and his appearance did not prepossess me, nor can I say he improved on acquaintance. Picture to yourself a mean, miserable-looking creature, with the aspect of a mangy cur and the mien of a snake, clothed in a filthy nightgown, with long greasy curls, and the dirt of a lifetime obscuring anything pleasing his look may ever have had, and you have "Gwaram," the sitter. I asked him for the usual supplies—fuel, grass, flour, barley, etc.; then for a messenger for Kachi; and lastly, for four or five camels, or horses or donkeys, or any animal that would carry a load, for mine were quite pumped. To all these requests he replied, "Ba chashm" (*i.e.*, most willingly), and then he left. I could have borne his absence with a patience worthy of a philosopher, but that everything for which I had asked was as absent as himself. After waiting in vain some time, I sent for one Veru, the Hindoo of the place, and through him procured the supplies I wanted, and later on several men of their own accord offered their services as messengers; selecting one of these I agreed with him to take, as far as Kachi, a letter for the officer commanding at Jacobabad, and ask the Khan's Naib to send it on to its destination. But still no tidings of any animals, and as it was now evening, I sent a message to the Ja-Nishin to ask him to come and let me know what was being done about the camels. He sent me back a pert reply, that nothing was being done, and that there was nothing to do, there being no camels in the district or horses either, and that with reference to coming to me, he had work and could not be interrupted. I was thus thrown on my own resources, but as it was too late to do anything that evening, I had to wait till the morning, when, believing Gwaram's word, I made an arrangement with a man to supply me with two bullocks, which would carry the heaviest part of my things, while the poor camels were dragged on to Bapao, where it was said others would be procurable. I had hardly done this when eight or ten horses were brought up and offered me; and to finish an unpleasant subject, in the first five minutes after starting I counted two herds of camels, with from twenty to thirty in each. Sohraf is described by one traveller as a lovely valley, by another as a desolate plain,—the difference being of course to be accounted for by supposing the digestions of both were not in an equally healthy condition; and if I am asked to decide between them, I must incline to the former, notwithstanding the scant civility I had received at the place. The climate was in every way so delicious, and I was in such excellent health myself, that I cannot say a word against the place. Truth, however, bids me add, that Zaman's cities and gardens were of a very diminutive size.

We got off on the 17th about twelve, and found the road very good into Angira, a distance of fifteen miles. It ascended slightly to pass over an undulation which divides the drainage going to the Sohraf river direct from that which joins it lower down; and just beyond it we crossed a considerable ravine, called the Tarki, which came from a hill of the same name to the east. It had no water in its bed, but on the right bank a little canal took a plentiful supply to the village of Dand, and on the left a karez had been cut to irrigate some fields to the west. After traversing several undulations we at last, at the twelfth mile, crossed a watershed dividing the drainage of the Teghab system from that of the Mula, and then we descended into a circular plain, surrounded by hills, called Angira. Dand, the village through which we had passed, belonged to one Nurdin Mingal, who subsequently figured as a rebel of some note in the latter-day troubled politics of Kalat, and who was eventually put to death by order of the Khan.

Angira is very little lower than Sohraf, and consequently has very much the same sort of climate. It has a very considerable space of arable land, only about one-third of which is, however, cultivated. There is an abundant supply of water from the surrounding hills, notwithstanding which advantage there are no settled inhabitants in the place. There are two or three hovels scattered about the fields, but when we went to see if anybody would help us to some wood and grass, etc., we found them untenanted.

Umid Ali, my new guide, however, got on to his pony, and after an hour or so unearthed a wild Brahui, who made himself very useful in bringing in firewood, and in going off to his camp for milk.

This man, Umid Ali, was a Hindustani, who professed to have almost forgotten his native language, and he certainly seemed to understand Brahui better. His account was that he was a native of Delhi, and had been here about twenty years; rather a suspicious date for the self-expatriation of a Delhi Walah. However, the time has long past, and bygones are bygones in reference to the mutiny, so I did not care to ask more. He was riding a very smart blood-looking little mare, and I noticed other animals of the same kind in the valley. The breed seems one that is very capable of improvement.

On the 18th March I started about six a.m., going nearly due east, and gradually turned more north. We passed a great deal of excellent arable land, all lying waste, and at the fourth mile came to running water in the river bed which had been dry above, and then we passed a camp of nomads on the left. We had now fairly entered the Mula route, as the stream which runs past Angira is the source of the river down which the road lies. I had wished very much to go and see one of the Ghor-bastas, or infidel buildings, of which I had heard so much, and there was said to be one between this and Lakorian on the Baghwana road; but on enquiry as to the distance I came to the conclusion I could not spare the time which would have been necessary to visit it, and if I had gone on to Baghwana I should have had to make a long detour by Khozdar, before I could get back into the Mula again. So leaving these reputed wonders for another time, I started. The road went the whole way along the bank or down the bed of the river, and was naturally very stony. The river at this point has a small stream of running water, which however disappears again before Bapao is approached. I went on to this latter village, which is off the regular road, in order to make some arrangements about camels. On arrival I was very civilly saluted by a nice-looking old man, with a beard of many hues, whom I afterwards learnt was Mazar Khan Zehri. On my informing him of my wants, he at once said he would be glad to furnish any number of animals I required, and it turned out he was on the point of sending his own camels down to Kachi for loads, so my arrival was as opportune for him as for me. He also supplied me with a lot of green corn, which was a great luxury to my starved beasts. As, however, the promised quadrupeds did not turn up till it was getting late, I determined to go on, and leave Umid Ali to bring them after me when they had finished their feed; so putting a few necessaries on my horse, we started, guided by a small boy, who for his years proved one of the best walkers I have seen. We passed through, or on, the skirts of pretty considerable plains, all composed of good arable ground, though covered with stones and for the most part uncultivated. I suppose the fact is there is no population, else these fine plains would not be left bare. This and others I have passed through since crossing the Tazinan range would support in comfort ten times their present population, while the more barren parts and the hills would still remain for the grazing of their camels and sheep. No part of the road is worth mentioning till the Pisi defile is reached at ten miles from Bapao. The hills are steep, but at a considerable distance off, and till the above point there is no semblance of a pass, while the road is good though stony.

The Pisi defile is caused by the hills on either side throwing out spurs which nearly meet. It is one mile in length and only about thirty yards wide, though in one place it is not more than thirty feet. The road is in the bed of the river, and is much obstructed by boulders; as also it sometimes takes to climbing up the sides, it is generally very bad. On either side rise steep perpendicular cliffs for about one hundred feet. No doubt to a front attack in the old approved manner of taking the bull by the horns, this defile would be very strong; and this is the way non-military travellers generally look at these places. I am, however, surprised to see that Colonel Neil Campbell, who reported on the route in 1840, seems to consider it very strong, saying an enemy by merely throwing down a few stones might render it impracticable. All I can say is that, so far from regarding it in this light, I am of opinion that this defile is not tenable unless held by a very large force. For, though there is no other road, as the surrounding hills are practicable for infantry, the evacuation of the defile could be forced on an enemy unless he held these heights; also, I may be wrong, but even with the awe-inspiring influence of approaching darkness, it did not strike me as the place to detain a decent General a couple of days.

We got through just as evening was setting in, and as my small boy said the "bent" (cultivation) called Pisi was still three or four miles on, I pulled up on the first bit of tolerably level ground above the river we reached. After we had got pretty well settled, I discovered we were in the middle of a graveyard. I thought of Leyden's stirring lines on the graves of my ancestors, and the night was favourable to the calling up a vision of offended Brahui bones rising, and, after due sorting, getting themselves together, and sternly warning me to be gone. There was a faint moon, enough to show the deep black shadows of the surrounding cliffs; the night breeze was sighing; the water of the river could just be heard between the lulls of the wind, rippling gently along; and all else was still, black, and lonely. However, by this time I had got my blanket out, and my head was on my saddle, and I was about as comfortable as one can be with a boulder in the small of one's back; at all events I was not inclined to move for the ghosts of all the departed Brahuis who had gained or lost paradise. Yet, as I was lying, I saw the sudden flare of a fire over the hill-top, and this reminded me that I was quite alone, except the boy and my cook; which latter, though a very good hand at a stew, was not much to be relied on in a fight; so I thought it just as well to have my gun handy; and for us all to keep together and quiet. The Brahui is, as far as I have seen of him, the most inoffensive race of highlanders imaginable, but temptation is what does all the mischief in this world, and if a few of them should happen to find a lone Faringi by himself in the middle of their hills on a dark night, it was quite in reason to suppose that a sudden itching for that Faringi's property might seize them; so it was better not to tempt them. We waited a couple of hours on the hill-side in the dark; then my people came, and I felt valiant enough to light a fire, and hungry enough to long for my dinner. This, however, I did not get till ten; and meanwhile, to prevent the time passing heavily, and just as I had got my bedding spread out, a smart shower of rain came on and tried to wet everything; but I was too old a soldier to be caught napping in this way, and before any harm had been done I had all my paraphernalia rolled up and covered with my waterproof, and I sat patiently in my great-coat on the top thereof. Finding it could do no harm here, the rain went on down the pass, to an accompaniment of thunder. This reminded me how lucky we had been in the matter of rain all the time

I had been sleeping in the open without a tent, nearly forty days, during which period we had only been incommoded with two slight showers.

19th.—During the night Umid Ali came up with the other camels, though I was too sleepy to take much notice of them, and in the morning we got off again. The road, as before, followed the river, and as far as Goram Bawat, sixteen miles, there was only one place where the hills closed in enough to warrant the term defile. Every two or three miles there was an opening, with a strip of good land therein, either on one side of the river or another; so that an outline of the route here would resemble a string of sausages, the sausages being the Bents, or cultivation, in the open parts, and the tying of the same representing where the hills close in between each opening. The names of these Bents are Pisi, Chari, Bel Kondi, Mordana, Dardalu, Patki, and Goram Bawat.

As far as the Mordana Bent, there is scarcely any fuel or forage, though everywhere an abundance of coarse thatching grass; but beyond there is in each opening a good deal of both. At Bel Kondi I was pleased to see on the right bank of the river what Umid Ali said was a Ghor-basta, just like all the other "Bastas" in the country. This one simply consisted of a number of terraces built up on the face of the hill. They did not give me the idea that they were made either for the object of irrigation or cultivation, or for purposes of defence, but they simply looked as if the hill side had been terraced to afford space for dwellings, either permanent or temporary. And the position of them above the river, yet close to it, favoured this view. In this case it could not have been for irrigational purposes that the "basta" was made, since there the river was immediately below, with an inexhaustible supply of water; nor could it have been to bring more ground into cultivation, because even supposing every inch of the level ground below to have been cultivated, and more to have been required for the support of the population, they would natura lly have taken the next best sites and prepared these. Whereas here there were several large terraces that might have been turned to account —"Un-Ghor-basted," if I may coin a word; while the few insignificant terraces I have mentioned are so prepared. The most natural inference is, that this was the site chosen for the dwellings of the cultivators of the valley below. The theory of their being erected for defensive purposes is also not in the least borne out by the analogies of the case. For the most ancient worthy, even of prehistoric times, must have had sufficient knowledge of the art of war to know that if his enemy can get on to a hill immediately above his village and lob big stones on to the heads of his beloved wife and children, the site of that village is, in a military sense, defective. However, I don't pretend to arrive at any conclusion from only seeing one—and that probably a small one—of these Ghor-bastas.

Mordana is the largest of the openings through which we passed, and there is a good deal of cultivation in it, but no settled inhabitants. At Patki, there is quite a jungle of the pretty "patki" tree, which is something like the "Sisu."

I reached Goram Bawat about eleven, and was disappointed at not catching an itinerant blacksmith whom I had hunted for two days, but he, like a Will-o'-the-wisp, had evaded me. They said here he had gone to Peshtkana; I earnestly longed to find him, as if not my horse would soon be dead lame, I having run quite out of nails for his shoes.

I meant to have gone on again in the evening, but the camel men declined to stir; I thought at first this was an attempt to get me to proceed by single marches, but on explanation I found they were willing to go as far as I wished during the twenty-four hours, but wanted to travel at night, in order that their camels might have the day for grazing. As journeying at night would hardly suit my surveying operations, though in other respects I liked the idea well enough, we came to a compromise, that we were to start very early in the morning, before daylight, and finish the whole stage right through. I agreed to this, meaning to let them go off with the camels while I stayed behind till daylight and then caught them up.

On the 20th my things started at four, and I sat over a fire till daylight. Soon after leaving the Goram Bawat valley, the hills closed in on both sides. After going about two and a half miles we passed a halting-place called Lakeh Tokao, where there is water, fuel, forage, and grass, and in one and a half miles further a road to the left to Baghwana by Badoi, up the bed of a ravine which comes in from behind the Koh-i-Bug. The road now enters the small open valley of Peshtkana, the hills on the left going off east. It is two miles broad, and is covered with a jungle of tamarisk and other trees; but all is one mass of boulders, without any cultivation or cultivable land. Pushing on about half-way down this valley, we came to a clearly defined road which went up a parallel valley by Pandran to Kalat in five days, but it is said to be much worse than that on which we were. The Peshtkana valley is about five miles long, and almost immediately after leaving it the hills again close in on both sides, and form sheer walls of smooth white limestone rock almost perpendicular. These are perfectly impracticable from the pass side, but every few hundred yards the walls are broken by little gullies, and going up one of these I found that they are connected with the bounding ranges on both sides by spurs, and that they could be ascended from this direction; but inasmuch as the walls are commanded at short ranges by the above-mentioned ridges, and the tops of them are so sharp that it would be almost all a man could do to balance himself there, I don't think this bit of the pass is as strong, defensively, as it looks. These walls are called by the natives the "Dandan" or teeth, and they are very like gigantic teeth set up at intervals.

The road at this part is simply execrable, being all over huge stones and boulders, and my poor horse, having lost all his shoes, became dead lame, and I had to walk or sit on a baggage camel, an excruciating and undignified mode of proceeding I did not appreciate. We passed two places on the road where a halt could have been made, viz., at the shrine of Pir Lotu and at Dodandan; but I pushed on to the open valley of Nar, where the Mula river gives a turn to the north-east. Here there is a good deal of cultivable land on both sides of the stream, and much grass, fuel, and camel forage. There are roads thence to Khozdar and Khahk. I was sorry I had not time to explore a track over the hills to the east of the Nar valley direct into the plains of Sind, as the northern turn which the Mula river takes adds a great deal to the distance of that route.

On the 21st I got off at five a.m., and went down the bed of the river for some four miles, when it turned due north, and two miles further we came to Usui, a halting-place with abundance of everything. Just as I got up to this spot I found to my dismay that I had lost my spurs, which when I had to take to walking I had unfastened and strapped, as I thought, securely to my sword-hilt. As I would not have lost these for worlds, I had to trudge back and look for them, and just as we got to the turn in the river I came up with a party of travellers, and luckily found they had picked them up. I was delighted. I had had these spurs ever since I came to India, twenty years before, and had never had another pair. I should be afraid to say how many thousand miles I had ridden in them.

Beyond Usui, two miles, the road again turned south through a narrow defile to the shrine of Pir Laka, where there was a white-domed tomb, surrounded with beautiful trees, very picturesquely situated, with a certain amount of cultivation. After passing the shrine the road wound north-east, which direction it kept till we had cleared the pass. The road was throughout quite execrable, all over boulders, and after passing Khakori and Kharzan, two openings in the defile, I was precious glad to get to Hatachi, a considerable village with a good deal of cultivation. I put up in a delightful little garden of pomegranates, the shade of which was most welcome after my painful trudge from Nar. The gradient of the whole of the Mula pass is almost imperceptible the whole way from Sohraf.

Next day, the 22nd of March, we got off at five, and in half an hour came to some caves high up in the cliff overhead, on the left, called Koh-i-Khazana, which, according to Umid Ali, were supposed to contain treasure; and in an hour after came to the Bent-i-jah cultivation, a narrow strip on the left bank which extended for about one mile and a half. Passing this, two miles on, we came to a long slope of gravel and boulders which jutted out from a ravine on the left, and we had to make a detour to get round this. We then, four miles further, passed a large graveyard, called Paniwan. For three hours more we continued down the bed of the river, the most painful marching I can conceive, till we got to an open space with a good expanse of cultivation. Here, as at every halting-place since Angira, I had a most delicious bath in the deep pools of the river, some of which are very deep and long, so that I got capital swims in them.

On the 23rd, getting off at five, we went straight down the pass to Dahan-i-Dara, which I reached in three miles; after this the hills opened right and left, and in five hours I got to Pir Chata in the open plains. Here I was induced to take Umid Ali's pony, and rode the rest of the distance to Gandava in great comfort, arriving in the afternoon. The sensation of getting rid of the eternal boulders was most pleasing, and I can liken it to nothing better than to coming into a smooth harbour after having been out in a small boat in a rough chopping sea. Arrived at the camp of Major Sandeman, my troubles were over. I have nothing more of travel to record, and my pen fails me to do justice to the hearty hospitality I received from all,—the tub, the champagne cup, the easy chair, the delightful converse with my fellows, the sheets! As I got between them, having successfully accomplished my journey, I said, "This doth make amends," and slept the sleep of the just.

CHAPTER XI.

A SOLDIER'S END.

When Captain Lockwood left me on the 4th of March he went from Lal Khan Chah to a halting-place seventeen and a half miles distant, north by east, in five hours.

The road went for two miles in an east by north direction, over a stony plain, and up the left bank of the Dewana Khor to where it divides into two branches. This ravine runs close under the east end of the Koh-i-Sultan, and forms a "hamun" in the desert. The road follows the northern one to where he halted. From two miles from Lal Khan Chah the track followed the stony bed of the Nulla, ascending almost imperceptibly. The valley of the Nulla varies from fifty to four hundred yards in breadth, shut in by bare black hills from fifty to one hundred and fifty feet high, on the western edge of the Naru range. Two miles from where he halted, the road reached the western edge of the hills, and the country to the left was clear of hills, the view being shut in by sand ridges. There was good water in several places in the Nulla bed, and some wells about five feet deep: the road, by clearing and a little opening out, could be made practicable for artillery, though the last four miles were over heavy sand. Patkok, about four miles on, is the proper halting-place, but he was unable to reach it.

On the 5th March he went to a halting-place south of Rabat, a distance of seventeen miles, in five hours, north-east.

The road followed the sandy bed of the ravine on the south for one mile, when it arrived at its head. It then turned slightly to the left, and crossed some high ground with the Naru hills on the right, when it descended some two hundred feet by a stony path, and for five miles crossed a sandy plain covered with gravel and stones, when it entered the Sorgaza ravine, where there was a spring of very excellent water. The road then followed this ravine for two miles, over rather heavy sand. Then leaving the Nulla, it went for two miles again over very heavy sand, and for a further two miles over gravel and sand, when it entered the Marak Khor, where there was a well four feet deep, with slightly salt water. The Marak here was fifty yards broad, the banks being twenty feet deep, and steep, and the bottom gravelly. The road then passed for nearly four miles over sand, when it turned to the right and crossed a sand ridge fifty feet high, where the going was very heavy; two miles further on Captain Lockwood halted. The guide mistook the road; he ought to have gone to Rabat, three miles north-east, where there is water, in place of the spot selected, which did not boast a supply of the precious liquid; neither was there any camel-grazing, though plenty of fuel from dead "ta-gaz." No difficulty for travelling in this march, except the heaviness of the sand. To the north of this bivouac lay the Malik Dokand hill, not far to the north and north-west of which were the halting-places of Galachah and Sukaluk, where there is good water. These are the last places where there are any springs till the Helmand is reached.

On the 6th of March Lockwood went to Kia Chah, nineteen miles, in five hours forty minutes, in a direction a little north of east.

The road went, for nearly two miles, east over fine sand, when it crossed the Rabat Khor, coming from the hills on the right. This ravine was shallow, with a stony bed, three hundred yards broad. One mile and a half on he passed another ravine from the right, and then went over a stony ridge and into the Sognak Khor (four miles from halting-place). There was a small pool here of bad green water. Passing this, one and a half miles on he crossed the Galuri Khor from the right, and immediately after found a well-marked track, leading from Rabat, *viâ* Salea and Basalani, to Dalbandin. At three miles and a half further he joined the proper road from Rabat to Chageh. The road here ascended to higher ground, and after a mile a track went off to the right *viâ* Chilgazi, to Dalbandin. One mile further a shallow ravine, two hundred yards broad, running from Siadik to the north, was crossed, and three and a half miles on he passed close under a black rocky hill called Mushkani. Three miles to the left was a high red sand-ridge, on the other side of which, bearing 35°, the guide said was the Mammu halting-place. The road then went nearly straight to his halting-place, over a level stony plain one mile broad, with low bare stony hills on either side. The water at the halting-place was got from wells in the bed two feet deep, and was slightly salt. The camel grazing was better than before, but still bad; fuel was plentiful. The whole of this march was over gravel and stones: going good: no obstacle to heavy vehicles. Bar. 25·2.

He passed some flocks on the road, the owners of which bolted, but returned on finding it was not a raiding party. They were from Deshu on the Helmand, and had come *viâ* Galachah, and said that for five days the sheep had been without water.

On the 7th March Lockwood went to Barab Chah, sixteen miles, in five hours thirteen minutes.

The road ran south-east, over stony mounds. At three-quarters of a mile, a ravine from the left, forty yards broad, was crossed. At two miles, the road cleared stony mounds and descended to the Samoli ravine (one hundred yards broad, steep, stony banks, fifteen feet high), which it crossed; and at three miles joined the Bulu, Kuchen, and Galachah road; at four and a half passing close under a hill to the left end of a spur from Samoli. In one and a half miles farther it crossed a shallow ravine (fifty yards broad) from the left, *i.e.*, from the spur of Samoli. Here the road gently descended down a pebbly valley half a mile broad, shut in by low stony hills, and then turning slightly to the left gently ascended a similar plain for five miles, when it turned a little to the left up another valley to where he halted. The road was everywhere practicable. The water at the halting-place was slightly salt, from the bed of a ravine, and was procured from a hole a foot deep. There was some "gaz" camel-grazing here. On the road he passed three large flocks of sheep, which had come from the Helmand.

On the 8th March he went *viâ* Bulu to Tumpa

Gaz, twenty-three miles south-west; six hours forty-five minutes.

The road at first was east by north, very gently ascending obliquely across a stony plain for three and a half miles, when it entered low hills and turned slightly to the left, still ascending. At four and a half miles from the halting-place it arrived at the head of a ravine, which it entered and descended rather steeply for a mile. A little clearing and levelling would be here required to make the route passable. Then leaving the ravine to the right, it turned to the left, and, for a little over two miles, passed over a very gently-ascending, gravelly plain, with low hills each side, when it commenced gently to descend down a stony valley, four hundred to five hundred yards broad, with fifty to a hundred feet hills on either side. After five miles the valley narrowed to a hundred yards, the hills on either side being nearly perpendicular, and the road circuitous. Three miles on he arrived at a spring of excellent water, called Bulu. From here the road still followed the ravine for a mile south; then for four miles south-east, to Tumpa Gaz, where there were some few tamarisk bushes in the bed where he halted. There was neither grass nor water, but fuel was plentiful, and tamarisk for camel-grazing. The road on this march would require a little making in places to render it practicable, being the whole way over black stone and gravel. From Barab Chah the guide took him a great deal too much north, the proper line running nearly due east straight across the plain, as shown in the map. The road, however, was badly marked, there seeming to be little or no traffic on it. He found a great many "chikor" in the Bulu ravine, and stalked an "urial," but did not get a shot. Bar 25·75.

A road joins here from Lal Khan Chah as follows:—

Lal Khan Chah.	
Gwan-i-Shero :	water, gaz, camel-grazing.
Huki	,, ,, ,,
Talaran	running water ,,
Dozana	water; cultivation on this (Tumpa Gaz) march.
Chageh.	

Loaded camels can go this road with difficulty, and it is in hills the whole way. It is, however, the only other road, besides the one by which he came from Lal Khan Chah, to Chageh.

On the 9th March, 1877, Captain Lockwood went to Chageh, twenty-nine miles east, in nine hours fifteen minutes.

The track, leaving the Bulu ravine to the right, ran on to Dalbandin, going east over a stony plain, with low hills one and a half miles to the right, and a higher range the same distance to the left. At four miles there was a very small spring of water, called Kala Kurd, followed by a rocky ravine, the bed of which the road followed for a mile, when it turned to the right. At three miles from the water he entered a low broken range of hills across the front, and passed a place for penning sheep, called Poshab-i-parzonigi. A little over two miles on he reached Ziarat-i-Pir-i-dari, consisting of only a heap of stones. Immediately afterwards he cleared the low range of hills, and, crossing a gravelly plain for three miles, descended into a ravine called Dozana, one hundred and fifty yards broad, with steep hills on either side. Here there was a strong spring of good water, and a little cultivation. The road then followed the bed of this ravine for one and a half miles, when it left it to the right and crossed a stony plain to a hill, at the foot of which was a small pool of water, called Ab-i-Farang. The track now followed the skirt of this hill to its end, when it ran nearly straight into Chageh fort, leaving a low isolated hill half a mile to the left, seven miles before arriving. The whole march was over black, irregular ground, with low, bare, stony hills on either side. A very little trouble where there are ravines would make it useable.

On the 10th of March he halted at Chageh. Dilasa Khan Sanjarani and Yali Khan, respectively the cousin and son of Sarfaraz Khan, came in from their flocks to see him. The former was a respectable-looking Baloch, the latter a lad of about twenty, not much of a specimen of humanity. Both were very civil, and anxious to assist him. They said for three generations they had been under the Khan of Kalat.

The following roads go to the Helmand from Chageh:—

I.	II.	III.
Dozanan.	Same as I. to Shoraki	Lashkarab
Kala Kurd.	Kuchen	Karwan rah
Bulu.	Mushkani	Safea well
Shoraki.	Rabat	Razani
Arbu.	Sukaluk	Chah-i-Nawab Khan
Desert; no water	Desert	Desert; no water
Landi on Helmand.	Desert	Bagat, or Benadar
	Palaluk	

Chageh consists of a square mud-built fort on a level plain, with thirty or forty tamarisk-built huts round it, with a couple of wells of good water twenty feet deep. There were two Hindoos here, trading in wool and dates. The surrounding plain is covered with "ta-gaz," "karech," and "trat," which are excellent grazing for camel. The head man is Sarfaraz Khan Sanjarani, but he was away at Kala-i-Pat on the Helmand. His cousin, Mustafa Khan, and his sons, Yali Khan and Muhammad Shah, were, however, present. It is said they can raise a thousand matchlocks from the district. The country appeared quite safe, and the people seen were unarmed.

On the 11th March he made another halt. Early in the morning Mustafa Khan Sanjarani came in to salaam. He was a good-looking Baloch of about thirty-five, and was very civil and obliging, and went next day with Lockwood as far as Zarala. He gave Lockwood the following genealogical tree :

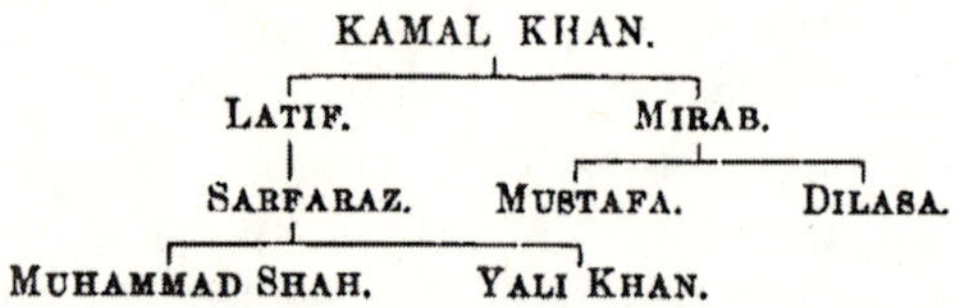

On the 11th March Lockwood proceeded to Koh-i-Pasht, seventeen and a half miles, in five hours ten minutes. The track went south, over "pat" covered with camel thorn and grass, owing to the recent rain. Leaving the Hamun of the Lora river two or three miles to the left for six miles, it crossed a shallow sandy ravine (fifty yards broad) called Shah-i-Salar (the same as crossed between Chageh and Tampa Gaz, and there called Dozanan). It then turned more east, and ran straight to some tamarisk jungle in the bed of the ravine from Poshab-i-parzonigi, here called Zarala, where there was a pool of very dirty rain water, where he filled his waterskins. During this part of the march the Hamun was close to the left. From Zarala the road circled to avoid the Hamun, which goes due east, when it ran straight to the foot of the Koh-i-Gau, a low stony hill visible from Chageh. There was no water at this halting-place, but excellent camel-grazing was found, and a little fuel. The whole march was level, over "pat" covered with camel thorn and grass, which gave the plain a pleasant appearance. There was no obstacle for wheeled carriages anywhere on the march, and water could be got in numerous places by digging a few feet.

On the 12th March he went to Saisar, twenty-five miles, in seven hours twenty-seven minutes, north-east.

The track went east with a little south, to avoid the Hamun on the left, which was muddy, and then crossed its most southern extremity for six miles. It then went straight on the Pulchota or Mekh-i-Rustam, a conical rock three or four hundred feet high, with lofty sand-mounds on its southern side. The road then turned more north, straight to Saisar. The first six miles across the Hamun were perfectly bare, over light brown soil slightly covered with saltpetre, the rest being gravel and sand, and good going all the way. On the right, about two to three miles distant, during the whole march, was a ridge fifty to a hundred feet high, separating the Hamun from the Dalbandin plain. Twenty to twenty-five miles beyond this was seen the high range of Ras Koh, north of Kharan. Far away to the left, twenty-five to thirty miles distant, was the north-east extremity of the Naru range. During the latter part of the march, five or six miles to the left, running parallel to the road, was a line of jungle which, according to the guide, marked the course of the Lora river from Pishin. No water was passed on the road, but it can be got near the surface by digging. No obstacle blocked the path the whole way. At the halting-place there was good camel-grazing, and water from a pool two hundred to three hundred yards in diameter, behind a sand-mound. A great many "obara" and a few hares were seen, but no people or flocks.

On the 13th March Captain Lockwood went to a halting-place south of the Lora Hamun, twenty-two miles, six hours twenty-five minutes, east.

The road went east, skirting the south side of the Hamun, with sand twenty feet high on the right, and mud cut up into pools of water on the left. At seven miles it crossed a sand-ridge, and turned more to the right up a branch of the Hamun, with sand on both sides. Continuing thus for four miles, it then crossed another sand-ridge and descended to a well called Tal, twenty feet deep, with stinking water. After another mile it crossed a neck of land and followed the south skirt of a "jhil" (swamp) covered with coarse and very green grass. Following this for four miles, it went round its eastern edge and followed a sand-valley for two miles to where he halted. There was no water at his halting-place, but there was good camel "ta-gaz" grazing all the march. The road was good the whole way, but very heavy over sand-ridges. He found a flock of Mingal sheep and goats at the halting-place. To the north-west was another halting-place called Mahabat.

On the 14th March Lockwood marched to a halting-place called Jabba, twenty-one miles north-east. The road went in nearly a straight line the whole way between two parallel sand-ridges twenty to fifty feet high, over "pat" and firm sand. At one mile he passed a well of water called Mahabat, one mile to his left behind a sand-ridge. At two and a half miles he reached Jandum, where there was water two miles to the left, the other side of a sand-ridge; and at eleven miles from his last bivouac he came to Lala, a pool of water fifty yards in diameter, by the side of a sand-ridge close to the road. The track for five miles on from this was over flat "pat" that had recently been under water. At sixteen miles a stream of water running south-west, skirted with tamarisk jungle, was passed, and at eighteen miles he arrived at a "jhil," a quarter of a mile broad, between sand-hills. This extended on the left of the road for three miles to where he halted. There was a sand-ridge a mile or so broad to the left of the road the whole way, on the other side of which was an extensive plain drained by the Lora river. To the right, and one to three miles distant, was a low stony ridge, in places buried in sand, one hundred to two hundred feet high, which separated his route from the continuation of the Dalbindan plain, through which I passed. The road was practicable all the way, but would be very heavy going in places where the sand is deep. There was a track in places, but the guide mostly followed a line on the Nushki hills. He passed several Mingal flocks, which, after the recent rain, had come out for grazing from the latter locality. There was good camel grazing the whole march, and plenty of fuel, but there was no fodder for horses between Nushki and Chageh. Thousands of "kulin" were seen, as well as a few hares and one wild fowl in the "jhils." All the water passed is dependent on rain, and dries up in dry seasons, when wells are dug when necessary.

On the 15th March he reached Nushki in twenty miles, north-east.

The road ran nearly straight the whole way. After one and a half miles the track arrives at a jhil five hundred yards broad, in sand-mounds, the road skirting the south bank of this for one and three-quarter miles, where it ended. The road then for three miles passed over sand-mounds twenty to fifty feet high, when it cleared them, and ran over "pat" between sand-ridges half a mile on either side for four and a half miles, when a track leaves to the right to Bagak. From this the road gradually descended for a little over a mile, when it crossed broad high sand-ridges for three miles. It then passed over cultivation and sand-ridges to the Nushki village four miles further. It would be necessary here to pick the road round the sand-ridges, but this could be done.

Nushki is inhabited by Rukshanis and Mingals. The former are subdivided into Jamaldini and Bahadini. The head man of the Mingals is Rahman Khan, and the Jamaldini chief is Dad Karim, while Alam Khan rules the Bahadini. These two divisions have a couple of forts, and are always fighting, mustering about two hundred matchlocks each. The Mingals are a stronger tribe, and at this time of the year are scattered grazing in the desert between this and Chageh. The Khan's Darogha, by name Lashko, was very civil, and got everything (camels, flour, etc.) wanted. Rahman Khan Mingal had gone out to the Dagh to graze his flocks, and had taken the five or six Banyas that are here with him. Nushki supplies nothing except cattle. A little wheat is grown, but barely sufficient for the wants of the district. Water is plentiful from the Khaisar river, which has a small stream of running water utilized to turn four water-mills.

On the 16th March he made a short march to a halting-place four miles off to the east, in one hour twenty-three minutes. The track followed the left bank of the Khaisar river, here a quarter of a mile broad, with a shallow pebbly bottom. At half a mile it passed between two forts a quarter of a mile distant,—that to the right belonging to the Jamaldinis, and that to the left to the Bahadinis. One and a half miles distant to the left was the Mingal fort and settlement, each fort having a cluster of one hundred to two hundred mud huts round it. At two miles he passed through a low ridge of hills, and leaving Khwaj, a Mahomedan shrine (and old Nushki) on a mound close on the left, immediately after he passed on the same side a water-mill with two large trees. From this the road followed the small stream that turns the mill, and circles to the left of the Kuti hill close to the left, with the river Khaisar half a mile to the right, running in a stony plain.

On the 17th March he went to Galangar, sixteen and a half miles, east, in five and a half hours.

After one mile over a stony plain the road crossed the Khaisar nulla, which emerged from the hills close to the left, and entered bare stony hills, gradually ascending. At one and three-quarter miles he passed Ziarat-i-Mir Haibat, a heap of stones, on the left. The track from here wound in high ground among low hills for four and a half miles, when it crossed a plain called Kum-i-Murid, two miles broad, and extending three or four miles on the right and left, and draining to the Khaisar. Having crossed this plain it again entered low hills, following the valley of a ravine three hundred yards broad, shut in by fifty to one hundred feet hills, called Kishingi. After following this for one mile it emerged on to another plain called Alunj-i-damag, which it crossed to a heap of stones named Talkhi, and again entered low hills one hundred to two hundred feet high, winding amongst them for three miles, when it passed Ziarat-i-Pir Langu, and descended some fifty feet to the bed of a large shallow nulla draining to the Khaisar. The road then wound up this for one mile, and arrived at Galangar, a pool thirty yards by ten yards, with a slight stream, the water of which was good. Camel-grazing here was bad, only "narian" and "buta" being procurable,—and these his Mekran camels would not eat,—and there was no fuel. The road is fairly practicable, except the part from where the track first enters the hills to the Kum-i-Murid plain (four miles), which would require a good deal of making, though the gradient was everywhere easy. He passed five or six flocks of sheep and goats, each five hundred to six hundred in number; also a caravan of eight camels going from Shikarpur to Nushki.

On the 18th March he went to Kardagaf, eighteen miles north-east, in six hours five minutes.

For the first three miles the road passed up the nulla, over stony ground, shut in by fifty to one hundred feet bare stony hills four hundred yards on either side. Here a track diverged to the right, *viâ* Gurgina and Mungacha, to Kalat. About three miles farther on the road quitted the main nulla to the left, and, going up a branch, arrived at its head, four miles on, when it crossed a low kotal; then, gently descending, it crossed obliquely the Gurgina valley, which drains to the Khaisar. To the kotal the road was stony; from there it changed to a white light soil. The valley was extensively cultivated from dams of rain water. The road then, in four and a half miles, crossed the Gurgina valley and forded the nulla that drains it here, a stream, twenty yards broad and one deep, of brackish water. It then passed a low hill twenty or thirty feet above the valley, and descended to the Kardagaf valley, running straight to the village of the same name in five miles, over light soil, through "banded" cultivation.

Kardagaf consists of forty or fifty mud houses, inhabited by Sarpara and Rodanis. The head man of the latter came and saw Lockwood, and was civil in getting his supplies. He said they could muster five hundred matchlock men out of the valley, but probably not more than half that number could be collected. The whole country was covered with a shrub called "dranna," which his camels would not eat, though there was no other food for them. Water was procured from streams from Karez, three miles off in the hills to the east. No difficulty for heavy vehicles this march.

On the 19th March Lockwood went to a halting-place beyond Baraz, seventeen miles, five hours forty-seven minutes.

The track went straight north over "pat" and gravel covered with "dranna," down the Kardagaf valley, three miles broad, and shut in on the east by hills two hundred to three hundred feet high, on the west by a lower ridge. At two miles he passed a mound fifty feet high close on the left; and three-quarters of a mile on a road to Kandahar appeared in sight, going straight down the valley. The Baraz track now turned half right towards the eastern hills, at the foot of which it arrived in six and a half miles from Kardagaf. The road then ran east of a low ridge separating it from the plain on the left with the main range to the right, and over undulating stony ground full of ravines till twelve miles from Kardagaf, when it entered the Baraz nulla, where there was a weak spring of water. The path then wound up this nulla to its head, where, crossing a kotal, it descended for fifteen minutes down another nulla to a plain gently sloping north-east. It then proceeded straight to where he halted. There was no water here, but only "dranna" for the camels, and no fuel. The track was good going the whole way, except from where it entered the hills to the east foot of the kotal, which would require a little making. There was a hard frost here during the night. From the top of the kotal a road jutted out to the left, going to Quetta.

On the 20th March he went to Mastung Fort, thirteen miles.

The track passed nearly due east over a plain sloping east by north. At three-quarters of a mile it ran close under the end of a ridge to the left, and at two miles crossed a nulla (Sharin Ab) with a stream of sweet water, ten yards broad, six inches deep. Three miles from Mastung the road lay between ruined houses and trees close on the left. The country on both sides was extensively cultivated, and the road was everywhere good.

On the 21st March he went to Alladin's Well, twenty-one miles north-east, in six hours fifty-four minutes.

Leaving Mastung, the road stretched north-east for four miles over light sandy soil, cut up by ravines. It then entered a gorge, one mile broad, between stony hills two hundred or three hundred feet high; the ground, also, became more stony. Here a track diverged to Teri on the left, and Kalat, *viâ* Mungacha, on the right. Following this gorge, which gradually narrowed to five hundred yards, the road turned more north, and at seven miles from Mastung passed up a nulla to the right, the head of which it reached in less than a quarter of a mile, when it descended by a steep zigzag to the Dasht-i-Badaulat. The length of this pass was about two miles, and it would require a good deal of labour to make it practicable for any but light vehicles. The road then crossed the Dasht-i-Badaulat in a north-easterly direction to Darwaza, where it joined the Bolan road from Dadur to Quetta.

He turned south for two miles to get water at Alladin Chah. From this point his road was along the regular Bolan route, down which he came to Jacobabad, where he arrived the day after my appearance there, viz., on the 27th of March.

On his arrival he found that, having heard a steamer was to leave next morning from Sakar for Multan, I had proceeded on my way. He hastened on, but was too late to catch the steamer. Not, however, to be done, he crossed the river and managed to get on to the engine of a material train which was just starting, and caught us up at our first night's halt, arriving late at night. I was of course delighted to see him, and he appeared in excellent spirits; but next morning, when he woke, he called my attention to the swollen state of his ankles. I thought it was owing to his having got into a bad state of blood from the indifferent food he had eaten, and trusted that a little good living would put him all right; but, alas! he only got worse. He went up in my Department to Mari, but he never picked up. Dropsy and Bright's disease set in, and after struggling against these for some long months he eventually died.

Poor Dick Lockwood! His loss to me and the numerous friends to whom his unvarying cheeriness had endeared him, can never be made up; and I know no one of his standing who could not have been better spared to the service. Through the kindness of General Roberts I had just got him appointed to the Quartermaster-General's Department. In this, there can be little doubt, he would have served in the Affghan campaign which broke out shortly after, and so he would have got all he wanted to make him one of the foremost men in the Indian Army. But what is the good of repining? He has gone from us, it is true; but he carries with him to the "great beyond" the love of all who knew him, and the respect of all who served with him. Many a better known man, when it comes to the last, would give all his honours for that.

FINIS.

APPENDICES.

APPENDIX A.—ROUTES.

ROUTE I.*—SONMIANI TO BANDAR KAMAL KHAN.

Shek Raj, 18½ *miles*.

THE road is very good. Soon after leaving there is a heavy sand ridge to be crossed, and at the sixth mile another heavier one. At 14 miles come to a halting place (Churrun). The road then is pretty good and goes along a stream, and lastly through rough jungle and crosses the Purali river (which is here 30 yards broad and 3 feet deep).

Water procurable from wells in bed of river, 6 to 8 feet deep.

No grass procurable, but forage abundant.

Ootul 11½ *miles*—30 *miles*.

The road is very good the whole way, and goes through a low jungle for 8½ miles; it then crosses the Kulhulli ravine, and goes along its right bank for half a mile, then through rough thick jungle of caper and tamarisk for 1½ miles, and the last one mile lies through rough narrow lanes between two hamlets.

Some "kurbi" † procurable here for horses, but no grass. Forage excellent and abundant.

Water from seven wells 60 feet deep.

---

* In the routes in this report the word "forage" is always meant to imply camel forage, "grass" being used for horse and mule forage.

† Stalks of Indian corn and other grain used as fodder.

Bochiri River, 12½ *miles*—42½ *miles.*

The road is very good the whole way, only requiring a little work to improve it for artillery. Several ravines are crossed, viz. at 1¾ and 2¼ miles the Kulhulli (240 yards broad); at 7¼ miles the Jurruk; at 8 miles the Loiwarrow; at 8¼ miles the Kipperwulli; and at 11½ miles the Ghar (60 yards broad).

Good water procurable from two wells. Forage abundant; no grass.

Bochupir, 8¼ *miles*—50¾ miles.

The road is extremely good the whole way; throughout easy to find, from its going through rough jungle, which at times is extremely thick. It crosses many ravines, viz. at half mile the Bochiri ravine; at 2¼ miles the Sukun river; and at 5¼ miles the shallow and dry bed of the Wuriur.

The water here is thick but good from a well. Forage abundant, but no grass.

Dund, 8½ *miles*—59¼ *miles.*

The road is pretty good, being merely a camel track through rough tamarisk jungle and over deserted fields.

Water from one well; forage procurable.

Bela, 8½ *miles*—67¾ *miles.*

The road is very good all the way. Here water is sweet and plentiful, and some supplies would be procurable as there are a large number of Hindoo shops. The country round is highly cultivated and studded with villages.

Sar-i-Asiah, 11¼ *miles*—79 *miles.*

The road goes through narrow lanes of brushwood jungle (which would have to be widened) for 3 miles; then it goes over a plain passing south of Sunjuri at 3 miles, Turruru at 4 miles, and a mill at 8½ miles. At 6¾ miles it goes into the bed of the Purali river and up it for 2 miles and then over a plain, the part in the river being rather rough from small stones.

Excellent water from a running stream; grass plentiful, but forage scarce.

Purali River, 9½ *miles*—88½ *miles*.

The road is very good, and goes nearly the whole way along the left bank of Purali river, at first over open country; the hills to the east a considerable way off; at 4½ miles pass a singular-looking hill called Runnur Cheri; at 7 miles it enters the bed of the Purali river and goes through rough thick jungle for a quarter mile, and continues up it to the end of the march. Camp on right bank of river among jungle.

Water is plentiful and excellent; and fuel, forage, and grass are abundant.

Sullow River, 16¾ *miles*—105¼ *miles*.

The road on the whole is excellent. One quarter mile after starting the Kohun river joins the Purali, and the road goes up the former (for 10½ miles), whose bed is a splendidly smooth road, with high precipitous banks. At only one place would there be any difficulty for heavy vehicles, viz. at the Trupp-i-Kohun, which is much narrower than any part of the Bolan Pass, being only 10 or 12 feet wide, and crossed by rough fragments of rock, leaving the Kohun ravine at its head; it goes over a plain for 3 miles to the Pinj ravine, up which it goes to within a quarter of a mile of the end of the march.

Water is good and abundant in the bed of the Sullow river; and grass, forage, and fuel are abundant.

Kanegi, 13 *miles*—118¼ *miles*.

The road is fair, but requires some improvement, as it mostly runs through narrow defiles; 300 yards after leaving it enters the Miran Kushta ravine, and goes up its bed for 3 miles, then leaving it, it crosses a small but very rough hill in 1½ miles, when it regains this ravine and goes up its bed for three quarters of a mile further. The road then zig-zags up a hill, and then for a short distance lies over level ground, and then zig-zaging down the hill enters the Aranweri ravine (at 7¼ miles). It then continues in the bed of this ravine winding about a great deal for one mile, when leaving it crosses over pretty good ground and enters it again by a bad piece of road. Going down its bed now for 3 furlongs, it leaves it at 10½ miles and goes over open ground for three-quarter mile into the bed of the Kanegi ravine, up which it goes for 1¾ miles to the halting place.

Here water is scarce from wells dug in the ravine; forage and fuel are plentiful, and some coarse grass is procurable.

Burran Luk, 7¾ miles—126 miles.

This is a fatiguing march, going for 3½ miles up and down the ravine bed, the ascent and descent of which are very steep; and then over very undulating ground.

Water here is extremely good from the Tullardir river. Forage is scarce; no fuel; some coarse grass.

Hussun Pir, 7½ miles—133½ miles.

The road has to cross the Burran Luk pass, which is nothing more than a couple of stony water-courses up and down a very ordinary hill; the ascent, though steep, is only about 200 feet, and the descent is very trifling. The ascent commences at once from the last halting place, and at the top the road goes through a rough and extremely narrow cleft in the rocks for about 150 yards, and is then gradual to the top (1¼ miles). Here two roads meet, one goes direct down the pass, while the other goes off to the left. The latter is longer and is considered best, but there is not much to choose between them. The foot of the pass is reached in about 3 miles. (Here a road from Torkubur joins.) The road then enters the Dunnadir river, and is rough and bad, going along its bed for a mile. It then ascends out of it by a difficult path, and is very good to the halting place. At six miles from the last halting place the road goes through a rough narrow pass, through which the Oornatch river flows, and this has to be crossed at this point.

Water very good from holes in the Oornatch river. Coarse grass and forage procurable.

Oornatch, 6 miles—139½ miles.

The road is good the whole way, though in some places the jungle would require to be cleared.

Water here is very good, and is procured from the bed of the river; forage and some "kurbi" are procurable.

Gaito, 8¼ miles—147¾ miles.

The road is bad on the whole. At first for two miles it is fair, then comes the Sanjaru-ka-kund defile which is so intersected by ridges of rock as to be utterly impracticable for vehicles, and it would require great labour to make it useful. The road then goes over smooth ground for about half a mile, when it descends the steep bank of the Parechi river and enters the Parechi-tankh defile. This is half a mile long and consists of the river bed which is contracted to about 40 yards in width, and in some places, for a short distance, it is only 12 or 15 feet broad. The bed is covered with very large stones, which however would not be any very great impediment to carriages. Then the river bed widens, and the road is very good; at six miles pass a small post called Surtulli Kund.

The water here is extremely salt, but a small quantity of good water is procurable near a spring on the southern edge of the Gaito Hill. Fuel, forage, and grass procurable in small quantities.

Gaz, 9 *miles*—156¾ *miles.*

The road winds very much in the bed of the Parechi river, and is shut in the whole way by hills varying in height. It is not very bad and would be practicable, though in many places the soft steep banks require sloping.

The water here is good and is procurable from the river. Forage, fuel, and grass procurable. Camping ground very confined.

Gurroah, 15 *miles*—171¾ *miles.*

The road is generally very good. It goes for five miles through ridges lying north and south, composed of parallel rows of enormous square stones, and then it crosses several parallel ridges of basalt lying east and west for another five miles. The road then comes to a spit called Purra (water and halting place), and here crosses at 10½ miles the Surmasung river from the left. Thence the road is good, the Gaz kund ravine at about 13½ miles, being a little rough.

The water in the river is saltish, but in the running stream which is conducted off for cultivation, it is very good. Fuel, forage, and grass are plentiful.

Hazar Gunji, 8½ *miles*—180¼ *miles.*

The road is pretty good in some places, the ground is broken and cut up by small ravines, and there is also a good deal of tamarisk jungle. At two miles pass the road to Khurma-i-istan, and at 4½ miles the foot of Fakir Muhammad. At 2¼ miles the road crosses the Surmasung river, and after going over undulating open ground, it then proceeds up its left bank for 5½ miles, and then crossing the river again arrives at the halting place.

Nal, 9¾ *miles*—190 *miles.*

The road is excellent all the way. It crosses the Surmasung river (here 500 yards broad) at 4¾ miles.

Water here is good from two streams. Some supplies and a little forage and grass are procurable.

Kharan, 80 *miles*—270 *miles.*

From Nal to Kharan there is a road which goes across the Besamur valley. I have not got any details of this route; it is probably about 80 miles, and is practicable for camels.

Jalwar, 25 *miles*—295 *miles.*

The road goes over a plain which is covered and obstructed by sand.

Water procurable from a spring in the ravine. Fuel and forage scarce.

Zarda, 15 *miles*—310 *miles.*

The road crosses a difficult pass called the Julwar Kund, which however is traversed by laden camels.

Water procurable from wells dug in ravine. Fuel and forage abundant.

Pirpochi, 12 *miles*—322 *miles.*

The road is stony, descending among hills.

There is only water here after rain. Fuel and forage, however, are abundant.

Band Khan Jahan, 18 *miles*—340 *miles.*

The road is quite good, but crosses some heavy sand-ridges.

Water, fuel, and forage abundant.

Total from Sonmiani to Bandar Kamal Khan, 636 miles.

ROUTE II.—ORMARAH TO PANJGUR.

This route was traversed in 1873 by Lieut.-Colonel Miles and also partly in 1877 by Captain Lockwood.

1. *Khor Basawal,* 20 *miles.*

The road goes all the way over a plain of sand-hills, tufted with bushes, along the Isthmus of Ormarah to a broad swampy ravine with deep muddy bottom; in crossing this it goes north-west over a sandy plain covered with camel forage to the Khor Basawal. Here there is a small hamlet with date trees, and a small muddy pool of water. The bed of the ravine is here very broad and open, but has no water in it. Camel forage is procurable, grass and fuel are scarce.

2. *Dost-i-Gwaram,* 14 *miles*—34 *miles.*

The road goes up the whole way along the sandy bed of the Bussawul river. Plenty of water is found in it in all seasons, but the bed is liable to spaits from the hills. The direction is west-north-west or west.

3. *Abgir,* 15 *miles*—49 *miles.*

The road goes up the Khor the whole way. At three miles pass Wakab, where there is a small stream running. There is considerable shrub vegetation in the bed. The surrounding hills are flat-topped clay ridges. Here is a supply of water from the bed of the river, and camel forage and fuel are procurable, also a little coarse grass.

4. *Khor Kasug Farosh,* 12 *miles*—61 *miles.*

The road is along the Khor, which becomes gradually narrower and shallower. It is extremely tortuous, and the bed is covered with round cobble stones, which make travelling very difficult for animals. There are frequent pools and springs of water in the bed. At three miles pass a place called Zorambent, and at twelve miles halt at a pool of rain-water in a tributary ravine of the above name, to the Basawal. Here there is fuel and forage.

5. *Belor*, 12 *miles*—73 *miles*.

The road is northerly, going along ravines and torrent beds full of large loose boulders, and is very difficult. At the end it is through hills, and a low water-shed is crossed which divides the drainage of the Kolwa valley from that of the Basawal. Water is plentiful from springs all the way.

6. *Nal*, 15¾ *miles*—88¾ *miles*.

The road first goes north by west for two miles among low hills when it issues into the Kolwa plains, which it crosses to nine miles. Then ascends a stony glacis to the Kuldan ravine, which it then follows for four miles, winding between low hills. Then leaving the ravine, it crosses a plain into Nal in one mile. Water from bed of ravines; fuel, forage, and grass procurable.

7. *Kil Khor*, 12¾ *miles*—101½ *miles*.

The road goes north over a long stony slope for one mile, and then crossing a small ravine enters the Kaldan ravine (150 yards wide), up which it winds for four miles, the ravine getting narrower till it is not more than six yards across, and is shut in on both sides by rocky hills. (Here running water.) Then leaving the Kaldan the road turns up a smaller ravine to the right, in some places only three feet broad with a rocky bottom which it follows for one mile, ascending gradually to the top of the Hotal Pass. The road then descends very steeply and is narrow for a quarter of a mile, when it becomes less steep going down a stony water-course for 2¾ miles further. Here it emerges into an open valley, two miles across which it crosses in north-east direction, and then passing some pools of water in a ravine reaches the halting place. Here water is plentiful in the bed of the ravine. Grass, fuel, and forage abundant around.

8. *Nafta Sham*, 18¾ *miles*—120¼ *miles*.

The road goes for three miles north among low hills, when it crosses a low pass with a small plain. Traversing this in three miles on, it comes to an opening in a low range, and going through this it enters the Dashta plain. Crossing this likewise in a north-west direction it comes to yet another ridge which divides it from the Kurpulla plain, which is also crossed. At the mile the road comes to a pool of water, which never dries up, called Meshkai-i-Kumb. The road then zig-zags through a ridge running east and west for one mile, when it enters the Gumbuk ravine (running water), which it follows for two miles. Then leaving this it crosses a stony valley to another ravine down which it winds for three quarters of a mile when it forsakes it for a third half a mile down which is the halting place. The road is quite good throughout and practicable for vehicles.

Water is procurable in the ravine in pools after rain, and by digging at other times; and fuel, forage, and grass are plentiful.

Wash Jaorkhan, 19¼ *miles*—139½ *miles.*

For a mile the road leads out west over stony ground, when it crosses a low stony pass into a stony plain, at the other side of which is the Zahin ravine (here 60 yards broad, rocky bottom, running water). Descending into this at second mile it follows it to the end of the Zahin hill. When it leaves the ravine and turning more to the left goes over broken stony ground between low rocky hills for 3½ miles. The road now enters the Mantur ravine, and winds along its bed for 4¼ miles between steep cliffs 200 feet high, which form a formidable defile. (Running water in this ravine, which does not dry up.) Clearing this defile the road goes nearly west for two miles (here road to Shahbaz), and at one mile on crosses a low watershed dividing the drainage of the Kil Khor from that of the Dasht plain. It now takes to the Kashi ravine down which it descends for 1½ miles, when leaving it goes over a plain and one mile on enters the Wash Jaorkhan ravine which it descends to the halting place. The road the whole way is between rocky hills, but it is good and easy.

Water excellent from a fort. Coarse grass, fuel, and forage procurable.

Thence to Dashtak, 40 *miles.*—179½ *miles.*

From Ormarah, there is no other route leading to the north till we reach Pusni. From Kulmat there certainly is a path which goes by the Jafari ravine and then into that of Basawal, but from that point it is the same as the foregoing, and besides that the anchorage off Kulmat is bad, the five-fathoms line being six miles off, it is not shorter or better than that from Ormarah. I now, therefore, turn to—

ROUTE III.—PUSNI TO PANJGUR.

1. *Dokani*, 19 *miles*.

The road after crossing the sand-hillock north of Pusni goes up the bed of the Shadi Khor, crossing and re-crossing several times for five miles, the hills for the last two miles closing in. It then gets on to high ground on the banks going from side to side. At nine miles pass small bit of cultivation called Gazdar (from here a road to Kalmat goes off). It then crosses to right bank, and in one mile passes Laz Bent,* a bit of cultivation between a hill called Koh-i-Sukhta and the ridge on the right. Leaving this it crosses to the left bank and again to the right at 13¼ miles, when it leaves the river which comes from the north-east. It then enters the Andorak hills (a range of low sharp parallel ridges with numerous low passes), and winding tortuously through them for three miles it emerges on an open plain extending for the next three miles up to the river again. (This gives a long sweep from Dokani to the east to get round the Andarok range.)

Here there is abundance of water, fuel, and forage, and a little grass is procurable. The whole of this march is thickly wooded, and a halt could be made anywhere after five miles from Pusni, below which the water is brackish.

2. *Gharki*, 16 *miles*—35 *miles*.

The road goes up the course of the Shadi River (passing Ghoramani Bent at three miles) for five miles to the junction of the Gharki Khor. (Here road goes on north-north-west to Pidark and Kej). Thence it continues up that ravine which is enclosed between high banks and low hills for 10 miles. A halt can be made almost anywhere, as fuel, forage, and water are abundant.

3. *Gwarko*, 17 *miles*—52 *miles*.

The road goes up the Gharki Khor and is quite easy all the way.

Water from "karez." Grass procurable in the neighbourhood.

---

* Cultivation.

4. *Talach Khor*, 17 *miles*—69 *miles*.

The road goes south-east over a stony glacis over the bank of the Dumma ravine for $2\frac{1}{2}$ miles. It then enters hills and winds through them for two miles when it again emerges into a stony plain over which it goes for two miles. It then again enters the skirt of the hills to the south of the Gwarko plain, and continues amongst them for the rest of the march nearly due east. The road lies between two ridges and is good, but cut up by ravines from that on the north which would require to be improved to make them practicable.

Water very precarious, but could be stored. No grass, and little forage procurable.

5. *Ispirod*, $17\frac{1}{4}$ *miles*—$86\frac{1}{4}$ *miles*.

The road goes north-east, and ascends gradually over broken stony ground shut in by hills for two miles. It then turns to the right and enters a ravine called Kokeni, which it ascends for two miles to the head of the Gwarko watershed. It next crosses a bleak stony plain for five miles when it comes to some low hills, and winding among them for $1\frac{1}{4}$ miles again emerges into a similar plain which it crosses for seven miles to the Ispirod ravine.

Grass and forage plentiful; water is precarious, but it could be stored in the bed of the ravine.

6. *Balgatar*, $17\frac{1}{2}$ *miles*—$103\frac{3}{4}$ *miles*.

The road crosses a stony, ravine-cut, plain for $5\frac{1}{2}$ miles to the Kil Khor (where are pools, fuel, forage, &c., here cross Kolwah road), crossing which it continues over the same description of ground for five miles when it enters the Kuttag ravine (here road from Sami and west joins in). It then goes up the ravine with low ridges on either side, the bed formed of fine gravel, with easy gradient, for $4\frac{1}{2}$ miles, when it suddenly turns up a small ravine for a few yards and then crosses the ridge by a very low pass. (For two miles on the south and one mile on north there is water running, but no fuel, forage, or grass.) It then descends quite easily for four miles. A halt can be made only where there is water, and this only the guides can tell with certainty. The supply is precarious, being in pools, but wells could be dug, and water would be procured 10 feet from surface. Here there is fuel, forage in small quantities, but no grass.

This is a suitable place for the collection of supplies which might be brought in small quantities from Kolwah on the east and from Sami on the west.

7. *Tush,* 13 *miles*—116¾ *miles.*

The road is quite good over a level plain, the last part with detached hills on both sides. This tract is, however, subject to inundation, and then there is a path which makes a long detour to the left reaching Tush in about 24 miles. A halt could be made half way.

Water abundant, no fuel, forage near, nor grass.

8. *Gwat-Kachum,* 10 *miles*—126¾ *miles.*

The road is quite easy the whole way winding along ravines and crossing low ridges. There is water at 2½ miles, and in the Koruchi and Hingul ravines. The space here is confined and stony, but water is always abundant. Fuel and forage have to be procured at a distance round. No grass.

9. *Gwani Khan,* 11½ *miles*—138¼ *miles.*

The road goes up a ravine for four miles, quite easy, then ascends slightly to get over the Choki Goran pass. Then it descends to the Lashkaran Khor (here good running water, fuel, and forage), which it goes up for 2½ miles. Leaving this it goes over a low ridge then up a narrow ravine and emerges after 3½ miles on to a high stony plain, which it crosses for one mile and then descends to the Gwani Khor.

Here there is always abundance of water. Some forage and "peesh" fuel is procurable, and a little grass.

10. *Wash Jaorkhan,* 15 *miles*—153¼ *miles.*

The road first goes up a ravine and then crosses an open gravelly plain in 3½ miles. It then goes up a ravine from the north winding about a good deal, and the ravine becoming narrower for two miles when it gets on to a spur and ascends the Goran pass at six miles. The ascent is easy, but the road might be improved, being narrow. The road then descends a ravine with hills on either side to the Wash Jaorkhan ravine seven miles.

Water in pools precarious; fuel, forage, no grass.

11. *Dashtak, 40 miles—193¼ miles.*

There is a road which goes down the above ravine. This has abundance of fuel, forage, and water in its bed. This route would avoid the detour into Panjgur. A depôt might be formed for supplies at Dashtak where there is abundance of fuel, forage, and water. Supplies in small quantities might be drawn in from Persian territory, Washak, and Panjgur.

ROUTE IV.—GWADUR TO PANJGUR.

Unfortunately there are no roads from Gwadur direct to the north, the steep Durrum range interposing itself between. The only routes therefore turn it either to the west or east.

A.—TALAR ROAD.

1. *Barambab.*

The road goes along the sea-shore to the Koh-i-Mehdi, then through low hills, and lastly over level plain. It is quite good throughout. The water supply here is precarious and brackish. Forage procurable. No fuel or grass.

2. *Kappar, 32½ miles.*

The road goes through low hills and is quite easy. Here water is scarce, but perennial and good. Fuel and forage procurable. No grass.

3. *Talar Pass, 21 miles—53½ miles.*

The road first goes over broken ridges of sandstone, and then over a perfectly level plain to the Pass.

Here there is an ample supply of water, and fuel and forage are procurable, but no grass.

4. *Amulani, 26 miles—79½ miles.*

The road goes up the bed of a ravine which forms the Talar ravine. This has very lofty and steep sides, and presents a remarkably bold and rugged appearance. It is narrow, and being subject to floods, is at times dangerous. The road then goes up the ravine, and at five miles crosses east and north some low arid hills of sandstone alternating with clay to the *Biri River* at 10 miles where there is water. It now crosses a ridge of sandstone hills and then goes over a plain of alluvial soil intersected by the rivers Shahid, Niluck, and Dudeh to Amulani. Here there are a few patches of cultivation, and water is found in pools, but as it is dependent on rain it is precarious. No fuel or forage are procurable here. When the water fails at Amulani the nearest water is the Dasht River, more than three miles to the west.

5. *Miri*, 22½ *miles*—102 *miles.*

The road first goes over a level plain for 12½ miles with no water on it and then enters a series of low hills which it crosses in a northerly direction, in 10 miles more.

Here all supplies are procurable in small quantities. Water, fuel, forage are abundant, and some grass.

6. *Girok Pass*, 15 *miles*—117 *miles.*

The road first goes over the Kej plain for five miles and is quite good. It then enters the Girok Pass. This is formed of the bed of a torrent, which at its mouth is covered with large boulders, but the track improves as one ascends. The gradient is very easy; the depth is not very long, but it is at present impracticable, though a few hours' labour bestowed on improving the road in the neighbourhood of the watershed would suffice to make the track passable. The water-supply is very scarce, and there is no fuel, forage, or grass.

7. *Boleda*, 24 *miles*—141 *miles.*

The road lies the whole way over a plain dotted here and there with low hills, and having its surface sparsely studded with a scant vegetation of camel-thorn and other shrubs. At the end it crosses the Ghish Khor.

Here water is very abundant, and some few supplies might be procured, and fuel and forage are procurable.

8. *Mudi Khor*, 9½ *miles*—150½ *miles.*

The road ascends the Mudi Khor ravine the whole way; the path is very narrow and slippery, and difficult for camels.

The water-supply here is plentiful, and fuel and grass are procurable, but camel forage is scarce.

9. *Kullug-Diz,* 25½ *miles*—176 *miles.*

The road goes still up the Mudi Khor till a watershed is crossed, and then it enters the bed of another torrent called the Shitab. (There is abundance of water, fuel, forage, and grass in its bed.) Going up this for some miles it then leaves it, and ascends steeply to a plateau, whence it is level into Diz.

10. *Well,* 8 *miles*—184 *miles.*

The road goes over a plain. Here there is a well with bad and little water; fuel and forage are procurable.

11. *Gwargo Khor,* 16 *miles*—200 *miles.*

From this the road turns north, and crossing some low hills to the west of Pimpiska reaches the Gwargo ravine. Here water is precarious, but wells dug would produce a supply. Fuel and forage are procurable, but no grass.

12. *Dashtak,* 16 *miles* —216 *miles.*

The road goes along the course of the Gwargo to its junction with the Rakshan at eight miles, and then down it to Mulli Gitan.

From this *vide* No. VII.

B.—The Faleri Route.

This is 40 miles to Seroki. It has nothing to recommend it, the only water between being at Ankora 13 miles, and Faleri 26 miles, and the supply is very precarious, being altogether dependent on rain. From Seroki the route follows the same line as No. IV. A. The road goes over a plain of whitish clay between distant ranges of barren hills. There is very little fuel or forage on this line.

By this route Gwadur to Dashtak is 217½ miles.

C.—The Tankh Route.

1. *Tankh,* 25 *miles.*

The road for 12 miles is north across a level sandy plain. At eight miles pass cultivation on right called Nigor; at 12 miles enter a low range of hills, which go through for two miles, the road being stony and bad, but not very steep.

Beyond this the whole of the road is level and easy over a barren country. Water scarce from well; no grass; forage and fuel abundant.

2. *Belar*, 21 *miles*—46 *miles*.

The road leads east between two ranges and over a barren country, but is quite easy all the way.

Water-supply fair; no supplies; fuel and forage procurable.

3. *Talar Pass*, 6 *miles*—52 *miles*.

The road leads over a hard barren country to the south entrance of the pass.

Thence *vide* No. IV. A.

By this route Gwadur to Dashtak is 216½ miles.

D.—The Durdan Route.

This is a northern route to the Dasht river; it is 37 miles, and has no more advantage than the others. There is a precarious supply of water on the road in pools, but no fuel or forage. It, however, reaches the Dasht river some 12 miles higher up than the route by Faleri.

From Dardan *vide* No. IV. A.

By this route Gwadur is 205 miles from Dashtak.

Route V.—The Dasht River to Panjgur.

We now come to the last available route to the west.

1. *Surian Jump*, 16 *miles*.

The Dasht river is navigable for boats for perhaps 10 miles, after which it is necessary to land on the left bank of the river, and march over the level plain to Surian Jump, where the first fresh water is procurable.

Here fuel and forage are abundant.

2. *Dumb*, 13 *miles*—29 *miles*.

The road goes north-east over a dusty plain covered with camel-scrub the whole way. At one mile pass Kuldan, at

$3\frac{1}{2}$ miles cross the Persian Telegraph line, $4\frac{1}{2}$ Seroki, $9\frac{1}{2}$ Kullatu. The latter part of the way the road is a good deal cut up by cultivation bunds.

Water from the river to the west. Fuel and forage abundant.

3. *Miting,* 15 *miles*—44 *miles.*

On leaving the road crosses to the right bank of the river, and then turns north-east for two miles, when it runs between low isolated mud-hills for three miles. It then recrosses to the left bank, and continues over the plain between the river and low hills on the right for $4\frac{1}{2}$ miles to the Saijdi ravine. Crossing this Dardan is passed $1\frac{1}{4}$ miles on (whence road to Gwadur). The road then takes to a narrow ravine, up which it goes for one mile, when it goes for one mile further over cultivation, and is much intersected by bunds, whence three miles on over hard plain to halting place.

Water from the river, and fuel and forage are abundant.

4. *Hasadin,* 19 *miles*—63 *miles.*

The road goes for the first quarter mile up the bed of the Dasht river. It then gets on to the left bank, and turns a little east to get clear of jungle near the bank, when it goes for seven miles over an open dusty plain covered with scrub jungle to Sadoi-Kullat. It then comes near the river and goes for four miles further along its bank, passing two villages, Darzam and Zaram, on the way. Now crossing to the right bank it keeps to it for two miles, when it again returns to the left, which it keeps for the last four miles.

Water, fuel, and forage abundant.

5. *Kuhak,* 20 *miles*—83 *miles.*

The road first goes up the bed of the river for three-quarters of a mile, when it ascends to the left bank, and continues along the rough jungle for three miles (pass south Kangari two miles on left). One mile further it crosses to the right bank, which it goes along for $4\frac{3}{4}$ miles to $7\frac{3}{4}$ miles (eight pass Matilab) when it again comes to the left bank. At $11\frac{1}{2}$ miles it recrosses to right which it keeps to the end. The whole road is over hard level plain.

Here water is plentiful in the river. Fuel, forage, and coarse grass abundant.

6, *Kuntadar,* 11½ *miles*—94½ *miles.*

Leaving Kuhak the road crosses to the left bank and goes north-east through thick tamarisk jungle for five miles. It then crosses the Kussar ravine from the right, and at six miles the Niling ravine. At ten miles cross to the right bank. The road is all level over hard clay soil much cut up in places by irrigation cuts and dams, and is all through heavy tamarisk jungle.

Water from a well good and abundant. No grass, but fuel and forage abundant.

7. *Kullatak,* 20 *miles*—114½ *miles.*

For the first six miles the direction is north-east to a range of hills which are crossed by an easy path, after which the direction is more east over barren stony ground. A few miles west of Kullatak the Kej river is crossed, and a fertile tract entered which is intersected by water-courses. Hence the road skirts date-groves to Kullatak.

Water-supply is plentiful and good, some supplies are procurable, and fuel and forage abundant.

8. *Girok Pass,* 14½ *miles*—129 *miles.*

The road goes over a stony plain to the south foot of the Girok Pass. This is a defile formed by the bed of a torrent. The surface at its mouth is very broken, being composed of large boulders, but the track improves afterwards. The gradient is very easy. The defile is not very long, but it is not practicable in its present state, though a few hours' labour would soon make it so.

The water-supply is scarce and somewhat precarious, and fuel and forage are scarcely procurable.

Thence *vide* Route No. IV. A.

By this route Dashtak is 230 miles.

I have named Panjgur in detailing the above routes, as the name is well known, but it will be seen that I bring all my routes up to the Dashtak ravine, which is at the extreme end of the Panjgur valley, if not quite out of it. There would be no advantage in going to any of the villages of Panjgur sufficient to compensate for the extra distance which must be traversed. At the junction of the Dasktak and Rakshan there is a fine open plain, which would form a good site for a depôt, and water, fuel, forage, and grass are abundant. The villages of Panjgur have not equal advantage in the last respect, and in the first it is much inferior, because all are surrounded by dense forests of date palm, which would make it very difficult to find a proper place for a depôt. Then there is no doubt that what supplies the valley afforded could quite easily be transported to Dashtak, while any that might reach from Boleda or the Persian districts could come there with greater facility.

From Panjgur there are two routes which lead to the north.

Route VI.

The first goes as follows from the village of Khodabadan in Panjgur.

1. *Hushtdia.*

The road goes north from the village of Khodabadan, over the plain of Panjgur, and then comes to the range called Bund-i-Panjgur, which bounds that valley on the north. It then crosses the range by a pass difficult for camels, and on the other side of the watershed is the halting place.

Here there is water, but very little forage or fuel, and no grass.

2. *Palantak.*

The road winds down a ravine amid low hills, and then comes to a defile in the Sabz Koh range. Here water, fuel, and forage are abundant.

3. *Lundu Sham.*

The road goes through a difficult defile, through which the Palantak water goes to the Bibi Lori stream, and it then comes to a low pass between these streams.

Here there is water sometimes after rain, but the supply is very precarious; fuel and forage are abundant.

4. *Bibi Lori.*

The road goes down the bed of this river the whole way.

Water precarious in pools, but might be procured if wells

were dug. Beyond either bank of the river is all sand. Here fuel, forage are plentiful, and some grass is procurable.

5. *Budu.*

The road goes down the sandy bed of the Bibi Lori to its junction with the Mashkel just below this place, which is where Pottinger crossed the Mashkel. Water, fuel, and forage abundant. Thence *vide* Route No. VII.

This route is shorter than the following, but has no other recommendation; there is a difficult pass on it, and the water-supply is precarious along the whole line.

Route VII.

The next is the route I followed, viz. from Dashtak.

1. *Kimli,* 13 *miles.*

The road goes over a level plain for four miles to the Dwanguz ravine. Here it goes under a fantastic hill, Koh-i-Sinj, and crosses the Rakshan, recrossing it again under the end of the Sinj ridge at 6½ miles (here road to Kuhak goes off). From this the road, when the river is low, continues to go down its bed, but at 2½ miles on it is confined between two low ridges forming a deep, which is impassable, so that we had to turn off to the right and cross a low ridge at nine miles. This effected, the road goes over an open plain for 2½ miles back to the Rakshan. It then goes down it for 1½ miles crossing and recrossing the stream when it ascends highish ground and then descends to the bed of the Mashkel, half a mile above its junction with the Rakshan. Here water, fuel, forage, and grass are abundant.

2. *Tump,* 15 *miles*—28 *miles.*

The road goes down the bed of the Mashkel to its junction with the Rakshan, and continues on in the same direction for one mile, to get round a low ridge between which and the Koh-i-Sabz is the entrance to the defile Tankh-i-Grawag. It then winds through this for the next ten miles crossing and recrossing the streams many times. When the river is up, this defile is impracticable owing to the deepness and swiftness of the river crossings. A road could be made so as to be above the flood mark, but it would be an expensive work. On emerging from the defile the road goes over a stony plain down the left bank of the river for four miles. Here water, fuel, and forage are abundant, and some grass is procurable.

(The other road by which the Tankh-i-Grawag can be turned is as follows:—The road goes west up the bed of the Mashkel river for four miles, and then between it and low hills on the north for 4½ miles. It then enters the Gazinda ravine and winds north-west in its bed for 5½ miles. Leaving this it enters another ravine amongst low hills, and keeping to it for two miles it issues on to a high plateau sloping down from the Siahan range. It then enters the Tump ravine and goes down its bed for four miles, when emerging from it, it goes over a long stony slope to the bank of the Mashkel at the above point. The distance by this line is not less than thirty miles, or forty-three miles from Dashtak.)

3. *Buzurg Gaz,* 21½ *miles*—49½ *miles.*

The road crosses the river and goes over a level plain for nine miles. It then goes between low clay ridges and down the bed of the Ooshturi Khor for three miles. It then turns north still down bed of a large ravine for a mile, and having got round a low clay ridge which runs parallel with the Mashkel it turns east and goes over a plain about 1½ to 2 miles from right bank of the river to the 17th mile. Now it goes between low clay ridges, again for two miles, and then down to the river at 20th mile. A halt may be made anywhere about here. I halted at the 21½ mile a little short of the Buzurg Gaz ravine.

Here water, fuel, forage, and grass are very abundant.

4. *Zorati,* 20 *miles*—69½ *miles.*

The road goes through thick tamarisk jungle for nearly a mile to Buzurg Gaz ravine, and crossing this it ascends a low clay hill, and then descends again to the river by the Zani ravine at the 4th mile. It then goes down the bed of the river, which now becomes stony, crossing and recrossing to the 9th mile, when the entrance of the Tankh-i-Zorati defile is reached. The road is of the same nature as that through the

Grawag defile, and the same remarks apply to it. The road is, if anything, easier. It is about eight miles through. At the exit the road turns sharp to the left up a small ravine (as the river forms here a long deep pool which is unfordable), and going over a low ridge descends to the bed of the Kuman Rud. Crossing this it goes over stony ground to the halting place at the 20th mile.

Here water, fuel, and forage are very abundant. The Tankh-i-Zorati can be turned by a pass which goes over the Siahan range from north of the Ooshturi Khor, but the pass is difficult for camels.

5. *Miańrud*, 22½ *miles*—92 *miles*.

The road crosses the river in the first mile, and then goes across a level gravelly plain between low ridges of clay leaving the river off to the north; at 7th mile come to the Shaneh cliff. (Here a road to Kharan.) Then go up the river bed for 2½ miles. Cross and go over high gravel plain on right bank to Chekulu, six miles on, whence the road goes down the stony bed of the river for six miles.

Here water is abundant; fuel and forage are scarce; no grass.

6. *Nullaf*, 14½ *miles*—106½ *miles*.

The road crosses to the right bank, and then goes over desert covered with black gravel to the junction of the Bibi Lori six miles. It then descends and goes up the sandy bed for two miles, when leaving it goes over heavy sand for six miles, passing Budu at the 9th mile. It then descends and crosses the river bed to Nullaf.

Here water is not certain in pool, but wells would produce any amount.

Fuel, forage, and grass are abundant here. The river, which has had a tendency to go east of north, turns north-west from Budu.

7. *Rekh Farang*, 17 *miles*—123½ *miles*.

The road is very heavy the whole way, as it either goes over the sandy bed of the river or climbs on to the bank, and goes over very heavy sand-hillocks to avoid quicksands with which the bed abounds.

Here water is precarious, but any amount could be produced by digging wells. Fuel and forage are abundant.

8. *Surguri*, 15 *miles*—138½ *miles*.

The road is better over harder sand than the former march. At three miles are some curious pillars, and a road to Jalk goes off. At 11 miles the Mashkel, which has now very little water in it, divides into two branches, the road going between them.

The same remarks as to water as in former stage. Fuel, forage, and grass abundant. The last part of this march is over good arable soil.

9. *Godar*, 11 *miles*—149½ *miles*.

The road goes over a good deal of arable land and up the Mairum Khor, and is quite easy all the way. The jungle on the road is everywhere very thick. Here there is a fine deep pool of water, which however might dry up.

Fuel, forage, and grass are very abundant. This is an important site, from it roads go to Chageh, Jalk, Naru, Talab, and Kharan. It would be a suitable place for a depôt, being the point where the river has to be left, and possessing soil which might be cultivated; stores might be collected and sheep maintained here.

10. *Meski*, 19 *miles*—168½ *miles*.

For the first mile the soil is good; then it begins to be encrusted with salt efflorescence, and this gets thicker and thicker till it becomes a veritable "kavir." This continues for the next 14 miles, the centre being the worst, but all being salt soil beyond hope.

(Three or four miles to the right is the salt bed called Wad-i-Sultan, where salt a foot thick is dug out and carried off by caravans.)

At about the 11th mile a sand-ridge is seen on the right, and this runs west-north-west till at the 14th mile it crosses the road. It is covered with "ta-gaz," and the part of it which crosses the road is called Gaz-i-Dowran. There is fuel and forage in small quantity here, but no water, but it is probable tanks might be formed. Thence the road goes on over sand covered with black gravel for 4½ miles, when it descends some 30 feet into a depression called God-i-Morjin. Here fuel and forage are abundant, but no water. This depression is connected with the Hamun of the Mashkel, and as it receives all the surplus water of the Nohli range, and a very considerable amount of drainage from the east Naru hills, there would certainly water be found here if wells were dug.

11. *Paniham,* 11 *miles*—179½ *miles.*

The road goes level over the depression for the first three miles, crossing half-way a considerable ravine called the Morjin, it then ascends out of it, and at 4½ miles (road over gravel) comes to a small pond of rain-water called Jai, where, though the supply is clearly precarious, the site is very suitable for the construction of tanks, the water being quite sweet. Beyond this still over sand covered with gravel. At about the 6th mile the road descends into the Kullundi Khor, which it crosses obliquely, and again gets on to the same sort of ground. Four miles further it descends again into the ravine, and going up it for three-quarters of a mile reaches Paniham. Here are half a dozen date-trees, and water is very abundant and good from wells in the bed. Fuel is scarce, and forage not very plentiful. Water also can be got at Kullundi, a spot with some date-trees also, three miles lower down; indeed it is probable water could be got anywhere in this ravine.

12. *Shandak Khor,* 40 *miles*—219½ *miles.*

From this to Shandak there is no water, and therefore water must be carried and a halt made wherever convenient. This is possible, as there is camel forage to a certain extent nearly anywhere, but almost no fuel. The road goes for four miles up the Paniham ravine, passing at three miles a place called Paniham Nowar, where there is plenty of fuel and forage, and where water could be got by digging a few feet. Thence it goes over a sandy waste covered with stones of all colours and sprinkled with camel scrub. The plain is intersected at intervals by shallow ravines which drain south-west; in these digging would probably not produce water, but the beds form very suitable sites for underground tanks. The last half of the march the sand is a little heavier, but is nowhere difficult, and the road goes through a series of curious sand crescents. In the Shandak ravine water can be procured in any quantity by digging wells. It is not very good, though quite drinkable.

Fuel and forage are plentiful here. In the hills near this are some nomads who could supply a few sheep, and a good road goes from this to the Helmund, from which it is probable some grain could be brought and stored here. For this reason a small depôt for the storage of whatever grain could be got might be formed here.

13. *Manzil*, 16 *miles*—235½ *miles*.

The road now turns north-west and goes over a succession of heavy sand-hills for seven miles to the Diwanak Khor. Here good water could be procured by digging wells in the bed, and fuel and forage is plentiful round about. From this a number of low easy hills are crossed, and at the 11th mile the Kolachi Nowar is reached. Here there is water after rain, and the site, being a depression, is very suitable for the construction of tanks. Thence going over a plain at the 13th mile, a low pass called the God-i-Goran is reached at 1½ miles on the bed of a ravine. Here, close to a shrine, is water in the bed. When I was there this was very stinking from long standing. Fresh wells would produce good water; if not, abundance of beautiful water can be got over a sand-ridge one mile to the north-west by scraping holes a few inches deep in the sand, and here fuel and forage are very plentiful.

14. *Amir Chah*, 43 *miles*—278½ *miles*.

From Manzil the road goes between low ridges and over heavy sand for nine miles, whence there are two roads. The northern goes outside the spurs of the Koh-i-Sultan range altogether, till near Amir Chah. There is not a drop of water on the road, which is over heavy sand-ridges all the way, and is 43 miles in length, but there is abundance of fuel and forage anywhere, so that if water is carried for the men, a halt can be made where convenient.

The other road is about the same distance, but it goes through the hills, and has water at 22 miles, and at other places a little off the road. This road may be described as follows: At three miles from the point where the road splits enter a ravine, in the bed of which water might be produced from wells, or at least tanks might be formed. Here there is fuel and forage. It then goes up this ravine for four miles; road very firm and good, and then leaving it crossing several spurs from the Koh-i-Sultan and several ravines, till at five miles it ascends a steep pass over the main range, and descends in half mile at a place called Chakul, where there is a small spring of excellent water. From the place where the road leaves the ravine, fuel and forage become scarce, till they almost cease at Chakul.

Thence the road goes down the Chakul ravine for 2½ miles, and going over an intervening terrace gets into a ravine coming from Koh-i-Kansuri, and gets up it to its head for 1½ miles, when it again ascends a steep pass, also over the main range. At two places, Washaf, about four miles down the ravine, and Gamichah in a dell a little to the left, there is water, but no fuel or forage. Having crossed this pass, a small bit of level is reached, where people coming for assafœtida usually encamp. This place is suitable for the formation of tanks, and there is plenty of fuel and forage on the sand-hills near. From this the road goes over heavy sand-ridges for eight miles, then it is easier, and in 11 miles it enters the hills, and crossing a low pass descends over sand to Amir Chah in seven miles or 18 miles from the Nowar. At Amir there is a well about 30 feet deep, at which my guide declared he had seen 2,000 animals watered. At all events the supply seems plentiful, and if the well was in regular use, the water would not be bad. As this is the last place where water is procurable, it would be advisable to have here very complete arrangements for the improvement of the supply. Here therefore several wells should be dug, and lower down the ravine tanks should be constructed to catch water from the ravine when in flood. The forage here is very good, and fuel is also abundant.

15. *Zirreh,* 85 *miles*—363½ *miles.*

From Amir Chah there are two ways (I cannot say roads) of getting to Zirreh. I went by one and came back by the other. The first is easily described. After crossing a heavy sand-ridge on leaving, it goes for 70 miles as straight as a die over a beautiful hard level surface composed of sand and black gravel. At the end to the right is the depression called God-i-Zirreh. Thence it turns more north and goes for 14 miles over a country with good arable land much encroached on by sand, and in the thickets of withered bushes bearing traces of having been thickly wooded. For the last mile it goes up the bed of the Shela, or drainage between Seistan and Zirreh. Here, at Godar-i-Shah, there is brackish water in the bed a couple of feet deep. Formerly when the Helmund came down water could have been procured in the Zirreh depression under 70 miles from Amir; but if this river is not permitted, as has been the case for the last 10 years, to flow to Zirreh, even the water now found may dry up altogether, as it has done lower down, and then by this line there would be no water for a distance of nearly 140 miles. At present at the Godur-i-Shah there is a plentiful supply of brackish yet quite drinkable water, and fuel and forage are abundant, yet even this last must in time cease if the water which aids its renovation is cut off altogether. Zirreh under adequate conditions of water-supply would form a suitable site for a depôt. Supplies could be concentrated here from the Helmund, and the soil around is sufficiently good to give reason for hope that some cultivation would be successful.

The other road from Zirreh to Amir Chah is the one by which I returned, and it is as follows:—

Amalaf, 50 *miles*.

The road for the first five miles goes over the plain south of the Shela, which is composed of good arable land, much mixed with patches of sand. It then goes for five miles over the heavy sand-ridge called Siah Rekh, which runs along the left of the route by which I came. It then goes down a ravine between high sand-hills for two miles, when it gets out into a large plain. (From this a road goes off to Kucha, watering place.) Thence the track lies over this plain, which is covered with stones which make it very difficult going for camels, and very trying for their feet. Over this it goes for thirty-two miles. There is no water anywhere, so that this must be carried. Wells dug in the Siah Rekh Nowar would probably produce water; if not, it is a very suitable spot for tanks, as it receives all the drainage of the hills for a long way, and there is plenty of fuel and forage near. There is scarcely any forage after the sand-ridge is left, and no fuel or grass. The road then enters the hills and goes up the Amalaf ravine between low hills for six miles. At Amalaf good water is procured from wells dug in the bed, and is only two or three feet below the surface. The supply could be increased to any extent. Forage is not plentiful here, but fuel is procurable.

2. *Amir Chah*, 57 *miles*.

Leaving Amalaf the road ascends among low hills, and crosses a watershed at 4½ miles. It then descends another ravine draining eventually north for two miles, when it leaves the ravine and crosses a bare plain for 4½ miles. It then goes over two or three small ridges, and passing Koh-i-Trashta Kurik, an isolated hill at 4½ miles, it gets on to sand which becomes heavier and heavier, till 10 miles on, close to the Koh-i-Dalil, it forms a very heavy ridge. There is not a drop of water anywhere on this route, and there is no fuel or forage till this sand is reached, therefore a halt should be made at the first convenient spot where there is forage. Tanks could be constructed in the bed of the ravines at about the 6th, 13th, and 17th miles, but it should be remembered there is no fuel or forage at these points. After passing the Koh-i-Dalil the ground improves, the sand being covered with black gravel. The road crosses two low ridges, and at the 8th mile comes to a sand-ridge, surmounting this in about one mile there is the same gravel plain intersected by low ridges for six miles on, and then keeping on the right of a low range nearly covered with sand, the track goes over very heavy sand-ridges for 3½ miles to Amir Chah.

Route VIII.

From this I have already described the roads back to Naru, and I will therefore turn to other roads which also lead to Zirreh. The first of these is the left road mentioned in my remarks above. Starting from the halting place I have named, Shamba Gum, one road is as follows :—

1. *Jolushan.*

The road keeps the left bank of the river, and gradually leaving it enters the bed of a ravine up which it goes with steep cliffs on either side to a steep and difficult pass over a low dip in the Siahan range. The pass is described as barely practicable for camels. The halting place is in the ravine on the north side. There is abundance of water here, but no fuel or forage.

2. *Norchah*, 29 *miles.*

The road is over a level plain covered with black gravel after emerging from the hill. Here there is sometimes water in pools, but the supply is very precarious. Fuel and forage are procurable.

3. *Askan, 20 miles.*

The road is over a plain covered with black gravel with patches of sand, last part over better soil. Here there are some date-trees, and formerly there was cultivation. Water is good and abundant from wells, and also fuel and forage.

4. *Ludgust,* 15 *miles.*

All over level country with date-trees and remains of cultivation. Here good water is abundant from wells, and fuel and forage is abundant.

Muksota.

This is a long march over a level plain. Water from wells good; fuel and forage procurable.

Gaz.

A short march over level plain. Well water good; fuel and forage procurable.

Gorani.

A short stage still over plain. Good water from wells.

Kumirah.

A long march. No water here, but fuel and forage are procurable.

Nodu.

A long stage. Water good from wells; fuel and forage procurable.

Talab.

A shorter stage. Water from the bed of a ravine, brackish; fuel and forage procurable.

Washaf.

A short stage. Water good; fuel and forage procurable.

Jujuck.

This stage is two long marches with no water. This place is in the hills. Water brackish from ravine; fuel and forage not very abundant.

Amalaf.

A short stage.

Thence to *Z*irreh *vide* No. VII.

A road goes from Mairum, Route No. VII., to Muksota on the above route. The distance is one long march without any water between. This route can also be reached from Godar to Golugah, and thence to Gorani or Gaz. All these are over a sandy plain with no water.

Route IX.

From Meski, Stage 10, Route No. VII., there is a more direct road to Amir Chah and Amalaf as follows :—

1. *Isatahir*, 12 *miles*.

The road goes north-west over the bed of the God-i-Morjin for six miles, then over high stony and gravel plain. Here there is excellent water in the ravine from wells. There are a few stunted date-palms here as at Paniham, and fuel and forage are abundant.

2. *Nehri*, 42 *miles*—54 *miles*.

This is a long stage without any water over a level sandy plain covered with stones and gravel. To the left is the Hamun of Talab or Kindi. The water here is very bad, only just drinkable, and fuel and forage are not abundant.

3. *Mushkija*, 12 *miles*—66 *miles*.

The road same as above; here pool of salt water; fuel and forage procurable.

4. *Amir Chah*, 13 *miles*—79 *miles*.

For the first four miles the road is over a plain, it then enters hills, and has to cross two passes, one of which is difficult for camels.

The road to Amalaf by this line goes west to Razai in 22 miles over a sandy plain. Here there is good water from wells in a ravine, but little fuel or forage. It then goes for about 11 miles towards a low pass in the range in front, crossing which it goes over sand, keeping to the left of the Koh-i-Dalil, and joins into the Amalaf route from Amir Chah at about the 16th mile.

By this line Mushkija to Amalaf is 54 miles without any water.

Route X.

There is a route which goes from Amalaf (Stage 16, Route VII.) to Seistan thus:—

1. *Kirtakur*, 15 *miles.*

The road comes out of the hills in four miles, and then goes along the stony glacis at foot of the hills. There is good water here from the ravine; fuel and forage are scarce.

2. *Kuchawur*, 12 *miles*—27 *miles.*

The road is pretty level along the foot of the Kucha Koh. Water is good from the bed of the ravine from wells. There is but little fuel or forage.

3. *Madano*, 40 *miles*—67 *miles.*

A very long stage, which goes along the foot of the hills the whole way. Good water is procured from wells in the bed of a ravine which drains to the Shela. Fuel and forage scarce.

4. *Hurmak*, 12 *miles*—79 *miles.*

Still along the foot of the hills; road stony; water from a spring excellent; fuel and forage scarce.

5. *Saif-ud-din Nowar*, 35 *miles*—114 *miles.*

The road leaves the hills and approaches the Shela plain, which has much good soil mixed with sand. There is some salt water at about twenty miles. Here the water is brackish from wells. Fuel and forage are abundant.

6. *Kundur*, 20 *miles*—134 *miles.*

The road goes along the Shela, sandy in places.

Thence the road is the same as that followed by Goldsmid's mission to Seistan.

Route XI.

From Talab there is another route which goes inside the hills as follows:—

1. *Sung-Ach*, 20 *miles.*

This is a long march along the Mirjawur ravine, the last part in the hills. There is no water here except after rain, but wells would produce some. Fuel and forage are plentiful.

2. *Mirjawur,* 20 *miles.*

The road goes up the ravine between hills. Here there is a bund and some cultivation; and good water is plentiful from the ravine. Forage and fuel are abundant.

3. *Bed,* 20 *miles.*

The road still goes up the ravine to Bed, which is at its head. There are hills on either side. Good water is abundant from wells in the ravine bed; and fuel and forage are plentiful.

4. *Dozaf,* 20 *miles.*

This march leaves the ravine, and ascending crosses a pass and then descends to another ravine, the drainage of which goes towards the Lar-Koh. Water is abundant from the ravine, and also fuel and forage.

5. *Tankh-i-Hurmak,* 12 *miles.*

The road goes over a plain, then over low hills. The water-supply comes from the river bed.

6. *Saif-ud-din Nowar.*

Vide route above.

I have mentioned a route which goes to the right from my route to Naru, but there are in fact three several roads which go off from it and make the Helmund at Pullalak, viz. :—

Route XII.

From Paniham or from Meski roads go to the Gat-i-Barote over the same sort of sandy plain as mentioned between Paniham and Shundak. The distance is not under forty miles, and there is no water, though some forage is procurable. At the Gat there is water from a spring, but fuel and forage are scarce.

Amuri Khor, 13 *miles.*

The road goes north from the Gat-i-Barote over a level stony plain to Wadi, and thence follows the route I came back by to the Amuri ravine. Here water can be procured by digging wells, and fuel and forage are very abundant.

Secondly, from about twelve miles beyond Paniham a track goes off north-east and makes for the Amuri Khor, going over the same sort of sandy plain covered with stones as was traversed by me between Paniham and Shundak. The distance is about twenty-eight miles, or forty from Paniham (all without water) to Chah Araban; here water, fuel, and forage. Water would therefore have to be carried. The route strikes into the Amuri just at its junction with the Dahna Khor, and thence follows my route up the bed of the Amuri for about five miles to the point where that ravine comes down from the north.

Amuri Dup, 8 *miles*.

The road goes up the bed of the Amuri as above. This is a very short march, but there is water, fuel, and forage in abundance.

Gund-i-Gowr.

A short march, all up the stony bed of the Amuri. Here water, fuel, and forage.

Wad Kuddu.

Not a long march. The road goes up the Amuri to near its head, then crosses a low pass, Wad Kuddu, over the main range. The halting place is at the north foot of the pass. Here there is water in a ravine which drains towards Mullik Rubbat, and fuel and forage are abundant.

Mustian Doni.

The stage is a short one, the road leaving the Kuddu ravine to the right and going over sand. Here good water is obtained from a well, and fuel and forage are plentiful.

Injirok.

Also a short stage, but over heavy sand-ridges. There is no water here, but fuel and forage is plentiful.

Sukaluk.

A short stage over heavy sand-ridges.

From this the Helmund is fifty miles over heavy sand, with no water on the way. It reaches the Helmund at Pullalak.

Route XIII.

The third route is called the Diwanak road, and it goes thus from Shundak.

Lal Khan Chah, 11 *miles*.

The road goes east for a mile and then over low easy hills to Lal Khan Chah, which is in the bed of the Diwanak ravine. Here water is procurable from wells in the bed of the ravine, and fuel and forage are abundant to the north.

Patko, 21 *miles*—32 *miles*.

The road goes for two miles over a stony plain up the left bank of the Diwanak ravine to where two branches meet. Going up the north one, it continues up its stony bed, ascending almost imperceptibly between bare black hills to its head at eighteen miles. It then turns to the left, and crossing the watershed descends by a stony path and then goes over a stony plain to Patkoi. Water from wells in ravine; fuel and forage abundant; no grass.

Jullejul, 12 *miles*—44 *miles*.

The road goes near the right bank of the Patkoi ravine over sandy country, and is level, but heavy in places. Water procurable from wells in ravine; fuel and forage abundant; no grass.

From Jullejul to Pullalak on the Helmund is 50 miles; all over sand, with no water.

There is a road which goes from Dizzak by Wash and Ladiz (Sarhadd), and so out by Madano to Saif-ud-din, and thence to Seistan. This must be the road Captain St. John mentions his having unsucessfully attempted to induce his camel-driver to take him. I have no more information regarding it, as I came across no Sarhaddis. This route is entirely through Persian territory, and, though there may be more water, the road is probably more difficult, and camel-forage and fuel are likely to be more scarce.

To make this section complete, it now only remains to give the route which leads from the various points on the Helmund given in the above routes to Herat.

These points are Landi, Pullalak, Rudbar, and Bandar Kamal Khan, and therefore it will be necessary to give the route XIV. from Landi, the point highest up on that river.

Kala Sabz, 22 *miles*.

The road is nearly due west. In three miles it clears the cultivation, and then enters on an undulating tract which slopes up to the sandy ridges extending between Khanishin and the river, and which is covered with coarse gravel and sprinkled with patches of camel-forage. At 11 miles it crosses a deep wide hollow which runs down to the river from the right and then passing over a ridge of sand-hills crosses another very deep and narrow ravine with sandy bottom, thence the road goes along near the bank of the river. Water plentiful from river. Fuel and forage very abundant.

Melgudur, 23 *miles*—45 *miles.*

The road is generally south-south-west, now and again striking the river at its successive turns to the south. For the first six or seven miles the ground is apt to be heavy after rain, whence it is good. Half way pass Mulakhan and two miles on Deshu. Water plentiful from river, and fuel and forage very abundant.

Lundi Barechi, 36 *miles*—81 *miles.*

The route is at first south-south-west and leads through wild uninhabited jungle for the whole distance. The road is a well-beaten track and passes a succession of deep bays of spongy saline alumin, and for the most part follows the course of the river; pass Abdulabad, Khojahali, Dasht Hadara, and Pullalak on the road. There is some cultivation here. Water abundant from river. Fuel and forage abundant.

Rudbar, 17 *miles*—98 *miles.*

After clearing the Lundi cultivation the path goes under some projecting desert cliffs. Beyond this it crosses the Rudbar canal and enters a wide gulf of level land and skirts the desert cliffs on the left. Then veering towards the river on the right, it crosses a bare pebbly tract to Rudbar. Here water, fuel, and forage abundant, and there is a considerable amount of cultivation.

Kala Jan Beg, 28 *miles*—126 *miles.*

The road runs nearly due west along the course of the river through a succession of ruins and canals. Here water, fuel, and forage are abundant.

Charburjak, 14 *miles*—140 *miles.*

The road runs west by north over a bare gravelly desert, dotted with ruins, for half the distance. Beyond this the surface is undulating and covered with brown pebbles. Here water, forage, and fuel are abundant.

Bandar Kamal Khan, 16 *miles*—156 *miles*.

The road is nearly due west, and for the first few miles crosses a sandy tract covered with mimosa and tamarisk. It then goes over a strip of bare pebbly ground along the course of the ancient Trakhun canal, now dry. The ruins of a small village are then passed and the road comes to the modern Trakhun canal, which is crossed by a rustic bridge, and then turning to the left through tamarisk jungle rises on the desert, over which it goes for a time and then descends on the Seistan plain, and a mile on reaches Bandar Kamal. Here water, fuel, and forage are abundant; some supplies procurable.

Dak-i-Dela, 14 *miles*—170 *miles*.

After clearing the cultivation round the fort the road runs north along the river by a beaten track on the verge of a wide, level, bare pebbly plain. Here water, fuel, and forage are abundant; also "kirta" grass.

Kubbur-i-Haji, 12 *miles*—182 *miles*.

The road runs nearly due north across the same sort of plain as in last march. Here fuel, forage, and water, and "kirta" are abundant.

Lash, 20 *miles*.

From Kubbur-i-Haji to Lash there is probably a route which leads direct. I have no details of the same, but it is possibly not more than 120 miles (Captain Lovett went from Chakhansur to Lash, which is 60 miles over a very desert country). Most likely there is water to be found for the digging.

Furrah, 50 *miles*.

This is all over a plain and follows the left bank of the Furrah road, the ground rising gradually the whole way. Here fuel, forage, water and grass are abundant, and some supplies procurable. From Furrah to Sabzawar the following is taken from a route by Ferrier, which, however, is very meagre.

Khush, 17½ *miles*.

Road over a plain, cross the Furrah road soon after leaving, lastly through fields. Here water.

Jeja, 24 *miles*.

The road goes for seven miles over a plain, it then crosses three canals from the Khush road, and becomes tortuous, rocky, and bad in a valley enclosed by high mountains. Here water, fuel, forage, and grass are abundant.

Sabzawar, 31 *miles*.

Crossing the river of Jeja, the road goes for an hour through mountains, and then for the rest of the way across a plain, following the course of the river the whole way. Here water, fuel, forage, and supplies are procurable.

From Sabzawar to Herat, the distance is about 85 miles.

Route XV.

West of the Dasht River there is a route which starts from Gwatar and goes up the Dashtiari River by Bahu Kullat, Sarbaz, and Mugguz, and then by a route through Paskoh and Sarhadd out by the route I have given in No. X. The first part of this road is well known to our officers as far as Mugguz, from this Haji Abdun Nubbi traversed it in 1839, and gave a meagre account of it. From Sarbaz a road goes to Bunpur.

Route XVI.

Next from Chabar there is the route to Bunpur followed by the adventurous Captain Grant in 1809, and in 1864 by Sir Frederic Goldsmid. From Bunpur there may be routes through Sarhadd to Seistan, but we have no knowledge whatever of them. The only routes we know towards Seistan are those of Captain Pottinger in 1810, and of Captain St. John in 1873, to Nurmashir, whence the road is the same as that followed by Sir Frederic Goldsmid on his mission to Seistan. It is evident, however, that these routes, though perhaps they may be practicable, have no advantage over those I have described before. From Jashk there is a circuitous route by the Fanoch pass to Bunpur. West of Jashk there are no routes to the north, all the country in that direction being entirely unknown, till we come to Minab.

ROUTE XVII.

Here the coast line is a very considerable distance to the north of the latitude of the Mekran Coast, and this, together with the fact that the country between this and Seistan is better populated and more productive than Persian Balochistan, should, in my opinion, give the preference to the route which goes by Minab to Bam and thence that to Seistan which was followed by Sir Frederic Goldsmid.

I will now turn to a consideration of the routes which lead from our frontier to Zirreh.

ROUTE XVIII.

The routes to be considered naturally divide themselves into two groups, 1st, those that must enter the mountains by the Bolan; 2nd, those that must enter by the Mulla. Of the former, the first route to which I would call attention is one which would take its start from Harand in the Ghazi District, and go through the Bugti hills to the Bolan. This route is the one by which the Punjab troops marched to Quettah, and is as follows:—

1. *Toba,* 18 *miles.*

The road crosses the plain to the west, and enters the bed of the Chachur ravine, up which it goes all the way. The bed is sandy and free from stones, except for the last two miles. Grass procurable, fuel abundant, water fair and plentiful.

2. *Bashka Bent,* 18 *miles.*

A somewhat difficult march, the road winds through somewhat high hills, those on the left bank being the loftiest. The bed is strewn with rocks and boulders. It is said to be impracticable in its present state, but it could easily be improved. Water procurable from stream. Grass and forage obtainable.

3. *Kalchas,* 20 *miles.*

The road still keeps to the bed of the Chachur, which as it nears the Shum plain opens out and becomes far less stony and winding. After about seven miles the country on either side is an open and grassy plain. Water, forage, and grass procurable.

4. *Dera Bugti,* 30 *miles.*

The road is bad over hills.

5. *Sungsila,* 12 *miles.*
6. *Chigerdi,* 14 *miles.*
7. *Sari,* 15 *miles.*
8. *Lehri,* 19 *miles.*

Route XIX.

Leaving the regular Bolan route at a point called Darwaza at the entrance of the Dasht-i-Badaulat, which is 60 miles from Dadur, there is a direct route thence to Mustung by which Captain Lockwood came down.

Mustung, 21 *miles*—310 *miles from Mittunkot.*

From Darwaza the route to Shalkot goes north-west, that to Mustung south-west. It first crosses the south portion of the Dasht-i-Badaulat, and then ascends by a steep zigzag a low pass, from this it descends to the bed of a ravine which it keeps, and then entering a gorge between stony hills 200 to 300 feet high, which at first is not more than a quarter of a mile broad, but which gradually widens to one mile, the road being rather stony. Keeping this for three miles it then gets on to a plain cut up by ravines, and goes over a light sandy soil right into Mustung.

Baraly, 13 *miles*—323 *miles.*

The road is throughout quite good over a plain sloping east by north, at first cultivated. At three miles pass some ruined houses; at 11 miles crosses the Shirin Ab ravine; and at 12¼ pass close under the end of a ridge. No water procurable, and fuel and forage scarce.

Kurdagaf, 17 *miles*—340 *miles.*

The road is good generally except where it enters the hills, where it would require making to render it practicable. At first it goes over a plain sloping gently to north-east to a ravine, which it ascends for 15 minutes to a pass (from here a road goes to Shalkot), from which it descends to the Barung ravine to the fifth mile. (Here small spring of water.) It then goes for 5½ miles over undulating stony ground a good deal cut up by ravines (to the east of a low ridge and with the main range on the left) to some hills. It then goes up the Kurdagaf valley, over a gravel plain covered with the camel scrub, to the halting place at 4¼ miles, the road to Kundwah goes off to the right. There is water here from Karez; no fuel or forage, but the "drauna" bush.

Gullangur, 18 *miles*—358 *miles.*

The road goes for five miles across the Kurdagaf valley over light soil through cultivation. It then ascends a low hill to a stream (20 yards broad, one foot deep, brackish water) which it crosses. From this for 4½ miles it goes across the Gurgina valley (which drains to the Kaisar), which is composed of light soil, and is extensively cultivated, being irrigated by rain-water collected by dams. Arrived at the other side of the valley it crosses a low pass to a ravine which it descends for four miles to a larger ravine (the Gullangur drains to the Kaisar) and continues down it to the halting place. This ravine is somewhat stony, the bed 800 yards broad and shut in by low bare stony hills 50 to 100 feet high. Water good from pools in bed of ravine, very little forage, and no fuel.

Nushki, 18½ *miles*—376½ *miles.*

For the first mile the road goes down the Gullangur ravine. There is then an ascent of 50 feet to the Ziarat Pir Lunga, whence it winds among low hills, 100 to 200 feet high for three miles to a "cheda" called Tulkhi. It then crosses a plain called the Alunji Damag, and enters a ravine 300 yards broad called Kishing-i-Hasing, bounded by low hills 50 to 100 feet high, and keeps it for one mile. Emerging from this it crosses a plain (two by four miles) called Kum-i-Morid to some low hills, through which it then goes for 4½ miles to Ziarat-i-Mir Haibut. From this it descends gradually among low bare stony hills for three-quarters of a mile to the Kaisar river, which here converges from the hills to the right. Crossing this it goes for three miles over a stony plain to Nushki.

The road is practicable except through the hills between Kum-i-Morid and Zirrat Haibut which would require a good deal of making, though the gradient is easy. At Nushki, water, fuel, and forage are abundant, and a few supplies might be collected.

Halting place east of Jabba, 22 *miles*—398½ *miles.*

Leaving the site of old Nushki and the shrine of Khoja Muhammad close on the right, the road follows the left bank of the Kaisar river (quarter of a mile broad, shallow, pebbly bottom), and passes between two forts about a quarter of a mile distant. It then goes for four miles alternately over sand-ridges and cultivation, and for another three miles over broad high sand-ridges. It then ascends gradually for one mile where a road to Buggull goes off to the left, when it goes over hard sand and between sand-ridges (one mile apart) for 4½ miles, and then for three miles over sand-mounds 20 to 50 feet high, to a swamp (500 yards broad); skirting the south bank of this for 1¾ miles it goes for 1½ miles over firm sand to the halting place. Water procurable in pools after rain, and in dry weather by digging. Fuel and forage abundant; no grass.

Halting place west of Mahabbat, 21 *miles*—419½ *miles.*

The road is nearly straight the whole way between two parallel ridges, at three miles it comes to a swamp (quarter of a mile broad), and at five miles arrives at a stream of water running to the south-west and a tamarisk jungle. It then goes for five miles over a flat, liable to be inundated, to Lala, a pool of water 50 yards in diameter, and then over firm sand or hard soil; at 18½ miles pass Jandour, water two miles to the right beyond sand-ridge, and at 20 miles, well of Mahabbat one mile to the right. Water-supply good, fuel and forage abundant; no grass.

Saisar, 22 *miles*—441½ *miles.*

The road goes through a sand valley for two miles, it then goes for four miles round the edge of a swamp covered with coarse green grass, and crosses a neck of land for one mile to a well called Thull (20 feet deep, putrid water). From this it crosses a sand-ridge and then goes for four miles along a branch of the Lora Hamun. After which it crosses another sand-ridge and then skirts the south side of the Hamun, with a sand-ridge 20 feet on the left, and ground much cut up by pools of water on the right. Good water from a pool 250 yards in diameter, and fuel and forage are abundant.

Koh-i-Gow, 25 miles—466½ miles.

The road is good the whole way, and for 19 miles goes over gravel and hard sand, the last six miles over bare light-brown soil slightly covered with saltpetre. The hill called Pulchotta or Mikh-i-Rustum is passed on the road. On the left for the whole way, two or three miles distant, is a sand-ridge 50 to 100 feet high, which separates the Hamun from the Dalbundin plain, and during the first part of the march five or six miles off on the right, is a line of jungle running parallel with the road, which marks the course of the Lora river. There is no water here, but it can be got almost anywhere about by digging, but fuel and forage are very abundant.

Chageh, 17½ miles—484 miles.

The road is good throughout, being all over a level plain covered with camel-scrub and grass. Cross the Zuralla and Shah-i-Sular ravines, both dry. Here water, fuel, and forage are very abundant, and some sheep are procurable. *N.B.*—There is a direct road across the Hamun from Chageh to Nushki when it is dry.

Tumpa Gaz, 29 miles—513 miles.

The road is all over ground covered with black stones and is practicable, but a little making at the ravines would be advisable.

It goes first to a hill, at the foot of which is a small pool of water called Ab-i-Farang. It then crosses a stony plain to a ravine called Dokanan (150 yards broad with steep hills on either bank), which it follows for 1⅓ miles to a fine spring of good water with some cultivation. It next crosses a gravelly plain for three miles to a low range of hills, which it goes through to a shrine (Ziarat-i-pir-i-Darre). From this it goes through a low broken range of hills for two miles to a camp (called Pashab-i-Parzonigi), then for two more over a plain to a rocky ravine, which it follows for one mile to a spring of water (called Kulluh-i-Kurd), whence it goes over a stony plain for four miles to Tumpa Gaz with low hills 1½ miles to the left, and a higher ridge the same distance to the right.

This halting place is in the bed of the Bulu ravine, in which water is only procurable after rain or by digging, and there is no grass. Fuel and forage, however, are very abundant.

Barab Chah, 23 *miles*—539 *miles.*

The road goes straight across a plain over black stones and gravel. Water brackish from well in bed of ravine. Fuel and forage abundant. No grass.

Kiachah, 16 *miles*—555 *miles.*

The road goes over a stony plain, and then turns and gently descends a stony valley for five miles to a shallow ravine, where at 1½ miles more it passes close under a hill to the right, which is the end of a spur from the Samoli hill; 2½ miles on it crosses the Samoli ravine (100 yards broad, banks steep, 15 feet high), and 1¾ further another similar ravine.

The water here is procured from wells, two feet deep, dug in the bed of the ravine, and it is slightly salt. Fuel and forage not very plentiful; no grass.

Rabat, 19 *miles*—574 *miles.*

The road at first goes straight over a level stony plain for two miles to a black rocky hill called Mushkari, which it passes close on the left, and 2½ miles on crosses a shallow ravine called Siahdil. One mile from this a road to Dalbundur by Chehlguzeh goes off to the left, and one mile further it descends to the road to Rabat and Sukaluk. It then goes across a plain for 3½ miles to the Jognuk ravine (here a small pool, bad water). The road then goes over a stony ridge to another ravine to the left, then over a plain of firm sand crossing the Rabat ravine (300 yards broad, shallow, stony bed). Water procurable from bed of ravine by digging. No forage or grass near this camp; water from Rabat ravine.

Patkoi, 17 *miles*—591 *miles.*

The road is good all the way generally over firm ground, but crossing many sand-ridges. Water from bed of ravine. Fuel and forage procurable.

Lal Khan Chah, 21½ *miles*—612½ *miles.*

The road first goes over a heavy sand-ridge, then ascends and crosses an easy pass, from which it descends the Diwanak ravine, the whole way the bed of this is stony, and it is shut in by bare black hills 100 feet high. The path is practicable, but the pass would be better for a little improvement.

Water from wells in the bed of the river; fuel and forage procurable, and a little grass.

Darband, 17 *miles*—629½ *miles*.

The road ascends the bed of a branch of the Diwanak ravine, and then crossing a low pass goes for the rest of the way over very heavy sand. Here good water is procurable by digging three to four feet in the hollows; and fuel and forage are very abundant, but there is no grass.

From Darband the road goes over sand south-west for five miles, and then joins the road from Shundak to the west, which is described in Route No. VII.

The distance by this route to Bandar Kamal Khan is 818½ miles.

Route XX.

The next route would be from Kusmur along the line of the Sind Horse outposts to the mouth of the Bolan.

The stages on this route are—

1.	Drekan - - - -	12 miles.
2.	Toj - - - -	10 „
3.	Doda Khan-ke-got - -	14 „
4.	Goranari - - - -	12 „
5.	Ooch - - - -	20 „
6.	Shahpur - - - -	12 „
7.	Chuttar - - - -	12 „
8.	Pulagi - - - -	12 „
9.	Hahri - - - -	16 „
10.	Mull - - - -	26 „
11.	Mittri - - - -	10 „
12.	Dadur - - - -	14 „
	Total - - -	170 miles.

All these marches are over a hard dry plain which is above the Indus flood level. Water is scarce, but camel-forage is procurable; very little fuel or grass anywhere. Supplies to a certain extent could be got at the stages in Kachi.

From Dadur the road falls into the Bolan route described in the former route. From Kusmur to Bandar Kamal Khan therefore is 736½ miles.

Sukkur is the point of junction of the railway system from the Punjab and from Karachi, and is the most important flourishing town on the Lower Indus.

Unfortunately the country to the south of Jacobabad and Shikarpur and between those places is very liable to be flooded, but this is less to be regretted, because all the southern roads would not be available, owing to the mouth of the Mula lying to the north of the latitude of even the former.

Route XXI.

The next available road would be as follows from Sukkur:—

1, Lukki, 15 miles; 2, Shikarpur, 9 miles; 3, Humayun, 13½ miles; 4, Jacobabad, 12½ miles; 5, Rojan, 11 miles; 6, Burshori, 28 miles; 7, Kasim-ka-joke, 16 miles; 8, Bagh, 20 miles; 9, Haji-ka-Shuhr, 16 miles; 10, Mittri, 9 miles; 11, Dadur, 11 miles—total, 161 miles.

This route has the disadvantage of being liable to be flooded by the Indus as far as Rojan, otherwise during the dry season it is quite good, and as it passes through a cultivated country and such large towns as Sakar, Shikarpur, and Jacobabad, it is certainly preferable to the former route.

The distance from Sakar to Bandar Kamal by this route, therefore, is 713½ miles.

These are all the direct roads to the Bolan, and I now therefore turn to the roads which lead to the Mula Pass.

Route XXII.

The first is the ordinary road from Jacobabad which goes by Rojan, 11 miles; Burshori, 28 miles; Sunjurani, 13 miles; Gundawa, 13 miles; mouth of Mula, 19 miles—total from Sakar, 84 + 50 = 134 miles, whence the following route gives all the information.

The total distance from Sakar to Suraf by this road is 253 miles, and to Bandar Kamal Khan it is 711 miles.

Route XXIII.

The direct road from Jacobabad to the Mula, however, is as follows: 5, Rojan, 11 miles; 6, Rahman-ka-gurhi, 24 miles; 7, Abad, 12 miles; 8, Panjok, 12 miles; 9, Mula, 14 miles, or 50 + 73 = 123 miles, nine marches from Sakar. All this is over a hard dry plain, the last part in the bed of the Mula river being however very stony.

10. *Kohau,* 11 *miles*—134 *miles.*

The road goes along the bed of the river, which is frightfully stony for five miles; it then ascends and goes over a stony terrace from the left for one mile. The pass is about two to three miles wide at this point. It then gets gradually narrower till at the 7th mile the hills come close together, called Dahan-i-Durra, and continue so for a mile. The road then emerges into an open space, where there is an encamping ground; crossing this at the 9th mile the road goes over a terrace for nearly two miles to Kohau. This consists of terraces of cultivated ground on both sides of the river. Fuel, forage, and water are very abundant. The whole is very stony, but the gradient is very easy.

11. *Paniwan,* 9 *miles*—143 *miles.*

The road goes all the way up the bed of the river, which is very stony in parts, especially when leaving Kohau, where the defile closes in, and is very narrow. Here there is a high terrace on the right bank and some little cultivation. Fuel, forage, and water are very abundant.

12. *Huttachi,* 10 *miles*—153 *miles.*

The road keeps the right bank of the river, near foot of terrace, all over stones, and crosses a ravine from the left at starting, there passing a considerable grave-yard. It then has to keep still to right to avoid a glacis of boulders from a ravine on the right at 3½ miles. At 4½ miles it crosses the river to the left bank, and goes over better ground to Bent-i-jah, a patch of cultivation on the right. Here fuel, forage, and water are abundant. To this the defile is about one mile broad. It then commences to narrow till at 7½ miles the hills close in to 200 yards, and continue so for a mile. The hill on the right is called Koh-i-Khuzana; on both sides the heights are very steep. From this the valley gradually opens till the village of

Huttachi is reached. This is on the left bank, and here the valley is more than a mile broad. Here fuel, forage, and water are abundant, and some grass is procurable.

13. *Pir Lukka,* 11 *miles*—164 *miles.*

The road keeps to the left bank of the river and is good, over good soil with few stones. The valley widens to about two miles to main branch of the stream, going off to the right. At two miles pass a path which leads to Zedi; at three miles a ravine from the left, and at three and a half a halting place called Khurzan (where fuel, forage, and water are abundant, and some grass is procurable); at six miles another halting place, Khakori, very suitable for encamping a force. The valley after this gets narrower, the road worse, crossing the stream several times over stones, till at 11½ miles Pir Lukka is reached. This is a tomb with a patch of cultivation on the left bank. The heights are very commanding and impracticable here. Fuel, forage, and water are abundant, and grass also.

14. *Narr,* 11 *miles*—175 *miles.*

The road goes out behind the tomb and turns north for a mile, and then gradually resuming south direction at two miles. The road is very stony, and the hills at the turn come, in very steep cliffs, close up, leaving very little room, which would probably make the road impracticable during flood. (There is a foot-path from Pir Lukka, which turns this bit and joins into the other road at the 3½ miles). The road after passing this narrow defile keeps to the left bank, and at 6¼ miles comes to an open space with cultivation called Usuri. (Water, fuel, and forage procurable.) Over this it is less stony for a mile or two. It then gets back on the bed of the river, and is very stony for three miles. Here the road rounds a spur on the right and turns north going over good ground through thick tamarisk scrub for two miles. At Narr the valley again opens forming a triangle, the base of which is two miles, and the sides two and a half to three miles. A camp could be pitched anywhere, but close under the hills on the right is the best and highest ground. Here there is some cultivation, and fuel, water, and forage are very abundant, while grass is also procurable.

15. *Pusht Khana,* 10 *miles*—185 *miles.*

Soon after leaving, the hills close in and are not more than

200 yards apart for the next nine miles. On either hand they rise almost perpendicular with a smooth face like a wall, and are quite impracticable. At 4½ miles the Dodandan peaks are passed, at 5¾ the cultivation of the same name, and at nine the shrine of Pir Lutu, on the left bank, with a bit of cultivation. The road is over the stony bed, and is very trying for camels. The valley after this opens with jungle in the bed, and the road crosses the river several times; at twelve miles enter Pusht Khana valley and encamp. Fuel, forage and water are very abundant, and grass is procurable. This valley is the largest opening in the pass, and about five miles long by two and a half at the widest.

16. *Gwara Bana,* 9 *miles*—194 *miles.*

The road goes up and across the valley for four miles; the direct road to Kullat by Pundran goes off to the right at one mile. The river splits into two, three miles up, and the main branch goes round the east foot of the hills. The valley then narrows, and the road crosses the river over stones, passing a more open bit called Lukka. At Gwaram Bana, it is about three-quarters of a mile across with a good deal of jungle. Here water, fuel, and forage is abundant.

17. *Pisi Bent,* 9¼ *miles*—203¼ *miles.*

The road goes up the bed, sometimes over stones and then over earth where the valley opens a bit, and it is generally better. At two miles pass Patki cultivation and jungle; at four is Durdalu; at six Mordana, a large opening with cultivation and ruins; at seven Kondi a bit of cultivation, and at eight Bel, Chari Lambi, and another opening, till at 12 miles the opening Pisi Bent is reached. All these places are suitable for camping and have abundance of fuel, forage, and water.

18. *Jangi Jah*, 14 *miles*—217¼ *miles.*

The valley is about 500 yards wide, and gradually gets narrower till at 4½ miles the entrance to the Pisi Dara is reached. The road is very good, mostly over earth. The Pisi gorge is 1½ miles long, and it is formed by the hills on either side throwing out spurs, which here nearly meet. The bed of the river is generally about 80 or 90 feet broad, but in one place the cliffs close into not more than 30 feet. The cliffs on either side rise up perpendicularly for about 100 feet The road lies up the bed which is very much obstructed by huge boulders. This gorge would not be passable during a heavy flood.

Emerging from this defile the valley once more opens out, the road going up the bank of the river, which here has no water in it for five miles. It then hugs the hills on the left, and crosses an open plain of good soil, and crossing some low ridges arrives at Jangi Jah. At the 11th mile the road to Zehri by Gazan goes off right, and at 12 miles that to Buppow.

19. *Amjirah*, 10 *miles*—227¼ *miles*.

The road goes along the bed of the river the whole way (which at the third mile begins to have water in its bed). It is quite good, but stony in places. Fuel and forage, however, nearly cease after Pisi Bent.

20. *Suraf*, 14 *miles*—241¼ *miles*.

The road is quite good the whole way over undulating stony ground. Here water is abundant, but forage and grass are scarcely to be had.

21. *Dragi*, 16 *miles*—257¼ *miles*.

The road is quite good the whole way; at four and seven miles across a low ridge of sandy hills, then go across the Chehlbagu plain, which is stony on either side, but cultivated in the middle. Water in a ravine at about nine miles. Water at Dragi scarce but good, and any amount might be collected by previous arrangement. No fuel or forage or grass.

22. *Halting place below Tazinan Pass*, 20 *miles*—277¼ *miles*.

At the second mile the road crosses the Siah Kumb ridge by a pass which would require improving, thence it descends to the Siah Kumb cultivation; at the fourth mile, and at the sixth mile gets into hills. Thence it ascends and descends low hills continually and crosses numerous streams all of which drain to the north to the Budu. The road on the whole of this march requires much improvement, being very stony, narrow, and bad in many places. A halt could be made on any of these streams, all of which have abundance of good water, and in some of the larger ones, the Jumri and Zarchi, there is plenty of fuel, but nowhere is there any forage or grass.

23. *Tazinan ravine*, 22 *miles*—299¼ *miles*.

Immediately on leaving the last halting place there is a low but difficult pass to be crossed, then the road is pretty easy to beyond the crest of the Tazinan ridge, where a steep spur cuts across. The ascent of this is not very difficult, but the descent is almost impracticable for laden animals. From the north foot of this pass the road goes all the way down a difficult boulder-strewn ravine, which is very painful going for animals. A halt of course can be made anywhere almost where there is water, and this is in great abundance along the whole stage. There is, however, scarcely any fuel or forage east of the Tazinan ridge, west of it there is both, and also a good deal of coarse grass. At halting place, water, fuel and forage abundant, some grass procurable.

24. *Chasi*, 17 *miles*—316¼ *miles.*

The road goes down the Tazinan ravine to its junction with the Budu, and is quite easy. Crossing this river, which has a broad bed (about 400 yards) but no water (fuel and forage abundant), the road crosses numerous spurs of a low ridge to the Gwaragan ravine. Water abundant, but fuel and forage scarce on the road. Thence it goes over a long stony slope from the Koh Shaikh Husain crossing many deep ravines, the ascent and descent to which are steep and difficult. Guns could not be got over this stage without a good deal of improvement in the road. At Chasi there is a shrine, and water is abundant. Fuel and forage, however, are very scarce, and there is no grass.

25. *Padag-i-Pokdan*, 24 *miles*—340¼ *miles.*

From Chasi the road goes up a ravine for three miles to its head; it then crosses a low watershed, descending the Gani ravine for four miles to its junction with the Murrakan and then ascends this to its head six miles on. The ascent is not difficult, but the road is narrow and stony till (water just below the crest of the pass) the top of the Ali Suhuk Pass is reached. Thence the descent is very difficult indeed, the path winding among huge rocks for two miles. This part is nearly impracticable for camels.

Thence the road goes down a stony ravine and then over a stony glacis down into the plain, the first but very difficult going for camels, but getting better at the end.

At Padag there is a well of good water, but fuel and forage are scarce, and there is no grass. A halt could be made at the east foot of the Ali Suhuk Pass, but the ground is very confined.

(From Padag is about 30 miles over sand-ridges easy going to the Koh-i-Gow stage on the Nushki route, 396 miles. Thence to Robat is 104 miles, 500 miles, and across the desert by Sukalak to Pullalak is about 70 miles, and to Bandar Kamal is 76 miles. Total 646 miles. To Lash, 746; Farah, 796; Herat, 960.)

26. *Meski*, 16 *miles*—356¼ *miles*.

The road is quite good the whole way over firm soil; pass well at Chandran, at four miles and at one mile to right of 7th mile. At Meski water is procurable from a ravine from the Ras Koh to the south. Fuel and forage and some grass procurable.

27. *Konarak*, 11 *miles*—367¼ *miles*.

The road is excellent all the way; pass well at Chahsar; at one mile to right of 4th mile. Here water abundant from a large deep pond. Fuel and forage plentiful; some grass procurable.

28. *Namreg*, 11 *miles*—378¼ *miles*.

The road is quite good, crossing one or two sand-hills which are quite easy. Water from a large pool. Fuel, forage, and grass procurable.

29. *Pishuk*, 12 *miles*—391¼ *miles*.

The road excellent all the way. Pass some cultivation at five miles, and a camp at 6½ miles. At Pishuk some water, fuel, and forage abundant; some grass procurable.

30. *Band-i-Khan Jahan*, 12 *miles*—403¼ *miles*.

The road is excellent all the way. Water, fuel, and forage abundant; some grass procurable.

31. *Kani*, 13 *miles*—416¼ *miles*.

As above.

32. *Shorgil*, 16 *miles*—432¼ *miles*.

Road for 11 miles excellent. It then ascends and descends many low hills and is tedious, but not difficult. Water here precarious and brackish, any amount however could be collected. Fuel and forage procurable, and a little grass.

33. *Hamun Khor*, 15 *miles*—447¼ *miles*.

The road is good all the way for eight miles over a high stony plain. It then descends into the Pisi ravine and goes up it for four miles, then over a jungly plain to the Hamun. Here water very good and abundant. Fuel plentiful; forage not very good; no grass.

34. *Girim Khor*, 18 *miles*—465¼ *miles*.

The road is good over a stony plain for six miles. It then gets among low hills, and ascends and descends deep ravines frequently to the 11th mile to Lagujgarh (a halting place) in the Ghedan-pasti ravine (here salt water, scarcely any fuel or forage), and continuing so to the Jowri ravine at the 14th mile. (Here water good from well; fuel and forage procurable.) Then it is excellent over hard soil.

Here water abundant and good from wells in bed. Fuel and forage scarce; no grass.

35. *Amuri*, 16 *miles*—481¼ *miles*.

The road for 11 miles goes over a stony plain intersected by ravines, at the fifth mile pass a well in bed of ravine. From Wadi at the 11th mile go up a narrow ravine bounded by low hills for three miles, then cross a low pass, and turning, reach Amuri ravine in two miles. Here water can be got by digging in bed. Fuel and forage are very abundant, and some grass is procurable.

36. *Juli*, 16 *miles*—497¼ *miles*.

The road goes down the stony bed of the Amuri Khor for four miles, to near its junction with the Dahna (first mile up, water plentiful in bed, and three miles down a well called Chah Araban); thence it goes for seven miles a stony plain intersected by ravines to a well in bed of ravine from the Karzak Khor, called Chah Nilagun (where there is a little water). Then there is five miles more of the same sort of stony plain to the Juli ravine, about one mile up which in the hills there is a large pool said never to dry entirely. Fuel and forage here are scarce, and there is no grass.

37. *Shunduk, 9 miles*—506½ *miles.*

The road is easy but tedious; ascending and descending the ends of the spurs from the Naru range. Here water is procurable by digging in the bed of the ravine, and fuel and forage are very abundant; scarcely any grass.

The distance therefore from Sakar to Bandar Kamal is 677 miles.

This takes us to the point where the route from the sea joins that from the east.

It now only remains to note the routes which go off to the Helmand. And here I must note that every route which goes to the Helmand direct from Balochistan first goes to Nushki. There are routes from Kajah Fatulla to Hazar Juft, and from Pishin by Shorawak, Shorarud to Koh Khushnishin. From Shorawak south there is no route till those which go from Nushki are reached. One other point may here be noted, the tract immediately south of the Helmand has always been marked on all our maps a perfect blank. No doubt this has arisen from ignorance of the topography of this tract; yet after having been all over it, I can only say this blank space is quite correct, and must always remain vacant. From Seistan at least as far as Hazar Juft, beyond the strip of cultivation, which in some places stretches along the left bank of the Helmand, there is a strip of utterly irreclaimable desert, which varies from 40 to 60 miles in breadth. In all this vast tract, which covers an area of nearly 300 miles in length by 50 in breadth, there is not one drop of water, no animal life, all is a sea of sand, stretching in awful monotony of desolation. Therefore no one can get to the Helmand without crossing this tract, and therefore it is that all routes go off from one of two points, *viz.* Sukalak and Gullachah, which are the nearest spots at which water is found south of the river for near 300 miles.

The routes then which lead from the south to the Helmand are as follows:—From Gullachah (or Kalchi of Christie) a road goes by Gaimashki to Deshu on the Helmand about 60 miles. Again there is the road that Captain Christie went. From Sukalak roads go to either Landi Barech or Pullalak; the distance is about 50 miles.

APPENDIX B.

OBSERVATIONS IN REGARD TO THE BOUNDARIES OF BALOCHISTAN.

No boundary has ever been settled between Afghanistan and Balochistan, and though in 1870–72 a Commission visited Mekran and Seistan for the purpose of settling the limits of these districts which should form the frontier of Baloch and Persian in the first, and Persian and Afghan in the second; no line has, I believe, ever been demarcated between Baloch and Persian beyond Mekran.

Colonel Goldsmid appears to have laid down that "the line of frontier (between Afghan and Persian) from Kuhak to the hills south of Seistan should be so drawn as to include all cultivation on the bank of the river from the bund (Kuhak) upwards. The Malik Siah Koh peak on the chain of hills separating Seistan from the Kirman desert appears a fitting point."

So far the boundary is quite clear, and I have nothing to remark except that the peak named Malik Siah Koh in St. John's map is really named Lar Koh, the real Malik Siah Koh peak being over 20 miles further north. This, however, is not a matter of much importance.

From Malik Siah Koh there appears to have been no attempt to mark the boundary of Persia until the confines of Mekran are reached. It is true Captain St. John has drawn a line from that peak to the Mashkel river, but as that line is based on entirely erroneous geographical data, it cannot, of course, hold good; and as he himself expressly says in his report, that "north of the point where the Mashkel river issues from the hills between the Sianeh Koh and Koh-i-Sabz ranges, the frontier of Kalat is not defined," I regard this part of the frontier as undetermined.

This being so, the question arises, what should be the frontier, *i.e.* on grounds of right, or on plea of expediency. Of actual right, there is no doubt Persia had none in Balochistan at all prior to that accorded her by the above Boundary Commission, and as this Commission left the whole frontier beyond Malik Siah Koh an open question by not mentioning it at all, it is clear she can have acquired no further right simply owing to that omission. And on grounds of expediency, I consider Persia had better be made to keep to the north foot side of the Sianeh range. It would be very difficult, if not impossible, to settle a satisfactory boundary between the foot of this range and the Mashkel river, and to extend her frontier to that river under the altered data of its course which my exploration affords would be extremely inconvenient.

Persia has shown herself an adept in pushing forward at every point where her limit has not been clearly defined, or her advance stayed by a superior power, and there is little doubt in my mind that if the frontier I have recommended is not marked out to her as a limit, she will push further forward in the direction of Naru, Chageh, and Kharan, till some serious complication arises. As a matter of fact, a Persian force has already been to Gulugah, close to the Hamun of the Mashkel, and I believe she did once threaten to invade Kharan.

With regard to the little district of Kuhak, situated to the south of the Sianeh range. Persia has already, as far as she is able, settled its fate. After requesting the British Government to despatch a Boundary Commission and agreeing to abide by its decision, she has completely ignored that decree. It is a fact, that scarcely was Captain St. John's back turned than the Governors of Bunpur and Dizzah marched with a force and captured it. It is certainly most inexpedient that Kuhak should belong to Persia; for as long as she has it, so long will Azad Khan have reasonable ground for endeavouring to get it back, and so long must all hope of peace on this border be deferred.

Colonel Thuillier has drawn the green line (by which he marks Afghan territory) from Shalkot so as to include Chageh and Kharan, and everything on the north of the Koh-i-Sabz range right down to the Mashkel. Beyond that river, he takes it across the Sianeh range to Isfandal.

I need say no more of the part on the left bank of the Mashkel, as that has been duly considered in my foregoing remarks; but in regard to the others, I must add a few words. I suppose Kharan is included on the ground that the chief of that State declares himself tributary to Afghanistan; but if this plea is allowed, of course, it must also apply not only to what Colonel Thuillier has marked off, but to all the additional territory which is subject to Kharan, that is to say, Rakshan, a considerable part of Mashkai, both banks of the Budu river as far, at least, as Kalah Nimroz, and as far east as half way from Kharan to Gidar. All this is subject to Azad Khan, at least if the fact that no mouse in their limits dare squeak without Azad's leave implies subjection.

But the plea of being tributary to Afghanistan cannot hold good, without also allowing the same plea to Persia, or to the Khan of Kalat. The fact is, Azad Khan is quite ready to declare himself subject or tributary to anyone. He has no prejudices about consistency; like Dugald Dalgetty, he offers his allegiance wherever the return will be greatest. He has declared himself the slave of Shir Ali, just with the same amount of intention of adhering to his word as he has to the Khan of Kalat, and would to us, the Russians, or anyone else who offered him good enough terms.

The mere fact of Azad Khan's having declared himself at various times of his chequered career a subject of theirs, cannot entitle the Afghans to claim his allegiance, any more than if one of our Indian tributaries were to do so, and, therefore, if he is not really a subject of the Afghans or the Persians, he must be that of the Khan of Kalat. Even if there was a shadow of right in favour of an Afghan claim, it must give way before the fatal inexpediency of permitting such an arrangement. In my opinion there are but two courses open, either Azad Khan must acknowledge the Khan of Kalat unreservedly, and give up the Afghan allegiance completely, or he should be brought to his senses without delay.

On what grounds Chageh has been included in Afghanistan I cannot conceive. It is a large district, consisting of several sub-divisions, as Dalbundur, Chageh, Koh-i-Pusht, and Koh-i-Sunt, and is inhabited by the well-known Baloch tribes of Sanjaranis. I marched right through the south part of this district, and Captain Lockwood through the north, and the invariable answer we received to our inquiries as to whom they owned allegiance, was "the Khan Sahib."

With regard to the south boundary of Afghanistan, nothing has ever been settled. Major Sandeman is in a better position to speak regarding the part of it east of Shalkot than I am; but with regard to the west, I will now record my opinion as to how it should run. The country to the west is all desert, and there are no marked features by which to describe it, but the line should, I think, from Quetta dip gradually towards long. 65° and nearly to lat. 30°, and then rise again north to the Koh-i-Khushnishin on the banks of the Helmand. From this the real boundary of the Afghans should only go along the outer edge of the culturable land on the left bank of the Helmand as far as Rudbar, and then the river would be the boundary between Baloch and Afghan. If there be objections to this line, the boundary may be extended along the left bank to Bandar Kamal Khan, whence a line to the Malik Siah peak should be the limit.